D1625131

THE SYNERGY MYTH

ALSO BY HAROLD GENEEN

Managing (written with Alvin Moscow)

THE
SYNERGY
MYTH

and Other Ailments of Business Today

Harold Geneen
with Brent Bowers

St. Martin's Press ≈ New York

To June Hjelm, my most patient wife, who dislikes dedications—
or so she says—but who has put up with my idiosyncrasies for
more than two score years—and is still gently smiling.

And, to the memory of my mother, Aida Valentina DeCruciani,
born in Plymouth, England, of Tuscan parents and schooled by
Jesuits; she was a tower of unyielding principle and strength
throughout her life.
In a new world she raised her two children, followed her
career, and remained throughout her life of eighty-one years a
remarkably warm and youngish woman, and a role model of
courage for me.

THE SYNERGY MYTH

Copyright © 1997 by Harold Geneen. All rights reserved.
Printed in the United States of America. No part of this book
may be used or reproduced in any manner whatsoever without written permission except in the case of brief quotations
embodied in critical articles or reviews. For information,
address St. Martin's Press, 175 Fifth Avenue,
New York, N.Y. 10010.

Design by Richard Oriolo

Library of Congress Cataloging-in-Publication Data

Geneen, Harold.
    The synergy myth: and other ailments of business today /
Harold Geneen with Brent Bowers. —1st ed.
       p.   cm.
    ISBN 0-312-14724-4
    1. Industrial   management. 2. Business. I. Bowers,
Brent.
    II. Title.
    HD31.G396   1997
    658—dc20   96–42975

First edition: April 1997

10 9 8 7 6 5 4 3 2 1

One hour of life, crowded
to the full with glorious action,
and filled with noble risks,
is worth whole years of those mean observances
of paltry decorum.

—Sir Walter Scott

Contents

SECTION THREE: SLICING THE BALONEY

SECTION FOUR: A COLD LOOK AT SOME HOT ISSUES

People like to think of ''writing'' a book as though it were a smooth and stately act. Like a swan propelling itself across a quiet pond. It is anything but! ''Endless rewriting'' would be a more appropriate description. And so my acknowledgment of the tireless efforts of my administrative assistant, Cathy Farago, and secretary, Marie Serio, both of whom managed to make such repetition an ever nourishing diet.

So, too, to Barbara Hendra, my longtime editor, who never fears nor placates to make my efforts distinguishable from the endless flood of marketable copy.

And lastly, to some gifted liberal arts instructors that I was fortunate to encounter in my college years who sparked the interest of a business major in some far less purposeful areas like, for example—imagination.

Again, thanks.

Harold Geneen

Introduction:
If Somebody Says
"Synergy," Run!

There's a crisis in American business that many people don't like to talk about. It's the baloney crisis.

I may be eighty-seven years old, but I haven't really changed all that much since the days I ran ITT, building it up from a hodge-podge of little companies in Europe and Latin American to a $28 billion industrial empire.

I now work about ten hours a day instead of twelve or fourteen. But I still run companies. I still jet off to meetings—but to Connecticut instead of Europe. I still seize business opportunities. Money, however, has become a measure of accomplishment, not an objective in itself. But I still like to try new things. Like building up smaller companies. And this, of course, involves risk.

But baloney is baloney. And there's a lot of it today. For example, I am uncomfortable whenever I see a book on management purporting to reveal some new secret of business success. I once wrote a book entitled *Managing*. But the point of that book was that there is no secret, no magic formula. There are just the old-fashioned virtues of hard work, honesty, and risk taking. Remember them? I believed then, and still believe now, that it is important not to succumb to the latest management fad. Because fads tend to contain a lot of—you guessed it—baloney.

Ten years ago, we had Theory Z, which basically preached copying the Japanese. More recently, we've had Total Quality Management, "reengineering," and a host of others. I called my theory the G theory, which is that there is no valid theory.

Be wary of any rules or doctrinaire ideas. A lot of them are pure bunk. Take "mentoring." That is the theory that every budding manager needs a mentor—a wise corporate elder—to guide him through the maze of office politics.

Baloney. As a manager, or aspiring manager, you should read a lot, listen a lot, work a lot, and observe a lot. That way, you'll learn a lot, on your own. The last thing you want is somebody spoonfeeding you on the past—*his* past. The world changes too fast. You have to live it now.

And all the how-to tomes in the world will get you nowhere if you lack the gumption to take risks. It's probably the commonest failing of mankind, in part because it isn't ridiculed the way laziness is or reviled the way dishonesty is. Thus, the workplaces of America are filled with industrious and upright citizens on a treadmill to nowhere—because they are so intent on playing it safe.

In this book, I will argue in favor of taking the initiative rather than clinging to the same old routine; of being decisive rather than forever deferring to some higher authority; of exposing yourself to failure rather than making peace with mediocrity; in short, of seizing opportunities instead of forever retreating from them.

One thing I won't advocate or defend on any grounds is a carcinogenic slice of baloney called "synergy," the most screwball buzzword of the past decade. It has a phony sound to it, as though it were made up. Say it out loud. Don't you feel a little embarrassed? Yet, it has become almost obligatory to trot it out to describe the wonderful future of a corporate merger or the brilliance of a corporate strategy. It has entered the vocabulary of book reviewers, advertisers, sports announcers, and (God help us) politicians.

It's a fancy label that means whatever the speaker or writer wants it to mean, which is to say it doesn't mean anything at all. I can't figure out why so many people have fallen in love with such an awful-sounding word. It supposedly comes from two Greek words meaning "together" and "work." You might say that the combination of those two words, *syn* and *ergon,* lacks synergy. To my mind, "synergy" ought to derive from the words "synthetic" and "energy"—in other words, fake vitality.

People who use the word synergy are really saying: "We've run out of sensible ideas and are chasing will-o'-the-wisps, so we might as well try to hide that under some ultrasophisticated language." Or they're saying: "This is the 1990s. Plainspokenness and common sense are out. Hype is in." Or else they're hoping: "Maybe there's an easy solution to our problems after all."

What is synergy? It is alleged to be some sort of alchemy whereby the whole becomes greater than its parts. You combine A and B and C and get the magic potion D. But simply mixing elements together rarely does much good and sometimes is a pretty bad idea. If you toss a nickel, a quarter, and a dime into a box, you get forty cents. No magic there. If you mix beef broth, lemon juice, and flour, you don't get magic, you get a mess. If you mix red and blue, you get purple—a happy outcome if you like purple but not so happy if you don't. If a car has three wheels and you add a fourth—now *that* is synergy. But if you add two more, all you get is an extra expense.

Some things don't mix. What kind of synergy would you get if you merged the Broadway hits *The Phantom of the Opera* and *The King and I?* What is the synergy of a fishing rod and a sewing machine?

There's never been a synergy that has lasted very long, except maybe George Washington and the cherry tree or Santa Claus and his sled. And the first of those is a myth and the second is a fairy tale.

True synergy is the rarest thing in the world. It can happen, but not at the rate that a casual reading of the business press would have you believe. It occurs when one entity that behaves in one way and another entity that behaves in another way merge into a third entity that starts behaving in an entirely new way. For the most part, the phenomenon is limited to chemical laboratories.

The world has gone nuts on the hidden gold of synergy. Nobody thinks about a grandiose plan without thinking about synergy. So should we do away with the concept? Never! People would just invent some other equally ridiculous buzzword. It could be worse; people could be saying "symbiosis," another crackpot term that a terrorist group once twisted around and used in its name, "the Symbionese Liberation Army." You haven't heard from them lately, have you?

When people say "synergy," they usually mean productive use of assets or efficient allocation of manpower and resources. And that requires sitting down and studying the situation—looking at all the steps in a process and either improving them, eliminating them, or combining them. And that, of course, requires hard work, determination, and strategic thinking; in a word, strong management.

Let's turn to another piece of modern-day flimflammery: the notion that the industrial conglomerate is dead. Finished. Why? Because it's too unwieldy. It's a mishmash of unrelated companies. It lacks coherence. It lacks "synergy" among its component parts.

Far better, the current conventional wisdom has it, to strip away extraneous ventures that have accumulated over the years and return to the *core* business. And corporations are falling all over themselves to do just that. "Sears Roebuck spun off its $9 billion controlling stake in its huge Allstate Insurance subsidiary, a move that will complete the firm's return to its retailing roots," says a recent newspaper story.

Well, this back-to-basics movement is for the birds. I listened to the chairman and CEO of a Fortune 500 company push the conglomerates-are-dead line a few years ago with the cliché "Shoemaker, stick to your last." In other words, he is saying that a shoemaker should stick to making shoes and everybody else should stick to whatever he or she knows best. But I never made shoes. I did make companies perform. And like musical instruments, companies perform better in concert.

Admittedly, I have a stake in defending the conglomerate. Some people suggest I practically invented it in its modern form. I was once called America's greatest conglomerateur. (I guess that's a compliment.) Rest assured, however, that this praise is offset by less flattering characterizations that have been directed my way over the years.

At ITT, we acquired hundreds of companies and lumped them together into twenty-five or thirty divisions. At any one time, we might have ten or fifteen divisions moving forward and ten or fifteen digging in. But that gave us a choice of opportunity, a choice of where to put our efforts; and we'd put them in the companies we knew were growing at that moment.

You can't do that with a steel mill. Or an auto company or a wood-pulp mill. A shoemaker can't do it, either. But we had hotels, automobile equipment, wood pulp, semiconductors, telecommunications equipment, cosmetics, baked goods. You name it, we had it.

And not only does a big mix like that let you throw all your energies into the winning propositions; it also lets you develop managers better. You can move them around from company to company so that each one gains from the experience of the others. That's what our open management meetings accomplished.

There aren't many conglomerates left, I'll grant you that. When the *Wall Street Journal* publishes its quarterly corporate performance results, it lists 679 companies by category and subcategory. Under basic materials, you'll find steel companies, aluminum companies, and so forth. Under technology, you'll find computer companies, biotechnology companies, and so on.

And tucked away at the very bottom of the far-right column you'll find this tiny section entitled "Conglomerates." There are no subcategories. Until recently, just four companies were listed: General Electric, ITT, Teledyne, and Textron. Pretty good companies, I'd say.

Take General Electric. In 1994, its GE Credit arm supplied about 80 percent of its profit. But GE also makes aerospace equipment, toasters, and many other products. At some point, GE Credit may get its butt kicked. But by then, something else—toasters maybe—will be going up.

It's clear that General Electric's chairman, Jack Welch, understands the fundamental advantages of a conglomerate. It's the theory of the mutual fund: Go where the corn grows tallest, but spread your risk.

ITT, for all its high-tech expertise, sold white bread. And there came times when wheat prices went down and bread prices went up, and we could raise prices and increase profits. And if wheat prices went up and bread prices went down, our large volume made us competitive in a tough market. All the while, we came up with some new ideas for an old market. Twinkies, for example. And we had a lot of different markets. Meantime, General Motors lives and dies by the sale of one thing: motor vehicles.

So why do conglomerates have a bad name? Simple. For a while, people were putting together conglomerates that weren't conglomerates. They were holding companies that resulted from stock deals. They were run as a loose collection of businesses, not a tight-knit group with an integrated management.

I don't know if conglomerates really are a dying breed. But if they are, it's because nobody wants to work on them the way you have to work on them. It is the hard way because you have to run many different businesses. But that becomes an advantage.

If you run a conglomerate right, you can do great things. One day a guy came into my office at about 5 P.M. He ran a company that made lawn fertilizer. Somebody was trying to take him over and he didn't like his suitor and wondered if we were interested.

We talked. One hour and twenty minutes later, I said, "Okay. We'll buy." We paid about $75 million. It was and is successful and growing. You couldn't do that if you weren't a conglomerate. What the hell did we know about lawn fertilizer? But we did know a good deal when we saw one. And we knew we had management people good enough to make a profit. We knew we had the research and development to fix anything that might be wrong with the fertilizer. We also had engineering staffs, marketing specialists—a full team of specialists to see that it got sold—and at a profit.

We had a style of operating. We could absorb a unit like that, and easily fit it to our operating approach, because we were geared to running new businesses as well as our "core." That's the flexibility of the conglomerate.

Everybody talks about the wonderful things Lou Gerstner is doing at IBM. Well, he has got the stock price up. You can't argue with that. But I don't think Gerstner would have spent ten seconds with that lawn-fertilizer fellow. I made a $75 million decision in about one hour and twenty minutes. And I didn't need the information superhighway to do it.

The risk paid off. The conglomerate is the ideal vehicle for exploiting the rich possibilities of risk taking without jeopardizing the corporation's survival. If risk is a bucking bronco, a conglomerate is the best way to enjoy the ride.

Let me repeat something I said earlier: Running a company is fun. It's also a game. And sometimes you can think of it as a leisure activity, much as golf, and crossword puzzles, and bridge, and rock climbing are leisure activities. Why can't running a business be just as much a challenge as those pursuits? In fact, it's much more challenging, much riskier, and thus much more fun. In a way, I suppose, you could say I've been enjoying all this for much of my life. Will Rogers said he never met a man he didn't like. Well, I never met a business that I didn't find interesting.

Any job should be fun. I'd go even further and say you should have fun doing anything in life. I've had a lot of fun writing this book, for example, and I hope you have fun reading it. And if running a company is fun, running a conglomerate can be even more fun. All kinds of unexpected opportunities open up. When I bought Sheraton Hotels, we inherited a little company in Detroit that made auto parts. (I think Sheraton owned that company so it could enter a car in the Indianapolis 500.)

Well, we started adding units. We bought companies in the United States, Germany, England, and Italy that made brakes, brake pads, steering gears, lights, and other parts for cars. We combined them into a single entity, and today that auto-parts company has 30 percent of the world's nonskid-brake market and total revenues of more than $6 billion. And it started from almost nothing. That's what a conglomerate does.

This holds a lesson for little companies, too. In a word, diversify. I was up in New Hampshire not long ago. I have twelve thousand acres of woods up there. It's great hunting, and I make a little money selling timber. I didn't like the price the local sawmills were paying, so I built my own sawmill. It does very well. It's my conglomerate training. Whenever I see an opportunity to grow a company, I take it—and most of them make money.

Not far from my property in New Hampshire there was a company that once had the world's monopoly on the spindles used in sewing machines. Little wooden bobbins. The Japanese came along and made plastic bobbins. Overnight, the company went out of business. The buildings are still there—empty. A small company; a small story. Maybe it should have gone into lawn fertilizer.

Shoemaker, stick to your last? Baloney. Yet that axiom, in essence, is repeated so often that many people accept it as gospel.

Let me review a few other suspect commandments of the 1990s workplace. I would nominate each one for the baloney-of-the-month award.

- **BALONEY:** Networking is all-important to your career. In an age of corporate downsizing, you could well be out of your job tomorrow. If that happens, you'll need to call on a vast network of friends, associates, colleagues, and other resources to help you relaunch your career.

- **REALITY:** Maybe, if you lose your job, somebody you know will put you in touch with somebody else who just might steer you to an interview with somebody else for perhaps an uninspiring job at an uninspiring company. If you're into humiliation, this could work out for you. But I'd suggest something else: Go out and look for trouble. Go to places other people shun because the business has serious problems and might be going down the tubes. Look for businesses that were once successful and that still make promising products but that through inept management or unforeseen circumstances are struggling. That's a more risky course than signing up with a big, bureaucratic Fortune 500 company. But that's where the real opportunities are, too.

  Years ago, I talked to a company called Freeport Sulfur about a job. The problem was, they controlled a large part of the world's sulfur supply. A sort of shared monopoly. They were so profitable, they really didn't need anybody. I turned down their offer and went to Raytheon—a company that needed somebody—particularly, at that time, somebody like me.

- **BALONEY:** Managers should nurture workers and strive to make the workplace a caring environment.

- **REALITY:** Managers should inspire workers and help them strive to make the company a profitable place. That way, people will keep their jobs and get raises, bonuses, and other perks for working hard and showing initiative, and share in the spoils. What could be more caring than that? My goal at ITT was always to make the people around me successful. I guess you could call that a caring approach, but it also achieved my goals. You'll help them, but if everybody pitches in, there is something for everyone to share. You lead people a little—you push them a bit, and you're the catalyst. You hold people to high standards for their own good. Much better than holding their hands.

- **BALONEY:** Corporations should show "social responsibility." (I even read somewhere about the "synergy" between traditional management and high-minded idealism.)

- **REALITY:** While managers should be encouraged to get involved in local volunteer work, they should never allow themselves to divert their attention away from their core corporate responsibilities. I remember how the chairman of a Fortune 500 company used to go around the country making speeches about management. A worthy cause, but his prolonged absences from the job he was being paid to perform nearly ruined the company. But my theory is that the best community relations in the world, and the clearest expression of social responsibility, is to provide steady, well-paying jobs.

- **BALONEY:** A company's board of directors will always stand guard over its best interests.

- **REALITY:** While many of them do, all too frequently the directors are too subservient to the chief executive. Perhaps without realizing it, they lose their impartiality. And even if they don't, how alert will they be when things start going wrong? They might meet for two hours every month; but do they realize the limits of how much they can accomplish in that amount of time? Besides, there's little risk to them if management's decisions turn out to be greatly inadequate. They might even reward what will turn out to be lousy decisions with big bonuses.

  I once took part in a discussion that the accounting firm Touche Ross was broadcasting to its clients on the responsibilities of corporate boards. As we talked, it became clear that the biggest single weakness of the system was the difficulty boards had in getting at all the facts. By the time boards at troubled companies realized there was a crisis, it was often too late.

  Afterward, I asked a Touche partner why the firm didn't offer a service to bridge that gap. For a fee, it could offer to study a company's operations and identify problems that might otherwise escape the board's notice, I pointed out.

  After all, the board has to get most of its information from the CEO, who's often also the chairman of the board. And he may even think everything is just great. But a paid outside accountant with an assignment from the board to review and offer opinions would often pick up on a disaster in the making before it was too late.

  But the Touche Ross partner told me: We've been offering that service. But no board wants to buy it. As long as boards have a comfortable relationship with the CEOs, the question is never asked: Should we make an independent review?

Of course, if a CEO botches things badly enough, the board will be forced at some point to dump him for both their own and the shareholders' benefit. Better that they had taken the initiative early on to question him more rigorously. Sure, they'll risk upsetting the applecart, annoying their colleagues, and frustrating the CEO. But it's a risk worth taking.

It is interesting to note that since I had that conversation with the Touche partner, many big accounting firms have sprouted flourishing management-consulting businesses. It's progress. But even so, their studies are ordered by, and presented to, the CEO. Presumably, the board still only knows what they are told.

- **BALONEY:** The corporation is an ideal breeding ground for entrepreneurs.

- **REALITY:** Corporate refugees often do become entrepreneurs. But generally, corporate managers are a different type. The entrepreneur is a special breed: He is built to run his own show, be his own boss, take his own risks. A corporate manager, by contrast, depends on his corporation to supply all his needs, from office space and secretarial help to departments on product development, marketing, and the like, and of course, his paycheck. He is usually the furthest thing from an entrepreneur.

At one company I was with, we created a separate R & D subsidiary and told the people they could develop and market their own products as if they were the owners. But the whole thing backfired. What we did was to hive off our most intelligent people, and while they were very good at what they did, they were not prepared to go it on their own.

But just ask any entrepreneur whether the risks he runs are worth taking. You might as well ask basketball champion Michael Jordan whether it's worth trying for three-pointers from so far out. So what if the entrepreneur stumbles, or Michael Jordan misses? They'll try again. Entrepreneurs can't conceive of doing anything else; they are running their own show, and they're enjoying it.

- **BALONEY:** The customer is always right.

- **REALITY:** He's wrong as often as he's right. Only you never tell him he's wrong because it doesn't usually pay to.

- **BALONEY:** The information superhighway will draw the peoples of the world together into a common human family. In the words of one enthusiast: "E-mail will someday unite us all in a shared state of epistolary bliss."

- **REALITY:** The information superhighway will transform American business, no question about it. You can sit down at your PC, hook up to a phone line, and tap into an endless number of data banks out there. Sports nuts can scroll through baseball statistics going back to the caveman. You can also swap greetings with friends and join "bulletin boards" and exchange messages with strangers about the topic of your choice, from chess to fine dining. This huge, seamless web of electronic data is known as the Internet. It is bound to increase the productivity of the American economy, give us a competitive edge against our foreign trading partners, and maybe even raise our standard of living.

  But let's not get carried away. The information superhighway is a tool, perhaps as revolutionary an innovation as the printing press or the telephone, but a tool nonetheless. A lot of it will be a guy in New Jersey sitting in his room talking to a guy in Iceland about the weather. It will also open up a huge opportunity to waste your time. You ought to go back to the beginning of the television era and read some of the claims people made for that new technological wonder.

  Will the information superhighway make people wiser or happier? I doubt it. You might be able to introduce yourself to your future wife on the information superhighway, but you can't hold hands with her on it. You'll have to fall in love the old-fashioned way. And you'll have to learn all the important things the old-fashioned way, too. You won't gain the courage to take risks from an on-line service; that inspiration comes from the heart.

  And here's a business canon that I've saved for last.

- **BALONEY:** If your job is at all demanding, sooner or later, you will burn out.

- **REALITY:** If you love your job, you'll never burn out. I used to do some shooting. Today, I can close my eyes and see the colors of the forest where I hunted. I can see the pheasant I shot. And I can see the ocean waters and streams where I fished, and the fish I caught. Those memories come back in such vivid detail, it is as if the events were taking place before my eyes. And the reason is that I was so intensely interested in what I was doing. That's the key: being intensely interested in what you're doing. It may not keep you going forever, but it will come as close as is possible on this earth. As the seventeenth-century English philosopher Richard Cumberland said, "It is better to wear out than to rust out."

Maybe that's why I've so far lived to a ripe old age. And to think I was once a two-packs-a-day, ham-and-eggs, extra-sugar-in-the-coffee man. And my heaviest exercise was lugging suitcases full of company reports back and forth to Europe. Several hundred reports would hit my desk every month in those days. And I would read every one of them. I'd underline them in red ink and write notes in the columns.

Some people accuse me of being a workaholic. I plead guilty. It's an addiction I picked up during the depression. I remember once being out of work and living on bread and taffy for two weeks. At that time, you could buy a pound of taffy for nine cents and get a second pound for a penny. So I ate bread and taffy. It was the cheapest fuel I could find. I finally got a job selling books door-to-door. I carried sixty pounds of books around in a gladstone bag. Hard work, but it got me back on meat and potatoes. You try living on bread and sugar for two weeks. You'll sell books door-to-door, too, for a square meal. The work ethic thrives on a hungry stomach.

I have nothing against folks who play shuffleboard in their Florida retirement communities. It's just that I'd rather spend my time turning around troubled companies. Such as Gunther International up in Connecticut. It makes the best finishing equipment in the world. Gunther's machines can take tens of thousands of different documents, staple them together, fold them and insert various combinations into envelopes, seal the envelopes, stamp them, and spin them into ready-to-deliver mail bins in a few hours. And it will record exactly what is being sent to whom in a computer. We had 1994 sales of around $10 million while our big competitors, Bell & Howell and Pitney

Bowes, had sales in the billions of dollars. But we're growing. This is a lot more fun than shuffleboard.

Yet, before I came along, the company was about to go belly-up. Dozens of jobs would have been lost. Those jobs are now relatively secure. It's up to us. To the men and women who hold them, I'm not a workaholic. I'm just plain Harold, the guy who still underlines the company reports in red ink to keep the bottom line in the black.

After my first book, *Managing,* came out in 1984, I decided that someday I would have to write a second book. Anybody can write one book. You have to write at least two before you can call yourself an author.

You'll find some commonsense notions in this book—but no lists of rules for getting ahead, no collection of canons for achieving fortune and fame. There are too many management compendiums around. Maybe you've read *Seven Habits of Highly Successful People.* Or *Transforming the Organization,* with its "Four Rs" of reframing, restructuring, revitalization, and renewal.

Such formulas remind me of the nostrums of the old-time improvement societies for curing people's backaches and restoring their appetites, or the hopeful prescriptions for better health, satisfaction, reading pleasure, or whatever that you find today in magazine articles. God save us from such lists.

I've been observing the business world for seventy years, beginning as a page on the New York Stock Exchange in 1926 and ending—well, it hasn't ended yet. Just last week, I was rummaging through Gunther's sales literature. I came up with a few ways to improve it.

I've gained some insights into what makes the business world tick. I've acquired what passes for wisdom, I suppose, though not the sort you can capture in a slogan or a catalog of dos and don'ts. If I had to try to summarize my thinking in one sentence, I'd write something like: "Work hard, have fun, take risks, and when you fall flat on your face, as the adage goes, just pick yourself up, brush yourself off, and move on."

I've tried to pack as much horse sense as possible into this book as an antidote to the horse you-know-what that passes for wisdom in some books and business schools. Some of the thoughts I dwell on might not seem to have all that much to do with business. For example, you might wonder why I've been dwelling so much in this introductory chapter on having fun and why I even wrote a chapter on the topic.

The answer is that business is an integral part of our lives, and the attitudes you bring to your job determine how well you will perform at it. If you don't approach your work with the notion you're going to have some fun doing it, you're heading for a pretty dull existence and probably less success than someone who can joyfully rip through it and smile at the problems at the same time.

PROSPERING

IN THE WORKPLACE

Go Ahead, Jump!

It was a hot fall day in 1932, the nation was in the grip of a terrible economic disease called the Great Depression, and I was nervous as hell.

I had recently gotten a job selling classified ads in the suburbs for the *New York World Telegram*. I had no training in how to sell anything. But I was broke and hungry, and so I found myself pacing up and down the main street of a little town on Long Island, puffing Lucky Strikes and trying to screw up the courage to walk into a local real estate office and exhort the scowling figure within to invest a few bucks in the power of the press.

For a full fifteen minutes, I walked back and forth past his door. Finally, I made my move. Boldly, I strode inside and stood before him.

He looked up at me quizzically. His face hardened as he sized up my skinny twenty-two-year-old frame and my nervous smile. "Yeah?" he asked coldly.

"Ah, I was wondering, perhaps, if you might be interested in, that is, willing to consider, taking out some classified ads. . . ."

"No!" he barked, and turned back to his paperwork.

"Thank you, thank you," I said, truly grateful at this chance for escape. I stumbled out into the street, filled with a mixture of remorse and relief.

It was an inauspicious beginning, but it was a beginning. I had taken the first step that became a crucial habit to getting ahead in any undertaking in the future. I had put myself on the spot.

If I have learned anything in my eighty-seven years, it is: Put yourself on the spot. Then get yourself off it. It is the surest road to success, because it relies on self-motivation.

Put another way, I had discovered that one way to succeed is to force yourself into a situation where you *have* to succeed or fail. In this instance, I failed. But, if you keep putting yourself on the spot, you will become so determined not to fail that you will eventually succeed.

Taking such risks puts you in good company. Remember the American Revolution? "We mutually pledge to each other our Lives, our Fortunes and our Sacred Honor." Those were not idle words. The founders of this country were indeed risking their lives. They had no illusions: Were they to fail in their grand enterprise, they would be hanged.

They took the risk, and they won the greatest prize in the history of nations, the birth of the United States of America.

Courage is nothing more than taking a risk for a good cause. Taking a risk for a poor cause—greed, say, as in excessive gambling or ill-considered speculation—isn't courage; it's damned foolishness. True courage means facing odds with composure. Something inside you says: If I believe in it—and it is worthwhile—I can't walk away from it.

If you put yourself on the spot, you'll work your way off. In the process, you'll gain the self-confidence to put yourself on the spot for higher stakes the next time. And so on, until you reach your full ability. When I was working for the *World Telegram,* I soon stopped fleeing at the word "No." I made my first sale, then a bigger sale. Before long, I was selling display ads, and my commissions shot up from ten dollars a week to one hundred dollars, a princely sum in the depression.

In the end, no matter how inhospitable my prospective client was, I'd always find a chance to say, "I agree with you." Then I'd sit down and offer him a cigarette. And the real job of selling had just begun.

In the corporate world, one of the biggest risks you can take is to stand up to your boss. It's worth it if you're standing up for your rights. How you do it is important. Stay calm. Be firm. And don't get emotional.

During the war, I worked for American Can's wartime subsidiary, Amertorp. For a while, it was our nation's main manufacturer of aerial torpedoes. I was the chief accountant at Amertorp's two plants, one in Chicago and one in St. Louis, each of which employed about ten thousand people. It meant a heck of a lot of train travel. For most people, that was the only way to get around during the war years. Almost every week, I'd take the train to St. Louis to talk with people at the plant there, then hop another train to go to Washington to reassure the Bureau of Ordnance that everything was okay, or hear from them that everything wasn't okay, then take another train to American Can's New York headquarters to report to the senior executives, then grab another train back to Chicago. It got a little tiresome bouncing around on the top (i.e., cheaper) berth of the Pullman.

I was earning about eight thousand dollars at the time. When the time came for our annual raises, I got four hundred dollars, as I recall. I had been expecting much more than that; I had essentially built an accounting system from scratch. The fact is, I didn't need a raise at all; it was the principle of the thing. I couldn't fathom why Amertorp would award such a small increase. It must be the same feeling a cabdriver has when he is tipped a quarter for a ten-dollar fare.

So the next time I was in New York, I walked into the office of my boss, who was head of the company and also a vice president of the can company. And I said, "I really don't need this raise. If that's all you can do for me, I'd rather not accept it." He just looked at me funny. And I turned and left. The next day, I returned to the plant in

Chicago, and my supervisor rushed up and asked, "What the hell did you do in New York?"

"What do you mean, what did I do?" I replied.

"Miller is burning up. He wants to see you," he said. Mr. Miller was my direct boss at Amertorp.

So I went to see Miller. Same question. "What the hell did you do in New York?" I answered truthfully. "I turned down my raise. I thought it was so small, it just didn't make any sense."

Miller just gaped at me. Finally, he said: "The boss just called from New York. He said he had just talked to you. And on further thought he said he had decided to increase all our raises significantly."

Before you attempt a confrontation like the one I have just described, though, remember: It's a risk. Sure, I had put myself on the spot; but I could have been fired on the spot. I knew that, and was willing to suffer the consequences. If I didn't like my situation, I would leave. That's what I did, again and again.

And why would I take those risks? Why would I go to the boss and say, "If this is all you think I'm worth, I'd rather not take it?" I didn't do it out of false pride. I did it out of a sense of integrity. It was something I owed to myself.

They say one of the secrets of Thomas Edison's ultimate success was his willingness to endure failure after failure to get where he was going. He bounced right back; he thought of his setbacks and his flopped experiments as opportunities to learn.

Ultimately, I left American Can. I had been promised a job "of significance" at the parent company after the war. But when I got there, the title they gave me was "expense clerk"—my reward for shepherding the finances and accounting of a major defense operation during the war. I went in to see the controller. I said, "I have been practically running the accounting of two torpedo plants, and this is my assignment?" Don't worry, he said, we'll fix everything—later. You've heard that word before, no doubt. It's poison.

After about three months, I mailed out a huge stack of résumés and got three jobs and took one at Bell & Howell. But never take foolish risks. If you come to a ten-foot-wide canyon, you'd better be pretty sure you can jump eleven feet, or else take the long path around.

The trapeze artist likes to have a net under him—just in case. The net makes him fearless. He performs brilliantly. At ITT, we liked to keep a net under our people. If a division chief stumbled, for example, our rigorous system for scrutinizing all operations would pick up the early warning signals and we would send in troubleshooters—not to wrest control from him but to help him set things aright. We also hired in-house consultants to keep tabs on each division and offer the boss advice for improving performance. Far from intimidating our managers, such controls gave them courage to take risks.

Risk-benefit analysis is usually easy. If it's a toss-up, I would be inclined to take the risk and rely on myself to achieve the benefit. But avoid foolish risks. If somebody offers you $10 million to go over Niagara Falls in a barrel, you'll probably need three seconds or less to estimate the downside, and then tell him what he can do with the $10 million.

However, if the risk is worth taking . . . *take it!*

Life itself is a risk, and one worth taking. Whole tomes have been written on the meaning of existence. No one has solved the riddle to the satisfaction of the general population, with the possible exception of the sage who announced, ''There's no such thing as a free lunch.''

Compared with getting up in the morning, all other risks are pretty trivial. And once you get up, almost everything you do holds some risk. As an anonymous poet wrote:

To laugh is to risk appearing the fool.
To weep is to risk appearing sentimental.
To reach out to another is to risk involvement.
To expose feelings is to risk exposing your true self.
To place your ideas, your dreams before the crowd is to risk
    their loss.
To love is to risk not being loved in return.
To hope is to risk despair.
To try is to risk failure.

Or, as Roberto Goizueta, Coca-Cola's CEO, put it, ''You can stumble only if you're moving.''

One thing you can be sure of: You will spend your life weighing risks, concentrating on the important ones, backing off from the foolish ones, seizing the promising ones, and accepting the dangerous but unavoidable ones with grace.

Taking risks enables you to escape the Peter Principle. That is the management ''law'' expounded by Laurence J. Peter and his coauthor, Raymond Hull, that says that everybody rises in an organization to his or her level of incompetence. Then they flail around, dependent on their secretaries and other underlings to make things work. "The cream rises until it sours," Mr. Peter wrote in his 1969 best-seller. "Every bureaucracy is inevitably made up entirely of people inadequate to their tasks."

But if you keep taking risks, you'll never reach your level of incompetence because you'll constantly be making yourself more competent. The Peter Principle doesn't make allowances for this human capacity for self-improvement. It doesn't understand how we can keep climbing higher and higher. Our willingness to take risks lets us do it. The air can get pretty thin, but our lungs will adjust.

Never give up. Keep slugging away. If Laurence J. Peter had given up, we never would have heard about the Peter Principle. He sent the manuscript to McGraw-Hill in 1964 and got a rejection notice that said: "I can foresee no commercial possibilities for such a book and consequently can offer no encouragement." He kept sending the manuscript out, and accumulated thirty more rejection slips. Finally, Hearst Trade Books paid him $2,500 for it and made an initial run of 10,000 copies. It ultimately sold more than 8 million.

It's always a risk to take a new job. It was certainly a risk for me to take a job with Bell & Howell, a company headed by Joe McNab in Chicago. He was tough. But once I accepted the risk and signed on as controller in 1946, I did what was needed to minimize the risk.

Mr. McNab told me to report to work first thing Monday. Sure, I said. But there was no way I was going to walk in cold. I got permission to go into the office over the weekend, and I sat at my desk from early Friday evening to late Sunday night, going through all the files.

Then, on Monday morning, I went in prepared.

One of the first things I noticed was that Bell & Howell was always late in getting its invoices out. I changed that. Mr. McNab only grunted.

One day he called me into his office. He was frustrated because the Office of Price Administration, which enforced price controls in the first years after the war, wouldn't let us raise prices on one of his new cameras.

"I need that price increase," he gruffly informed me. "Make it happen." The law only permitted price increases to cover some higher labor or materials costs, not overhead. We didn't qualify under that—but Mr. McNab's message was clear.

I swallowed hard. "Mr. McNab, I can't do that," I said.

I remember the fury he went into: I was to do what I was told! Who the hell did I think I was? The damned bureaucrats in Washington had no business dictating to the private sector. Nobody else was paying any attention to the Office of Price Administration, anyway, and besides, everybody knew the controls would be phased out soon.

I held my ground. I explained that I was a certified public accountant, and my ethical standards wouldn't let me fiddle with the figures. I truly didn't care whether my attitude made him mad. I had a counterproposal: I would go to Washington and argue with the bureaucracy and see what I could do for a legitimate price increase. Mr. McNab grudgingly agreed.

I spent several days at the Office of Price Administration, poring over documents with a government official. He gave me a fair hearing and was so impressed with the case I made that he authorized a price increase not just for one camera, but for the entire line.

I promptly called Mr. McNab from my hotel and told him he got his increase. "Except it's bigger than you asked for," I said. "And it's not just on one camera. It's on all of them."

Silence. Then an acknowledgment of my great triumph:

"Umph." That was all he said. Then he hung up. But after that, he treated me well, and when he found out he was dying, he wrote a sort of political testament saying that a fellow executive, Charles Percy, the future U.S. senator, should succeed him as president and that I, specifically, should be retained as controller.

That was not to be the last time I had to stand up for what I believed in, even if it meant putting my job on the line.

I left Bell & Howell after five years and went to Jones & Laughlin, the steel company. I would find myself in a similar situation there. The president was exasperated at the pay demands the internal railroad union was making in the mills. He refused to negotiate. The union only had a relatively small membership among the some thirty thousand mill employees, but they moved all the freight traffic within the mills. (These old integrated steel mills were each a couple of miles long, and they couldn't function without rail cars to move the heavy materials and finished products around.) Well, the union called a strike, but the boss ignored it and went to his summer home on Cape

Cod for a long weekend. Maybe he just assumed the strikers would give in.

At Jones & Laughlin, I had been promoted to controller. My former boss there was now in charge of the mills and was quite disturbed by this turn of events. "If we don't settle by early next week, we'll lose a month of canceled sales," he said to me. Yet he didn't want to call the boss, because he had a reputation for having a short temper.

I told him: "I have nothing to do with it." But he pointed out that the work stoppage could result in a heavy financial loss to the company. And I concluded it was my duty as controller to impress on the president the seriousness of the situation. In theory, he should have known, but he might have been unfamiliar with the delivery deadlines.

So I called him. He wasn't too happy to hear from me. But I explained my concerns.

He got a little huffy. "I know all that, of course," he said. But to my great relief, he got on the train the next morning and came back to Pittsburgh. The dispute was settled in about ten minutes. The month's sales were saved.

A week later, the president called me into his office. With him was our VP of sales. After a bit of inconsequential chitchat, he steered the conversation to the recent strike. "I was planning to come back and settle the damn thing anyway, right?" he asked, turning to the VP of sales. "Right," came the reply.

Well, I was glad I had called him. I could have ducked the issue with the argument it wasn't my job to call the boss at home. But I wouldn't have been able to respect myself if I had taken that way out.

I took the risk. The stakes were high to the company. There's an old saying: I seen my risk and I done it. As I think back, I had no other choice.

You're not going to get ahead without taking risks. And a risk is worth taking *if* the payoff is something you believe in and *if* you can live with the consequences of losing. I always followed the principle: I will take big risks for big stakes but not for little stakes.

After I left Jones & Laughlin, I spent three years at Raytheon, the big defense company in the Boston area, as executive vice president. I now had real authority—and plenty of self-confidence.

Charlie Adams ran the place. He had surrounded himself with "special assistants." There was a college professor who claimed to be a psychologist and went around asking people probing personal questions. He'd go back and tell his boss everything. Then there was a retired navy captain with a good heart but a pompous manner, and a fellow named Ernie who was bright enough but never seemed to do anything.

Anyway, one day I completed some very complicated negotiations with the navy on some troublesome contract performance. When I got back I found a note on my desk from Charlie asking me to see him. So I went to him and he proceeded to tell me what "I should have done." I recognized Ernie's voice in the admonition—and Ernie's lack of sound judgment in the advice.

So I just said, "Charlie, I don't ever want to argue with Ernie through you again." I walked out and took the weekend off. I felt there are some lines you have to cross to get your job done right.

Nor was I shy about asking blunt questions if I felt they were warranted. I believed I had a great future at Raytheon. After all, I had overhauled the company, closing a money-losing Chicago plant, instituting modern financial controls, and reorganizing management procedures. While I was doing all that, the stock shot up to seventy dollars from twenty. I was also handling the analysts and Wall Street.

But another one of Charlie's assistants started spreading the word that Geneen would never get the top job. So I went to see Charlie—and I didn't beat around the bush.

"Charlie," I said, "I just want to know, when you're ready to retire, if you're considering me as your successor."

His answer was abrupt and short—"I never make a commitment."

To which I responded with equal simplicity: "Fine. Thank you."

And I immediately began looking around for something else.

Was taking the top job at ITT a big risk? You bet it was! What did I know about running a multinational? But I could never have said no. I would have spent the next decade asking myself: "Why didn't you take it?"

I didn't get a whole lot of help from my predecessor at ITT, Edmond H. Leavey, a military general. After a couple of years on the job as a sort of caretaker CEO, he was due to retire.

Then, after taking more than a year to meet the board's request that he find a successor, he reported back that the ideal candidate was . . . himself. But the board had other ideas.

After I got the job, I went to see General Leavey. Our meeting was cordial and brief. He shook my hand warmly, introduced me to the other officers, wished me well, gave me his telephone number and the key to his office, and left forever. I don't remember ever seeing him again.

But I was finally on my own. ITT was now my responsibility. I guess you could say this was the challenge I had been moving toward since I had gone to work way back as a page on the stock exchange at the age of sixteen. And all of the work I had done, all of the jobs I had held, all of the risks I had taken, all of the efforts I had made were now on the line.

I had, incidentally, followed through on my cardinal rule: Go to where the trouble is, and they'll give you responsibility. ITT had incredible problems. I'm not going to kid myself; their desperation to solve them was the reason they hired me. And because it was so sprawled out all over the world, I'm not sure anyone grasped their seriousness. ITT had huge assets overseas—and nobody really knew more than the barest details about them.

Over the next eighteen years, I would put myself on the spot, and work my way off it, time and time again. One of the first things I did was to announce my intention of doubling profits within five years. So I was on the spot for five years with Wall Street! But I accomplished my goal.

Sosthenes Behn, the founder, had put together a great company, with more than $750 million in sales, and interests on all five continents. He had manufacturing plants in places as far-flung as Buenos Aires, Sydney, Johannesburg, Tokyo, and practically every major city in Western Europe.

But it was also a troubled company. In 1959, the ITT empire had only recently recovered many of the assets that it had lost in the war, and it still bore many of the problems that it had inherited from that conflict.

Some of the management might have thought they were going to be the next president and had suddenly seen their plans thwarted. One guy was a real agent provocateur who went around telling everybody why they should be dissatisfied. I got rid of him.

One guy who did support me 100 percent was Henri Busignies, a brilliant scientist that Behn had brought over from ITT's French lab. Few people have heard of Busignies, but he played a pivotal role in winning the war against Hitler. He invented the HUFFDUFF, shorthand for high-frequency direction finders, which used radio transmissions to pinpoint a submarine's location.

The HUFFDUFF shattered the one real threat the Nazis posed to Allied victory: the U-boats that would lie hidden for days beneath the shipping lanes and then ambush our support convoys. They inflicted horrific losses in the early days. Henri's HUFFDUFF was a radical new technology, capable of pinpointing the location of the subs when they surfaced to get air or to communicate. It all but obliterated the U-boat menace. After the war, I remember reading a book by a German admiral in which he stated that the HUFFDUFF's destruction of the U-boats was probably the turning point of the war.

That is what the unsung hero Henri Busignies contributed to Western civilization. I met him when he came to my office unannounced to tell me that he would have none of these early "games" and that I had his full support, for the simple reason that the company needed it. To me, he personifies the concept of "the risk worth taking." Unassuming, ordinary even, he commanded the heights of human endeavor.

Another Henry, who spelled his name the Anglo-Saxon way, was an indispensable guide and business interpreter for me in this period: Henry "Hank" Scudder. Hank was in charge of European operations and, though an American, had taken up English ways from his long sojourn overseas. I remember in particular the black umbrella that he carried everywhere—he called it a "bumbershoot"—and that he used for everything from a face-off weapon to a means of pointing out objects of interest.

After Henri and Henry, most of top management soon fell in line and I set out to learn more in a few months than you ordinarily could learn in a few years. In the 1980s, everybody was trying to "leverage" money. Well, as my experience in the 1950s showed, it is amazing how much leverage you can get from old-fashioned *hard work.*

First, I pored over all the statements, books, and reports that I could find in the home office. Then I spent three or four months traveling around the world or the ITT empire meeting the managements of the different companies. Then I started running it.

Where did I get my self-confidence? Experience. I had faced tough times before, at Bell & Howell, at Jones & Laughlin, at Raytheon, on that street in front of the real estate office on Long Island as little more than a kid in 1932. I had taken risks. I had gone where the trouble was. I had done my homework, and worked hard.

So I had the feeling: I've done this before. I can do it. I had put myself on the spot so many times that getting myself off it was second nature.

Does luck play a part in your career? It always plays a part—but you have to take the risks necessary to make luck happen. Luck in business is really talent plus hard work multiplied by your willingness to take a risk.

As golfer Lee Trevino was fond of saying, "The more I practice, the luckier I get." Baseball executive Branch Rickey used to say that luck was the "residue of design."

To be sure, for some people, the risk isn't worth taking. If somebody is forty-eight years old and has a wife and three kids and a good salary with a profit-sharing plan and a cottage by the shore, he won't want to take any chances that could jeopardize his good life.

There are lots of people like that. A former corporate executive named G. J. Meyer, who got "downsized" along with hundreds of thousands of other middle managers in the early nineties, put it this way in a book he wrote in 1995 entitled *Executive Blues:*

"I envy people who took fewer chances than I did and are now in the safe if charmless harbors that I set sail from years ago: the post office, the Navy, reporting jobs at daily papers. I also envy people who took more chances than I did and broke free of salaries and corporations and bull——. *I spend a lot of time wondering where I might be today if I had taken more chances.*" (Italics mine.)

People with a low tolerance for risk could specialize in fields where there will always be demand. Every company has to have accountants. Every company has to have a personnel director. Every company has to have salespeople. But even in those jobs, middle age may be the end of the road.

Taking a reasonable risk isn't just the way to get ahead in business. It's the formula for enjoying life. Victor Herbert wrote a song about "wonderful, wonderful Toyland" that makes the point you can't go back to your childhood, that you must face the harsh world alone. True enough; still, you can recapture some of the warmth of childhood, I believe, if you will take the risk of trusting other people.

So, go ahead: Take the risk. Put yourself on the spot. Today, I'm still putting myself on the spot. I have, for example, invested time, money, and reputation in a little company in Connecticut with a great product but a lot of problems. It employs about 140 people. Sometimes, when I fly up to the little town where it is located for a day of intensive discussions with the managers, and I read through all the latest reports, I feel that little quiver of concern that stalled me in front of the real estate office on Long Island so many years ago. A question starts to form: Is it worth it?

And then I say to myself, you're damned right, it is. This is what you do, Harold. You take charge. You fix things. You take risks, based on mutual trust between you and your employees. There is no guarantee you'll succeed, either. After all, you're now eighty-seven years old. But, what the hell, it's a risk worth taking.

2

The Theory of
the Conglomerate

Risk taking was hardly in my bones. At age sixteen, when most boys dream of becoming sports heroes or soldiers of fortune, I decided that I wanted to be an accountant.

"An accountant?" Arthur Wellington Taylor, the dean of New York University, where I was taking night classes, was flabbergasted. "That's pretty prosaic. Are you sure?"

"Positive," I replied. "It's solid."

I had reasons for seeking a steady livelihood: I had seen my er make and lose three fortunes. They would call him an entre- ur today. But that pace was tough on my mother. She was a courageous woman who got us kids through good schools and out into the world. As a result of her encouragement, I graduated two years early from a private boarding school. I was on my own now; and while 1926 was later to be called one of the years of "wonderful nonsense" that preceded the depression, my own circumstances had a wonderfully sobering effect on me.

As it turned out, accounting was just my first stop. Try as I might to take refuge in a safe profession, I ended up pursuing bigger dreams: taking on ever-bigger roles, running ever-bigger companies, and finally, building one of the biggest conglomerates ever, the International Telephone & Telegraph Company, later renamed simply ITT Corporation.

When I took over ITT in 1959, I recognized quickly its essential problem: 85 percent of our stockholders were in the United States and 90 percent of our assets were abroad, a lot of them in South America, where political instability made their future precarious. In fact, our American holdings were limited to a defense company and a small telephone-supply business.

Do you remember the old switchboards that looked like snakes climbing a wall? You've probably seen them in pictures. The operator made the connection by pulling out a rubber cord with a jack on it and poking it into a hole. That's what ITT made—and it was already dated. I can't recall any other product that amounted to anything.

Suddenly, I was in charge of this. And I discovered that around the world were strewn the pieces of the empire created by the legendary Colonel Sosthenes Behn. In South America, we owned eight operating telephone companies, each with its own telephone-equipment manufacturing subsidiary; telephone lines and wireless communications for a dozen countries, including all of the interior communications of Brazil; and several factories that manufactured telephone cable and television sets.

We also had telephone-equipment manufacturing operations all over Western Europe and in Australia, Japan, and South Africa. It was a much bigger company than Wall Street realized.

While it may have been an empire, nobody was really running it. I want you to get the picture: The European companies numbered close to fifty, yet they had no central headquarters. Their one contact with the parent company was an Anglicized American by the name of Hank Scudder, a one-man gang who spent most of his time traveling around Europe, Australia, and South Africa. His modus operandi was to invite executives from two or three ITT companies to get together in a hotel room to mull over ways they could build their markets, carry out development, and send their money into headquarters.

Imagine it. Three or four guys in an Antwerp hotel room asking: "When do we have our new telephone system? Who gets to sell our products in which export markets? Whose R and D developments will be adopted? And what, if anything, does New York expect us to do?" They are all running their own companies as they see fit, inventing their own strategies and jealously guarding their secrets.

Hank would write reports on those discussions, and require the subsidiaries to send him earnings results, but that was it. The ITT big shots in New York would travel to Europe once in a while, but they had no wish to be encumbered by gritty details of what ITT was doing there, much less in Latin America or places like Japan and the Philippines.

The war was still fresh in everybody's mind. The French were jealous of the Germans. The Germans were jealous of the French and the British. The Belgians were mad at all of them. The Italians kept their own counsel. Twenty European nationalities—and twenty posturings. And that's not even considering the South Africans, the Australians, the New Zealanders, the Latin Americans, and the Filipinos. It was quite a potpourri.

And everybody was reluctant to share research with one another. So here's a company of 136,000 people without any centralized supervision. This was the discord I inherited. Somehow, I had to join together these disparate elements into a working whole. That task—creating harmony from diversity—defines the mission of building a conglomerate.

We installed our new European headquarters in Belgium, a tiny country that was the most neutral meeting ground for former adversaries. For the same reason, NATO and the Common Market set up shop there. Brussels, the capital, is picturesque but dull. It has some of the finest restaurants in the world, but aside from eating and enjoying the splendor of the Grand' Place with its gold-scrolled facades, about all you can do there is work. And that's what we did.

After an early look around, I put the rationale for a conglomerate on a piece of paper to show our board of directors, and our course was set. It was a simple chart of our worldwide interests, but it starkly illustrated the imbalance between our U.S. and foreign holdings.

I reminded the directors of the vulnerability of our Latin American operations to political and economic instability. As for this country, I argued that the defense industry made an insufficient anchor for a multinational of our size and potential. It was too unpredictable, I said; you had to bid on new contracts every time, and you had to keep your R & D moving ahead of the state of the art just to stay in the competition. And even after you won a contract, the Feds would come in and cost-audit you and hold you to a low level of profit for the risk incurred.

Then I listed the businesses in the United States that we should try to get into. I remember detailing the advantages of owning an electric-utility company: They are guaranteed a return by the state boards that regulate them; the risk is exceedingly low; the financing is easy; the earnings growth is steady and the potential for growth is great. I also recommended the acquisition of a North American telephone company.

After all this, I proposed a strategy for growth: Reduce our risk in South America and use the earnings of our telephone companies in Europe to build up our U.S. operations, buying growth companies in a variety of fields to diversify our risk and to meet the concerns of the Justice Department's antitrust authorities.

That meant building a conglomerate. Not a holding company, but a real, integrated conglomerate, capable of growing by seizing opportunities. And that's what we did. We built an organization around functions, not products. We formed a group of very savvy people to make acquisitions. At the peak of our expansion we were buying an average of a company a week. In all, we bought more than three hundred companies, including Sheraton Hotels, Continental Baking, Avis Rent-a-Car, and Hartford Insurance.

All this buying represented a departure from ITT's traditional areas of expertise. What the hell did we know about the automotive industry? Nothing—except that it was big and bound to grow bigger. What did we know about hotels? Nothing—except that they would give us valuable visibility in the countries where we sold equipment. What did we know about the loan business? Nothing—except that it was historically a big moneymaker and didn't require a rocket scientist to run. One of the biggest loan companies in the United States at the time had been started by a Chicago trolley motorman lending money to fellow workers.

So we followed our instincts and we became a conglomerate.

As that happened, the competitive advantages of the conglomerate over the traditional corporation became increasingly obvious.

An ordinary corporation is more vulnerable to the vagaries of the marketplace and the dislocations of the economy. Say you're stuck in one field, such as steel. How are you going to grow? You have to try to steal market share from your competitors. That's a costly proposition; nobody gives up market share without a fight. Even a company on its last legs will fight like crazy and ruin the market for everybody. In sharp contrast, a conglomerate has unlimited opportunities. Nobody says, "We can't do that. It's outside our field of expertise." If necessary, you recruit or grow the expertise.

ITT became a dynamic company, ever changing, full of possibilities and surprises. We were into lipstick, garden tools, pumps, hotels, telephone equipment, finance, foods, vending machines, fire equipment, paper pulp and timber, large-scale underseas power and telephone cable, signaling equipment for railroads, Virginia smoked hams, pneumatic controls, boiler companies in Mexico, parking lots all over the United States, oil production and coal mining, publishing (including the *Who's Who* reference guide), a chain of restaurants in Chicago, rivets, Scott's grass seed and fertilizer, rayon pulp—you name it, the chances were that we either made it, marketed it, or managed it. One thing led to another. After we bought our brake company, we acquired makers of brake pads and other automobile accessories and merged them into it. Today, it racks up around $6 billion in sales annually.

Now compare this conglomerate to a company that manufactures nothing but safety pins. If it makes 100 billion safety pins this year, about all it can aspire to is to make 120 billion safety pins next year.

I spent five years in the Jones & Laughlin steel company in the early 1950s. I learned one thing: When steel is up, it's up. When it's down, it's down. And there's not a damn thing you can do about it. (Even one-product companies can prosper under the right leadership, of course. Look at Exxon Corporation: a giant company in a formerly depressed industry, yet its stock has beaten the overall market over the past decade.)

Even at Jones & Laughlin, my conglomerateur's instincts were at work. I noticed that the company's twin blast furnaces on the Monongahela River in Pittsburgh and at the Aliquippa Mill on the Ohio River five miles away disgorged enormous amounts of coal tar, which is used in making dyes, plastics, medicines, and paints. I thought: Why not refine it and make a range of new products? Even though I was the controller, not the marketing specialist, I wrote a detailed proposal for such an undertaking.

But Jones & Laughlin would have none of it. The steel industry in those days was run by macho types who lived and breathed steel and scorned the idea of moving into new areas. My project was killed. I believed that if it had been adopted, the company would have made millions—and, more important, discovered the possibilities for growth in other markets. Instead, it ended up with outmoded steel plants. Progress isn't something you can turn down.

The secret of the conglomerate is simple: It's a network of resources that you can use where you need them. The most important resource is human—managers trained to solve problems. In some areas, you may have to hold the line because the market isn't with you. In others, you can push ahead because the market is hot.

It is not at all the same thing as a holding company, which owns stakes in a broad variety of companies. A holding company is a passive investment vehicle. An ''operating conglomerate'' is a centrally managed company that gets deep into each of its operations. It allows a high degree of autonomy to the individual groups—but always subject to review and discipline from the top. The advantages of a conglomerate are great:

- OPPORTUNITY. A conglomerate lets you choose your field of competition. You aren't limited to buying just automotive parts companies, or food companies. You can buy into any industry and any company, anywhere, as long as it has a growing market and makes a good product—or one that you can improve.

- RISK MANAGEMENT. While I believe in taking risks, I also believe in making *smart* risks, and managing them closely. Conglomerates minimize the risks by spreading them, just as insurance companies do. We didn't just grab companies willy-nilly. There was a strategic plan. We always bought into industries that had above-average potential for growth and profitability. Beyond that core principal, we sought to balance our foreign and domestic earnings and to spread these among industrial, technical, and consumer products. A colleague once chided me: ''You worry about a lot of things that never happen.'' I replied:

"Did you ever stop to think that maybe that's why they *don't* happen?"

- **VERSATILITY.** Think of a conglomerate as a consulting firm that owns a bunch of companies. Company A knows how to make lightbulbs. Company B knows how to manage hotels. Company C knows how to sell insurance. Each has its own market and problems: Perhaps A's management doesn't know how to market its bulbs; B's management doesn't understand basic accounting; and C's management doesn't know how to structure its executive compensation packages to recruit and keep top talent. The conglomerate can transfer talent and resources from one unit to another, hire outside experts and form special groups with technical and marketing expertise to intervene in troubled divisions. In other words, the conglomerate's component parts can draw on the managerial resources of a huge corporation while exhibiting a nimbleness and innovativeness that are more characteristic of a small business.

- **SECURITY.** The nature of a conglomerate tends to protect it against two of corporate America's most unwelcome intruders: the takeover predator with his money and the U.S. Justice Department's antitrust division with its minions. The more acquisitions you make, the bigger you get, and the harder it is for another company to come after you. And, yet, being so diversified, you rarely if ever dominate a single industry and thus open yourself up for antitrust scrutiny.

No other form of corporate organization can beat the conglomerate for seizing growth opportunities. A conglomerate can buy any promising business—whether it's a bug-spray maker or a software designer—that has a salable product and a worthwhile market. (Ideally, it also will have operating costs and practices that can be improved on by you.) Its strong suit is *management,* which enables it to restructure an acquisition to increase its market and make it run more efficiently.

Forget the modern-day management mantra "Small is beautiful." For a conglomerate, big can be better, but *growing* both bigger and better is the key. Now we come to the heart of the matter. To run a conglomerate, you have to work hard and strive for continued growth. A lot of people over the years have put so-called conglomerates together, but they just added up the results and published them under a single name. I doubt if anybody else *managed* a conglomerate the way we did.

Management is the key. Competition isn't primarily between products or services or markets. It is essentially a contest between managements. And our management functioned more effectively than just about any other for one simple reason: We sat down and thrashed out our problems with a constancy and a rigor that nobody else tried to match.

Our top managers held one marathon meeting each month in Brussels and one in New York. We flew to Europe on two planes, a commercial aircraft and the company jet, so that if one went down we'd still have half our managers to run the show. The daily sessions ran from 9 A.M. to 11 P.M. or later. About 150 people would sit around a giant table, and each one would have a microphone in front of him. The table in New York was so huge that the city fire department ordered us to cut it into four parts, to create fire lanes.

You could hardly see through the haze of the cigarette smoke. Our dinner was a twenty-minute sandwich break. Everybody spoke openly. Anybody could question me or correct me. Where do you find that in corporate America today? Nowhere.

As we discussed each company, we'd flash its performance versus the division chief's projections up on a huge screen in the middle of the room. The goal was to improve by at least 10 percent each quarter over a year earlier. And all this was taking place while we were acquiring one company after another. All in all, we increased both earnings and revenues by about twentyfold in eighteen years, despite the oil shocks and recessions of the 1970s.

The chief executive of every division wrote his own report every month—and sent it to me and to every other division head. That's a lot of paper. I'd carry these reports around with me, in big tan suitcases. I read them all and annotated them and dog-eared the corners down. I still have twenty of those suitcases in my office, piled up against a wall, only now they are packed with material from the last two decades of my life as an entrepreneur.

A lot has been written about those meetings. One scribe recently characterized them as a "self-righteously bureaucratic style of management" where I "sweated" my managers. I also, by this account, enforced a dress code of "gray suits, white shirts, black ties and laced shoes." Baloney! The only dress code I enforced was to cover your butt with a strong performance. And let me just say one thing: It was because of those meetings that we built ITT from a $765 million company to a $28 billion company in eighteen years.

Underneath all the talk and number crunching something more important was going on: We were building trust in one another and learning how to put personal interests aside in order to reach a common goal. That's what really made it work. Contrary to the impressions of people who were not there, there was never any meanness in the proceedings, just a search for the facts. If somebody was missing his targets, we never got mad, or deprived him of his bonus. We'd say: "Look, you're working hard. But if you're not succeeding, we have a whole consulting group here to help." They had to learn to accept that help.

Those meetings were actually fun. Yes, *fun*. In the years since, I've gotten many letters from former ITT executives telling me those were the greatest years of their lives.

I came up with another management innovation that did wonders for our productivity: the product-line manager. It was actually a simple idea, like the wheel. And, like the wheel, it helped us roll ahead of our adversaries.

It worked like this: We'd hire a successful executive or consultant in the industry of a company we were acquiring and tell him, Find out what the competition is doing, then consult with the division chief and decide whether we need to do it, too.

Product-line managers were part of my passion for cross-checking. They would tell the division chiefs: Here's how you can do it better. The division chiefs didn't have to follow their advice; they just had to listen to it. The product-line managers could always appeal to senior management if they felt strongly about something, but they could never impose a decision.

Let me let you in on a little secret: Half the companies in the country today are conglomerates and don't even know it. Once you diversify, just a little bit, you're taking your first step toward conglomeration. If you continue along that path, you ultimately will have to hire that industry insider to independently monitor your acquisitions.

Conglomerates seem to be making a comeback, even if the name is rarely invoked anymore. Look at H. Wayne Huizenga's Republic Industries Inc. In little more than a year after he took over Republic in August 1995, it acquired nineteen companies, including Alamo Rent-a-Car, adding to its main business lines of burglar alarms and waste disposal.

Wayne, where's the synergy? Or what about HFS Inc.? It's been on a buying spree lately that has taken it into corporate relocation, mortgage brokering, fleet-vehicle management, and hotel franchising.

I return to an earlier proposition. Anybody can run a conglomerate if he or she puts together the right team. I used to worry about how we'd get to $2 billion from $1 billion, then how we'd get to $5 billion, then $10 billion, then $15 billion. It all evolved because we set up controls to let other people do it. In fact, once I had my management in place, I almost couldn't fail. I had too many smart people telling me what to do. It worked.

A comparison of the conglomerate with Warren Buffett, America's most successful investor, might be instructive. Warren Buffett doesn't have overhead of his own; he expects the companies he invests in to perform well. In other words, he buys into successful companies with successful managements. He doesn't involve himself in their day-to-day operations. His company, Berkshire Hathaway, is like a mutual fund. It diversifies its risk—and gets out of a bad investment by picking up the phone and selling.

You can't follow that policy with a conglomerate. Its job is to own *and operate* companies—ideally, through its strong, centralized management, to turn sows' ears into silk purses. A conglomerate couldn't buy the companies Mr. Buffett buys; it would cost a fortune. What it does instead is to create value by acquiring companies with good growth potential and then turn them around with superior management.

Today, when companies announce acquisitions or mergers, they're always talking about "synergies" and "the right fit" between similar companies, meaning, I guess, that their strengths and weaknesses complement each other.

The merger mania of the 1980s was mostly aimed at making a lot of people rich. It didn't do much to help the economy and it disrupted the lives of millions of common people. The mergers were financial transactions in which the shareholders and officers of one company made a fast buck by combining with a second. They were stock-market promotions, not management integration.

The current merger mania is supposedly different; companies are fusing to take advantage of their supposed synergies and to increase market share through acquisition rather than growth. In 1995, the dollar value of all the mergers was the biggest in history, and included Chase Manhattan Bank pairing with Chemical, Disney with Capital Cities/ABC, and Time Warner with Turner. I'm not a big fan of this round, either.

The sheer size of the combined balance sheets seems to evoke a feeling of confidence, usually followed by a litany of ingenious explanations detailing how this particular merger was an historic masterstroke that will guarantee a prosperous future forevermore.

The stock market may even reflect paper improvement. But it generally doesn't reflect improved long-term earnings growth—specifically, as measured per share. One would have to conclude that most combinations and their projected "synergistic" gains probably don't outlast the first annual meeting. But by then, everybody has forgotten. In short, there are damn few worthwhile combinations.

I note bank after bank cannibalizing the remaining banks and pointing with pride to the size of their accumulated capitalization and surpluses. This presumably boosts the confidence of their depositors and borrowers. It may be the result of an oversupply of banking outlets. It will surely result in a reduction in the number of employees. But it is doubtful that it will render more efficiency to the banking industry. There may be expense savings, but savings aren't growth.

It is suggested that takeover bids are more friendly these days. If so, it's probably because it has been found to be more economical to pay up front than to argue. But under no circumstances does this new congeniality add to earnings.

There's also the theory on the part of some analysts, particularly those who have taken positions, that today's mergers are more about building companies than breaking them up, more about making America competitive than making money. Somehow, I'd question this Pollyanna perspective. The size of the chief executive's salary and bonus remains one of the most compelling forces behind mergers. The bigger the company, after all, the greater the opportunity for increasing his compensation package.

Building companies, not breaking them up? Fine—but the focus should be on building them in a way that assures increased profits. Too often, that aspect is poorly considered. Putting American competitiveness ahead of making money? Even the merged companies' merged PR departments wouldn't try to foist that one on us.

Please don't apply the term "merger mania" to what we did at ITT. There was nothing manic about our program. It was steady and consistent. It had a single purpose: to supply superior management to rather ordinary companies that we picked up. The real growth wasn't just the addition of a new balance sheet to ours; it was the revitalization of a weakened company.

But a word of warning: I really believe that nobody could have accomplished what we did at ITT without a work ethic not to be believed. Honest, record-breaking performance, and the pride and carefully equated rewards that went with it. Please notice that the performance preceded the rewards, a factor greatly overlooked in many of our more recent tie-togethers.

At ITT, we were *not* looking for synergies. We did *not* spend time deciding whether a lightbulb company would make a good "fit." A lightbulb company is a lightbulb company, and you should run it as a lightbulb company.

We asked two simple questions: First, is the market worth going after? And second, with our management and technological resources, can we improve the company's product, expand its market, and increase its profit?

In general, we could tell pretty quickly if a company we were looking at had the potential for growth. We weren't hemmed in by a narrow definition of what ITT was. At one point, we felt that we were competing against General Electric. We were gaining on them. General Electric is also a conglomerate. It isn't generally considered one, or listed as one, because it started out in electricity, and its name suggests that that is where it remains.

What's in a name? GE has a credit company that accounted for 80 percent of its earnings in 1994, and it is also in lightbulbs, uranium, locomotives, aircraft engines, broadcasting, appliances, plastics, medical systems—practically anything you can think of. That's one impressive conglomerate. Today, of course, GE has grown vastly larger than ITT, with 1994 revenue of $60 billion compared with $23.6 billion at a greatly reduced ITT, and profit of $4.73 billion compared with $1.02 billion. It continued along the path of aggressive expansion while ITT slowed down as it matured and ultimately broke itself into three parts.

Growth makes all kinds of wonderful things happen. It delights the people who are part of the growth; it makes an impression on the outside world; it draws talent; it creates jobs and wealth and opportunities. At ITT, we were serious about our goal to get profits up by 10 percent every quarter. Guys would say, "Well, we're going to lose out in the first quarter and maybe the second but we'll make it up in the third and fourth." And we'd say bullfeathers to that. You've got to make it every quarter, or you'll never catch up.

One division chief once pleaded with us: Just leave me alone and even if I miss the target in the first couple of quarters I'll make up for it in the third and fourth quarters. If I don't, you can fire me. We replied: Sure, we can fire you. But by then, you may have lost $10 million. And it would be unfair to try to take that out of your paycheck. Unfair to us, that is!

I have this big Plexiglas cube in my office, a gift from ITT managers. It has fifty quarters embedded in the surfaces, one for each consecutive quarter of 10 percent-or-more earnings growth at ITT after I took charge. The press, the public, and just about everybody else, except ITT shareholders and employees, got bored with such steady, predictable growth.

We insisted on seeing how each division head was doing as we went along. But just making sure each division increased its profits wasn't enough. We wanted to increase the size of ITT itself through a sustained and reasoned acquisition program. Here's just a sampling:

Hartford Fire Insurance Company

We wanted to get into insurance because it is so huge and profitable, so we seized the opportunity to buy a 10 percent block in Hartford from a West Coast mutual fund. At first, Hartford's management gave us a cool reception, but ultimately supported our bid to acquire 100 percent in a transaction worth about $1.5 billion to fend off an intrusive third party. Alas, then we had to deal with the politicians! The Connecticut insurance commissioner, William Ross Cotter, had political ambitions. He came up with a carload of reasons for rejecting the deal. Before long, the papers were full of stories about this pirate who had sailed in from the high seas to seize control of one of the state's crown jewels. We finally won Cotter's approval by signing a sort of Bill of Rights for Hartford, under which we would build a hotel in Hartford, contribute to local charities, and so on. We ultimately paid something like $2.2 billion for the company, the biggest acquisition in insurance-industry history up until then. Mr. Cotter went on to become a congressman. In 1994, Hartford Insurance's revenue was more than $11 billion, and with a profit of $811 million, it accounted for over half of ITT's earnings. Under our guidance, Hartford developed superb, entrepreneurial management. It is a great example of what a conglomerate can do.

Sheraton Hotels

Another industry that proved extremely profitable to us was lodging. At one point, we bought a little group that franchised three or four Holiday Inns in Cleveland, but we sold it in order to buy a then-small chain, the Sheraton Hotel chain. It was put together by Ernie Henderson, who believed that the essential aspect of the hotel business was acquiring interesting real estate, with customers perhaps coming a close second. Today, Sheraton is the largest single hotel chain in the world. The hotel business is profitable enough, but its great advantage for ITT was that it also identified the company as a local citizen in all the world markets where we did business.

Auto Parts

And because of Sheraton, ITT got into auto parts. The hotel chain had a small automobile division run by a guy named Shirley Murphy, a car nut. Its main purpose—maybe its only purpose—was to enter a car called *Miss Sheraton* in the Indianapolis 500 every year. Because of Shirley, we took a look at the automobile industry and saw a lot of growth in auto parts. And we started buying companies that made auto parts, including one of only two American brake-line manufacturers. The returns were excellent. Then we bought a company in Germany, Teves, that made brakes. It so happened that a fellow in the company by the name of Otto Deppenauer was developing antiskid brakes. I remember Otto had a little open Ford, and he'd spray the skid pad with water and get you in the car and get it up to a good speed and then jam on the brakes. It would skid and turn around a few times. And then he would connect the automatic brakes that he was developing and he'd throw the same skid and go straight along.

Meanwhile, back at Teves, management kept trying to cut Otto's little antiskid project because it was costing them money with no apparent return on the horizon. The projected price of six hundred dollars for a set of brakes seemed way too high. But I had confidence in Otto. He was so earnest and seemed somehow defenseless. He was trying hard and he believed so strongly in what he was doing. Anyone could see he had integrity; you had to go a step further to have faith in his vision. But I wouldn't let them shut him down.

Today, ITT has something like 40 percent of the world market for antiskid brakes. We paid $80 million for the Teves brake company, one of several such acquisitions. In 1995, ITT's auto-parts division, starting from Shirley's racing car, was expected to generate revenues of over $5.4 billion.

This is what a conglomerate can do. The auto-parts division was welded together from many pieces. Welded together, not strung together, by a management with a strong focus, not just by some guy who's in charge.

Credit Companies

One of ITT's biggest moneymakers—before it was sold piecemeal in 1995 for a reported $6 billion—was ITT Credit. It grew from a $40 million investment in a little St. Louis personal-loan company called Aetna. The guy who was running it at the time, Dave Corwin, felt it was his calling to help people who were over their heads in debt by refinancing their borrowings at lower interest rates.

From $40 million to $6 billion! That's how a conglomerate works—if you work at it. And we worked at it. We kept buying, always targeting fields that we thought would grow. A sort of "working mutual fund," only we did the working.

Other Companies

We had two book companies. We bought a company that made under-the-street lighting and electrical distribution. We bought a big faucet company in Europe. (It's an amazing fact about faucet companies: They're all profitable. When in doubt, buy a faucet company.) We bought and ran Continental Baking Company, America's largest baker.

We bought a cosmetics company in the United Kingdom and two in the United States. We got into pumps. I guess I bought eight or nine pump companies, which all became a single international company. First, we bought Bell & Gosset, which made little pumps for hot-water radiator systems. We bought a company that made swimming pool pumps. We bought a company in Sweden that made submersible pumps. (By chance, it got to show its stuff when Chicago was hit with massive underground flooding. Boy, did those Swedish pumps pump!) It was a very steady industrial area. It had good margins; sales increased steadily, year by year; and there were no dominant players.

We bought several semiconductor companies, including one that was the last to make diodes. It was like owning the last company in America to make horseshoes—there wasn't much demand, but there wasn't any competition, either.

We bought an oil-and-gas company. We bought a coking-coal company. We bought a company called Pennsylvania Glass Sand from the founder. He owned a mountain of a particular grade of sand that is in high demand for making glass. All he had to do was refine it—he made a huge 50 percent profit margin. He sold it to me on the condition that if his son recovered from a motorcycle accident, I would let him run it. The young man did recover, and today, he runs the company—successfully.

We paid $40 million for Georgia Life Insurance Company, later renamed Abbey. It was sold a few years ago for $800 million. We went into the Rayonier pulp business. Not ordinary newspaper pulp, but cellulose pulp used in operating rooms, sanitary napkins, rayon, and certain kinds of textiles because it is so clean and consistent. We bought it because it was a raw-materials business and therefore a hedge against inflation, which was rampant at the time. We paid $300 million for Rayonier; it was spun off recently with a market value of about $800 million.

Sometimes, we started our own companies. For example, I was trying to buy Dun & Bradstreet and I noticed they made a lot of money on Yellow Pages. So we decided to do the same thing in Europe. Our telephone-equipment company in Belgium made a bid to the government telephone monopoly there to print its directory. They awarded us the contract. It was profitable from the start—and we made a much better directory. We then got into Yellow Pages in the Netherlands, Italy, and the United Kingdom. Eventually, the business spread all over Europe, Latin America, and the Far East. I'd guess it now makes $100 million a year. All this came out of a simple idea. A real example of building something from nothing.

Did we make mistakes? Sure. We bought Champion Lightbulb

in Boston to compete with General Electric. Bulbs represented a huge share of GE's profits, and we projected a growing demand in Europe. But we discovered too late that the scientific expertise in our labs, and the automatic machinery for making bulbs on the market, were no match for GE's. So we got out.

In about 1963, we offered $700 million for ABC. The bid was accepted but we had to delay the acquisition for two years because of delays in an antitrust investigation, and ultimately we dropped it. The Walt Disney Company in 1995 agreed to pay $19 billion for the same Capital Cities/ABC Incorporated, a merger that created the largest entertainment company in the world.

There were only a few industries we stayed away from: chemicals (frankly, I didn't know the difference between an alkaloid and a polymer and I didn't want to find out), airlines (too unpredictable), and movies.

Well, I did get interested enough in the movies to take a look at United Artists once. They made the James Bond movies, but that wasn't what interested me. What interested me was that out of the hundreds of films they had released over the years, only one had lost money. They made their real money on distribution. They made the distributors' profit on everything, even if the writer or producer lost out. I kept asking: How do you know your *next* Bond movie is going to make a large profit? And they kept saying: We don't. But count on it. In other words, trust to luck. That isn't a smart way to enter into risks. So I decided not to buy.

I remember looking at a highly successful company that made caskets and hospital beds. You couldn't tell me it didn't have a guaranteed customer base. But we decided that particular venture didn't make sense for us, so we passed.

Our basic formula was to look for companies (often troubled ones) with growth potential, offer to pay more for them than they were worth, and then fix them. Our stock was our currency. Preferred stock was our way of financing growth. So, we issued preferred series A, preferred series B, preferred series C, D, E, F, G, and so on, all the way up to T.

For those who criticize the theory of growth through acquisitions, I ask: Where would ITT be today if I hadn't undertaken it? The answer is clear. It would be nowhere. It probably wouldn't exist. Some other expansion-minded company would have swallowed it up.

Despite all its successes, the conglomerate was never quite

trusted. People didn't understand it. Why would a company buy a car-rental firm one week, a baking company the next, a pumps producer the next, a finance company the next, and so on? The CEO must be power-mad, or perhaps just mad.

Today, conglomerates have fallen into disrepute. The received wisdom is that they were dinosaurs, huge, unwieldy beasts doomed to extinction because they lacked nimbleness and focus. But I know that's not true. I have a word for that theory: Baloney! (Sanitized version.)

ITT is, of course, a much different company today. I *had* to create a conglomerate to save ITT. I had to make it grow to assure its independence. Rand Araskog, my successor, has operated under different conditions. He has focused on the core businesses. And he has made some excellent choices in selling off assets. ITT has realized over $15 billion from its divestitures. It was, for example, probably a good time to get out of telephones in Europe, given the fading loyalties of the government-owned telephone companies that we served and the growing competition within each country.

The truth is, running a conglomerate requires working harder than most people want to work and taking more risks than most people want to take. But it also brings rewards most people never dream of. At ITT, we lived a dream. The Justice Department stifled it with its ill-considered antitrust investigation in the late 1960s and stopped our U.S. acquisitions for ten years! And, after I left, the company veered onto a new course, emphasizing consolidation rather than growth. It has been split into three companies—a manufacturing company, an insurance company, and a hotel-and-entertainment company.

Often, I have felt the stab of frustration and regret, wondering what might have been. I think of the depression song:

Once I built a railroad, now it's done.
Brother, can you spare a dime?

I want to thank and honor all the people who joined me in pursuing the dream—who built up ITT and "made it race against time." In my time.

Thanks.

3

Doing Your Own Thing

I saw a bumper sticker the other day that read: "I Love My Boss. I Love My Job. I'm Self-Employed." That describes an entrepreneur to a T: somebody who cherishes above all else his independence. He just plain has to be in charge. He can't imagine reporting to any boss but himself.

The biggest fortunes in America are probably made by entrepreneurs. Think of Bill Gates, founder of Microsoft and the richest man in America today, with a fortune estimated by *Forbes* magazine at the end of 1996 at $18.5 billion. Think of Craig McCaw, who sold McCaw Cellular Communications Corporation to AT&T in 1994 for

$11.5 billion and made $800 million for himself on the deal. Think of Scott Cook, who was struggling to pay the telephone bills at his little start-up in the late 1980s and has since built that company, Intuit Incorporated, into the nation's number one maker of personal-financial software, with his stake worth several hundred million dollars. And think of James Clark, the chairman and biggest shareholder of Netscape Communications Corporation, the stock market sensation of 1995. The software company had never made a penny in profit and had sales of only $16.6 million in the first half of 1995, but when it went public in August, it soared to almost $75 from the offering price of $28, ended the day at $58, and was trading at around $157 in early 1996, making Mr. Clark a billionaire.

But, oddly enough, none of these men started their businesses to get rich. If money is your main goal, you probably aren't an entrepreneur. Because the more you care about money, the more cautious you become. And entrepreneurs are risk takers.

Mind you, between the pure entrepreneur and the corporate drone there are a lot of hybrids. For example, there is what I call the limited entrepreneur. He's the fellow who buys an easy-to-run business. It could be a franchise outlet such as a fast-food restaurant or a print shop where somebody else has written the format and supplies the expertise and the inventory. Or it could be an independent hardware store or some other mom-and-pop business that has always done well and will give him a steady income. Either way, the limited entrepreneur fulfills the dream of being his own boss but keeps risk at a minimum.

Then there is the quasi entrepreneur, who holds a salaried job but has one or two businesses on the side. For a long time, that was me. Even in my corporate role, I had the entrepreneurial urge to take charge. That moment came when I was named chief executive officer of ITT. And, from the beginning of my role as a corporate manager, I was doing deals on the side.

I'd like to make a stab at defining an entrepreneur and, by way of illustration, to describe my entrepreneurial side. But please don't consider this chapter a how-to guidebook; there are plenty of those gathering dust in the business section of your nearest bookstore. Rather, I'm hoping these reminiscences will illuminate what makes an entrepreneur tick, and perhaps show how much fun it is to run your own show.

The core characteristic of an entrepreneur is his or her (and more than half of new businesses are started by women) astuteness in discerning opportunity and alacrity in seizing it.

I see or read about this phenomenon again and again: the operating-room nurse who realizes a minor adjustment in the design of a surgical instrument would make it more effective; the salaried guy who organizes conferences for a company that specializes in that activity and then, suddenly, has a flash of inspiration: Hey, I could do this on my own! And I could do it better! And if I did, *I* would be making all the money. (Mind you, it isn't money that motivates such people, it is the chance to make a mark. But money is a pleasant side effect and a useful measurement of accomplishment.)

E. Ted Waitt, founder of Gateway 2000, says he got the idea for the company in 1985 as a sales clerk in a computer store. Customers were confused about which monitors went with which personal computers and with which printers. "I became fascinated with the idea that if you knew what you were talking about, you could sell somebody a three-thousand-dollar product over the phone in a twenty-minute conversation," he said. So he started Gateway to help customers put together complete systems. It had 1995 sales of $3.7 billion, up 36 percent from $2.7 billion the year before, and earnings of $173 million, almost double 1994's $95 million. Not bad.

Way back in the mid-1950s, I saw an opportunity in air. I bought an air-reduction plant that compressed air into nitrogen and oxygen. The oxygen would be mixed with acetylene for use in welding torches. My partner knew all about the oxygen business. It sure appealed to me, the notion that your basic raw material was the air you breathe. We had to pay for the cylinders that contained the oxygen and for their delivery, but the air, then as now, was free.

I made a little money on that deal. Then, in 1957, a partner and I bought a company in Crozet, Virginia, called Acme Visible Records, which made die-cut cards to keep inventory records and the like. The fellow who started it was getting close to retirement age. He wasn't interested in making his venture grow, even though he could have, easily. There's a tip for you: If you're shopping around for a bargain, look for owners who run thriving concerns but aren't making them grow because they just plain don't feel like it.

Another tip: Always pay a bit too much. Sound crazy? It's not. First of all, you'll get your quarry a lot faster. Try to lowball the owner, and you'll spend months of your valuable time niggling over nickels, and the prize may slip away.

We offered $12 million for Acme Visible, which was more than the owner was hoping for. About half a million of that was our own money. We completed the transaction quickly.

One of my conditions for joining ITT was that I'd get to keep my stake in Acme Visible. I'd go down to Virginia about once a month and check it out and hold management meetings.

And a few years later, we sold the company for nearly $60 million to American Tobacco. My partner and I each got about $5 million or $6 million out of it. Compare that to my first-year salary at ITT of about $150,000.

After I left ITT, I did a series of other deals. Why? Well, what do *you* plan to do when you become obsolete? Some people I know become active in their communities or get appointed to this or that nonprofit board. Hell, that's like playing poker for matchsticks. I say, throw some real money in!

Other people I know buy a second home in Florida and add a wing to their house in the Northeast. Still others want to golf and fish and hunt, activities they enjoyed in their working years but never had enough time to do properly. Fair enough. But it's not for me. I was a pretty ardent fisherman most of my life, but as I get older I'm no longer sure I really want to actually catch the creatures. I hate to think of myself as an equal adversary to this poor little fish.

I was heartened recently to read that the American Association of Retired Persons estimates that one in five of its members plan to start businesses or work for themselves.

Why am I still involved in running businesses at the age of eighty-seven? Because, simply, that's what I do. I've done it for half a century; I do it well; I love the challenges; I savor the accomplishments; most of all, I have fun.

Even today, I feel sparks of excitement as I read reports, study facts and figures, work the phone, and think about how I can make the companies I'm involved in more profitable and productive. I've probably been in and out of fifteen companies since I left ITT. I'm doing what I know how to do.

Like other entrepreneurs, I'm not in it for the money. No matter how much I make, it won't have an impact on my life. If I make an extra $5 million, the only thing I can do is give it to charity.

I just plain like to do deals. A bookcase behind my desk contains rows of loose-leaf notebooks crammed full with thousands of pages in all, detailing all of them. At my age, I've resigned myself to some sad facts: I'm never going to win a sailboat race. I won't become a skating champion. And, worst of all, I'll never beat Arnold Palmer at golf. Well, probably not. But I have a lot of experience in business, and I plan to keep drawing on it as long as I walk the green earth. (Arnold, no offense, but I understand your ProGroup maker of golf clubs and accessories went through a rough patch not so long ago.)

My first great post-ITT venture—an effort to sell three coke ovens for Allied-Chemical, the conglomerate—was a flat failure. Coke is coal from which most of the gases have been removed; it produces intense heat when burned and is used throughout the world in blast furnaces to make iron.

I must have spent nearly a year on that project. One of the ovens was in Ashland, Kentucky, one was across the river in Ohio, and the third was in Detroit. The idea was either to find a buyer or to organize a company to use the ovens to make coke for export.

Even back then, I had to deal with the environmental people. I'd drive to Frankfort, Kentucky, the state capital, and talk with them. The "smoke watchers," we called them. Anyway, this freelance selling job seemed like a propitious undertaking. Coke was extremely expensive in the United Kingdom and Germany at the time. Both countries had big steel mills. And I had a background in steel from my days at Jones & Laughlin in the early fifties.

Those coke ovens were worth $40 million apiece. All I had to do was sell them. But I never found a buyer. American companies were worried about the supply of coal: where I'd get it, how I'd ship it, whether it would make good coke, and so forth. The Europeans were shopping around. Meantime, the price of coke was faltering, in part, I think, because of talk that the Australians were going to get into the business.

So that entrepreneurial exploit was a bust. I worked on commission, meaning that if I had sold the ovens, I might have made a tidy little sum. Instead, I got nothing.

Still, I learned a lot. I almost made a sale to a company that had its own mines but wanted to stock coke from an outside source to save on the cost of raising and lowering production. In the end, though, it demurred.

I also picked up important information about the technology of coke storage, just in case I should ever run a coke oven: You dump it on the ground and calculate the loss factor.

And I also got to meet the governor of Kentucky and, better yet, his wife, a famous beauty. But I didn't get any money.

So I prowled around for a new opportunity. Understand, I was no J. P. Morgan, with billions in the bank, influence in Washington, and a huge staff at my command. I had left ITT with a grand total of $2 million, hardly a fortune even in those days. I represented myself. But I had resources much more valuable than that $2 million in seed money: I had experience and an eye for a deal. More important, I was willing to work ferociously hard to achieve my goals. More important still, I had confidence in myself.

Most important of all, I was willing to take a risk. So, despite my setback in coke, I got into an oil operation down in Louisiana. We had two shipyards and were refitting and rebuilding oil barges. We had some boats that serviced the offshore oil wells. Alas, when the oil business fell apart, our business fell apart. Strike two.

Was I discouraged? Not a damn bit. I was having fun. Besides, the essence of entrepreneurship is bouncing back from failure. You just keep trying. Japanese automobile magnate Soichiro Honda made the point in his usual trenchant style: ''Success represents the one percent of your work that results from the ninety-nine percent that is called failure.''

Again and again, you read about successful entrepreneurs whose early ventures were failures. Ask the founder of any successful company what he'd do if it went bust, and I can guarantee you what his answer will be: He'd start over.

With my next swing at the ball, I got a hit. I got into American Life, a life insurance company. Another fellow and I bought it from Occidental, out on the Coast. We ran it for about three years and sold it for a good profit. Somewhere in there, I got involved with another fellow in buying Leslie Fay, a dress outfit, in a leveraged buyout. (An LBO is a takeover financed by borrowed funds with the company's assets for security.) I made $10 million on that investment. My total investment: $50,000. What did I know about making dresses? Not a damn thing. But I knew a lot about numbers, balance sheets, and earnings trends. And about taking risks.

Maybe because I had pushed ITT into so many different industries, I pushed myself in all directions when I was on my own. I did a $160 million LBO of MPB Corporation, a maker of miniature precision ball bearings. The military was our main customer. Luckily, I got out before all the defense cutbacks, and made a profit of about $2 million.

I leveraged a $200,000 investment in a company called Finlay Fine Jewelry into a $15 million profit. I bought and sold a construction company called George Fuller, famous for building such New York City landmarks as the United Nations Building, the Plaza Hotel, and the triangular-shaped Flatiron Building. I got involved in numerous other ventures, from General Electric's life-insurance subsidiary to a fast-food chicken chain.

I had my setbacks, to be sure. I lost money on a New Hampshire dairy farm. The price of milk kept going down but the cost of supplies kept going up. The bottom line was that a rocky old farm in New England, with its long winters, couldn't compete with the giant farms in the Middle West, with their long summers.

Today, I have deals going in China, Russia, and other emerging markets. And I'm working hard to build up Gunther, the envelope-stuffing-equipment maker in Connecticut. It has first-rate R & D and a highly skilled workforce.

An entrepreneur grabs opportunities. I used to sell virgin pine from some woods I own in New Hampshire to a logger. The logger resold it to a sawmill for a sizable profit. The sawmill sawed the pine and sold the boards to a lumberyard, also for a profit.

There was an opening here, and I seized it. I built my own sawmill, right there on my land. I invested about $1 million. That was twenty years ago. Today, about ninety people work there. It's very profitable.

And it's going to get more profitable. I just bought seven thousand more acres with a partner, and I figure it has 17 million feet of pine timber on it. That's on top of the 12 million timber feet I already own and control. The way I see it, pine is going to go up. The U.S. government has practically closed off the West to logging, and demand for pine is booming in China and Thailand and other parts of Asia, and also in Europe.

But my opportunities didn't end with the sawmill. I noticed that it discarded a lot of wood. So I decided to make firewood out of it. It's a simple operation: You run the cast-off wood through a splitter, dry it in a kiln, package it, and sell it in supermarkets. It takes about as much expertise as setting up a car wash. And it pulls in $300,000 or $400,000 a year.

I also own a lumberyard in New Hampshire that specializes in building barns, all over New England.

I guess I've mentioned New Hampshire's rocky soil. It helped do in my dairy farm. But I've spotted an opportunity in rock, too. I've acquired a big stone deposit in New Hampshire and have begun extracting the reserves. An appraiser estimated their worth at $8 million.

My net worth today is substantial—certainly far greater than the kid who paid his way through the last couple of years of high school and sold classified ads in the depression ever dreamed. How did I do it? Opportunities come your way. You check them out. Some work out. Some don't.

For all my affection for entrepreneurs, I should urge some caution on my younger readers. Prepare yourself. First, get an MBA and then find a job in a corporation, the bigger the better. Sure, you want to be your own boss. But sacrifice that luxury for a few years so you can gain the experience that is vital to make your own business succeed. You should study for this the same way a medical student studies to become a doctor. After a couple of years learning the ropes at a big company, get a job in a small company to see how it works.

I'm on the board of a steak-house chain that two young men on Wall Street started. They knew all about raising money and putting deals together, but they didn't know much about the fast-food industry. So they worked for a summer, without pay, to learn the basics. In 1995, they decided to franchise. They've surpassed five hundred units and are growing fast.

All right. Now you're ready to make the big plunge. But wait: First, you have to have a good idea. That might take a year or five years to formulate. And meantime, you might decide you're in the wrong field. If that is the case, you should go back to square one— back to a big corporation in your new field of choice, then to another small company.

As you can see, I don't believe in rushing into things. However, once you've gained sufficient corporate experience, and assuming you're still determined to start or buy your own business, here are some guidelines to follow.

- Get a business owner or top corporate manager in the same field you're going into to give you a realistic evaluation of your business plan.

- Define your business. Ask yourself why you think it will be successful. Write down all the experience you have that justifies your optimism. Try to imagine some nasty surprises that will come your way. (Plenty will.) Ask yourself how you will deal with them.

- Do your homework. Figure out what your market is, what your costs will be, what your cash flow will be. Make a list of all your potential customers, and all your potential competitors.

- Plan carefully. Make realistic assumptions. What will your product contribute to the market? How quickly will your business grow? What will its profit margins be?

- If your market research tells you no, take no for an answer. Beware of falling in love with a product that consumers don't want. Don't try to foist another Edsel on the market. We called it the "pregnant Buick." This tendency to fall in love with a product nobody else wants is the biggest failing of the amateur inventor. There should be an entrepreneurial index. Some way of rating business ideas: A, B, C, D, and F. Then, the rule would be: Never touch anything below a B. Don't let your enthusiasms get the best of you.

- Raise capital in stages. The first test of an entrepreneur is whether he can recognize a good, capitalizable project. Then he should seek enough capital to prove his point. If he can prove his point, he should be able to attract enough additional capital to expand.

- Once you launch your business, don't bite off more than you can chew. If you raise $1 million, and have a great idea for a restaurant, don't open a chain of five restaurants. Start with one. Then build on its success. Work within your resources. Follow your plan. Don't stretch your resources too far.

- Hire adequate staff. Don't be afraid to bring in outside managers. Don't be a control freak. Or a nervous Nellie, fearful that the outsider, if she is smart enough, will steal your ideas.

- Be a tough negotiator. If you bring somebody into your company who asks for 20 percent, tell him: If you're that good, the company should grow fivefold within four years. So I'll give you 5 percent now, and that will be worth even more than the 20 percent you're asking in just four years.

Now, we're getting into the entrepreneur as manager. And we have to face an unsettling fact: A lot of entrepreneurs don't make it. Fewer than half of all start-ups survive for more than five years. It's sad to think of all those plucky men and women struggling to keep their businesses afloat. I think of them as valiant failures.

I guess that is one reason I call myself a quasi entrepreneur. I first operated in the protective cocoon of a big corporation. At ITT, we always had a checkbook in our back pocket. You could settle a lot of things just by ordering up people or resources. Big companies can handle big losses. Small companies can't. At a small company, you live close to the edge.

Still, as I've said, a true entrepreneur bounces back from failure. If all you lose is your time and your money, and if you hang on to your self-confidence, you'll be fine. It's like the popular saying goes: Pick yourself up, dust yourself off and get going.

Don't forget, either, that all the world admires somebody who won't quit. Even the most ardent Nixon haters have to admit: Here was a fighter who would never, never quit. Just be realistic, and anything but arrogant. And say to yourself: Here begins chapter 2. Thank God it isn't Chapter 11.

The same principles of perseverance and risk taking apply to the tough, but happy, question for the successful entrepreneur: To sell out, or not to sell out. As sure as bond yields go up when prices come down, somebody someday is going to come in your door and offer to buy you out. He'll make a sweet offer: You can be president and keep 10 percent or 20 percent. Think of it, he'll say; all that money, plus an important title, plus a big stake, and you can take a nice, long, well-deserved vacation.

Beneath the sweet talk there will be an implicit and not-so-sweet threat: Turn us down, and we will throw all of our resources into competing against you and running you into the ground. Now you have the real test of the entrepreneur. May I give some advice? Just say no.

Why? Otherwise, for the rest of your life, you'll keep asking yourself: Why did I do it and what would I have done with my company if I had turned the bid down?

The answer doesn't matter. Tell 'em to go to hell and tough it out. Having gone this far, don't discount your future. You'll never have the satisfaction of knowing where you could have gone unless you stick with it.

Tell them no. Then you're a true entrepreneur. A true entrepreneur isn't in it for the money, remember? Money is just the scoreboard. He isn't in it for the security. He is in it for the freedom to run his own show.

The word that comes to my mind is *bearings*. You're on your course. And you don't want to swing off course for money. What the hell's money?

There's an alternative to selling out to an acquisitive suitor, and that is going public. You want partners? Then bring the public in. Just remember one thing: The public is going to be a tougher taskmaster than you were on yourself. That's because you will now be responsible to your fellow shareholders as well as to yourself. It's almost like being the guardian of children.

On a less ambitious scale, you can make a private placement. You'll have a lot fewer investors than if you are listed on an exchange, but they will be a lot more focused on what you're doing. They won't hesitate to give you advice or ask you tough questions.

Either way, I'd say, don't rush into this. In fact, I urge you to resist the temptation for as long as possible. It would be better to sell 25 percent of your company for $70 million later on than to part with 70 percent of it for $25 million today.

Besides, going to Wall Street is like going to the dentist's office: You'll have to do it some day, but the experience is bound to be unpleasant. Those sophisticated wise guys have little respect for the entrepreneur. The whole idea of the Horatio Alger hero, the poor boy who pulls himself up by the bootstraps, is a joke to them.

You probably won't be able to resist Wall Street forever, though. Every Fortune 500 company was once just a start-up, just as every start-up was once just a dream.

You know, Americans love the little guy. I saw a survey not long ago that said one in four Americans distrust big business. It didn't say how many distrust big government, but the number would undoubtedly be as high or higher. But here's the kicker: Only 7 percent of Americans—one in fourteen—distrust small business.

To be sure, it is all too easy to glamorize small business. But keep in mind the goal of most small companies: To become big companies. I keep reading newspaper articles about how small businesses are creating all the jobs. But I rarely see hard evidence, just anecdotes, along the lines of: "While IBM was laying off two thousand people last month, little Techno-Wiz Incorporated was hiring twenty." But little companies lay off people, too, and a lot of them go under. And big companies go through periods of expansion.

Next time you read about the fading importance of the Fortune 500 companies, remember this figure: Their total revenues equal 63 percent of America's gross domestic product.

Furthermore, it isn't necessarily a positive thing if small companies expand at the expense of big companies. If General Electric decides to get rid of its trucking division to save on costs, you could say: "Gee, GE laid off five hundred people. But the independents gained five hundred. Wonderful." Consider, though, that the new employees at the small companies undoubtedly earn less money and enjoy fewer benefits than their counterparts at General Electric. Is that progress?

That said, the entrepreneur is probably the last great American folk hero, in the mold of the mythic figures from our nation's history: the pilgrim, the pioneer, the gold prospector, the cowboy, the inventor. In an age when comfort and security and risk aversion are rampant, he upholds the tradition of the rugged individualist striking out into unknown territory and living by his performance.

And, like the pitcher in the Ring Lardner short story whose real worth isn't his mastery of the game so much as the dreams he inspires in the kids on the sandlot, maybe the entrepreneur's greatest value isn't the jobs and wealth he creates, however sizable those may be.

Maybe his greatest gift is his appeal to the American imagination.

4

The Corporate Servant and the Hired Gun

Not everybody has the stomach to be an entrepreneur. And there is nothing wrong with admitting that you can't handle that level of risk—not now, anyway. Next year, maybe. Or a few years down the road, after you've squirreled away a nest egg to fall back on just in case your grand enterprise flops.

If you don't run your own show, of course, you'll have to play a part in somebody else's. What that means is that you'll be trading the freedom to do your own thing for economic security. In other words, you'll have to do what your boss tells you to do.

Even so, you'll have plenty of opportunity for adventure. Companies, after all, have as their purpose to make money. They are therefore on the lookout for imaginative risk takers—people who are forever exploring new ways of doing things, even if that means flouting tradition and questioning authority. Companies know that these innovators are their lifeblood.

That is why it is important to understand the two archetypes who inhabit the American business world, the corporate servant and the hired gun, and to choose early on which one you want to be. To my mind, it is no contest.

Corporate servitude used to be a respectable route to middle-class prosperity. Its practitioners are plodders. Shunning risk, they are drawn to companies that are big, successful, and a little bit fat, like the General Motors of bygone years. Why? Because they are *comfortable* there. (People in the industry used to call General Motors "Generous Motors.") The company is like family.

The corporate servant works hard (though not too hard), holds his tongue, and entrusts his future to others. He identifies with his company. His mind rarely wanders beyond its confines. He plans to stay in it until he retires. This kind of surrender soon snuffs out whatever sparks of ambition flicker in his heart.

You'll find these corporate servants everywhere, from the factory floor all the way up to the CEO's office. Their careers are fairly predictable. As long as the company is doing well, they are "safe."

And indeed, many corporate servants do well for themselves, at least for a while. As the years go by, their pay gets better, their benefits get more generous, and their vacations get longer. For the senior executives among them there are always enough stock-option grants to extinguish any yearnings for the entrepreneurial life.

But for all that, the corporate servant's life has a hollowness to it. One day he wakes up and realizes that he hasn't lived up to his earlier expectations of himself. And it is too late to do anything about it.

Sounds bleak. But it gets bleaker. You may have read about the "downsizing" of corporate America over the past decade. Call it restructuring, reengineering, or anything else, it has been a shocker, with millions of layoffs, most of them men in their thirties, forties, and fifties. And most of them good, old, reliable corporate servants.

To be blunt: As companies have gotten more cold-blooded, being a loyal corporate servant has become a losing game. You might as well work for a temporary-help agency. What's the difference between a nine-month contract that makes no bones about being what it is—an impersonal financial arrangement—and a ''lifelong commitment'' that can be broken at any moment?

But corporate servants who find themselves on the unemployment line would be wrong to place all the blame on capitalistic callousness. They are really victims of their own inertia. They chose stability over risk. They thought they had cut a bargain, but the other side panicked at the spectacle of increased competition and shrinking profits, and broke the unwritten compact.

True, most of the casualties are wounded, not dead. They find new jobs, albeit often lower-paying ones. Some drop out and make do. Those with special skills—lawyers, accountants, engineers, salespeople, and the like—may match their former salaries. A few specialists in high-demand occupations such as chemistry or biology might even come out ahead.

But the rank and file of these dispossessed will have no such luck. If I were in charge of overdue accounts payable in a small department at Kodak or IBM and got that proverbial pink slip under such circumstances, I'd be scared out of my wits.

Corporate servants will always be with us. And not just at Fortune 500 companies. Many family businesses keep people with the promise of big things to come: ''When I retire in twenty years, you can succeed me.'' Sometimes that happens. I've even seen the founders of small companies give everything away to their employees.

More commonly, though, an heir apparent toils in relative obscurity for the chance to run the show—and then a nephew is brought in at the last minute to take over. It happens again and again. If you want to trust your career to a family company, make sure all the kids and cousins and nieces and nephews and in-laws are accounted for.

It boils down to this: In building a career, playing it safe every step of the way is probably the riskiest path of all. If you have honest ambition, long-term goals, and some sort of timetable for achieving them, you have to move fast. You may not think of yourself as a drone, but unless you stay alert, you can slip into the habits of the corporate servant without even realizing it.

The years can fly by. The Bible gives us three score and ten years on this earth. The unforgiving realities of the business world allot us maybe two decades to prove ourselves. Your first jobs are apt to come your way by chance, even if you come equipped with an MBA. But whether you get them by chance or design, the real point is they are formative. You're not going to hit your stride until you're thirty-five.

Then, you'll have twenty years to make your play. Mind you, you should never give up, no matter how old you are. And the willingness to take risks will give you the same edge at eighty-five as it does at twenty-five; maybe a bigger edge, because you'll stand out more. But facts are facts, and if you've accomplished great things by the time you're forty-five, people will knock down doors to get you to work for them. If you haven't, nobody will knock down doors, but the ceiling might fall in on you. These mass layoffs of middle managers are no temporary phenomenon. So you've got to keep moving. You can be a big wheel one day, but if you stay too long in one spot, you'll soon be a flat tire.

Now we come to the second corporate type, the hired gun. Like the corporate servant, he serves his boss loyally. But unlike his more cautious cousin, the hired gun has an independent spirit, born of self-confidence. He disdains waiting games with uncertain outcomes. He insists on taking charge of his life, and he knows exactly where he wants to go.

In contrast to the corporate servant, the hired gun can move with ease from company to company. To some extent, he is a frustrated entrepreneur. Like the entrepreneur, he is on the alert for each new opportunity.

Throughout my career, I was a hired gun. I threw my heart and soul into any job I got, but I would leave in a minute if I felt I was being mistreated. Consider: I was a page and then a floor clerk on the New York Stock Exchange from 1926 until the Crash of 1929; an advertising salesman for the *New York World Telegram* in the early thirties; an accountant at Lybrand, Ross Brothers in the late thirties and early forties; the controller of American Can's weapons plants in the war years; a vice president and controller at Bell & Howell in the late forties; vice president and controller at Jones & Laughlin in the first half of the fifties; executive vice president of Raytheon in the second half; and finally CEO of ITT for nearly two decades starting in 1959. This represented five decades of seizing opportunities.

I always followed some basic rules:

- Try to stay in any job for at least three years. I usually lasted five years or longer. You will be learning throughout that period and developing a strong record. Whenever I left, it was because I realized I would not be able to achieve the responsibilities I sought as quickly as I wished. In other words, you can't sit there and wait for time to take care of you.

- When you do leave a company, try to go where there's trouble. You'll get a lot of responsibility. And you won't have much competition for your assignments. Because people generally avoid trouble. That's foolish. In your younger years, especially, go for the coin of experience. Gain that, and the coin of money will follow.

- The important thing is to step up and take the risk. Once you take the risk, you'll learn how to fix the problem. Finding the solution might push you to the limits of your potential.

Too many people adopt the corporate-servant mentality of clinging to their jobs at all costs. They are practically handcuffed to their desks. Cold fear holds them there—and yet that fear can be defeated by the heat of healthy ambition.

I never hesitated to switch companies if my path was blocked. It happened at American Can after the war ended. One day, I found myself in Penn Station in New York City with some time on my hands before my train arrived. So I stepped into a bookstore to browse through the racks.

A title caught my eye: *Pick Your Job—And Land It.* I bought it. Among other things, the book urged job seekers to use a Hooven typewriter, an advanced machine for the time. Its virtue was that it was able to type the same letter over and over automatically, making each copy look like an original. In those days, people sending out a large number of letters of application would often send carbon copies. It saved time, but it sent the wrong message to the prospective employer, telling him that he was only one among many.

After reading the book, I got a Moody's directory in the Chicago library, picked out about a hundred companies in the area that looked interesting, and sent letters to them all. Each letter was an "original," mind you, personally addressed to the recipient.

Well, I received six job offers. Coming up from the depression, I had never experienced anything quite so exhilarating. One of them was from an eclectic little company in Grand Rapids, Michigan, that made church pews. I thought about that for a while, but instead took a job at Bell & Howell as the new controller.

Oddly enough, that experience—of sending out a hundred applications and getting six firm offers—changed my life. I had achieved instant mobility. I no longer needed the Hooven typewriter, and I never worried again about whether I would be able to find a job. Of course, the higher up you go, the more difficult it becomes to land an even better job. But I discovered I could now control my own destiny.

I suppose I could have stayed with Bell & Howell. But the heir apparent, U.S. senator-to-be Charles Percy, was younger than me, and I decided the moment was ripe to ''seek new challenges.''

My willingness to risk the unknown paid off handsomely. I became controller at Jones & Laughlin, the steel company, at almost three times my former pay. Almost immediately, however, I became involved in a power struggle. My new employers had somehow neglected to mention that they were considering an internal candidate for the same job. If he were chosen, I would be his number two.

The safe reaction would have been to go along and hope for the best. But by now, safety was no longer part of my career equation. So I made a nonnegotiable demand: If you're not 100 percent satisfied with me, go ahead and look at other candidates, but only outside the company. After all, I pointed out, I had given up my previous position to fill a post that no one else at Jones and Laughlin had apparently been able to handle. I said: ''If you think there's someone within the company who is better than me, fine. Take him and I'll leave.'' There it was again: the willingness to risk my job to advance my interests.

It worked. They agreed to my terms. Just as I expected, there was little motivation for them to exert the time and energy and money to a drawn-out search outside the company. Three months later, they made me controller—the job I had been hired for in the first place.

In today's uncertain corporate environment, more and more young people are preparing themselves for careers as ''hired guns'' rather than corporate servants by getting MBAs, a sort of corporate transfer ticket. Every university's got a business school these days, it seems. I checked with the American Assembly of Collegiate Schools of Business, and was informed that the number of accredited business schools in the United States has more than doubled since 1972, to 315, and the number of people getting MBAs has nearly *tripled* in roughly the same period, to eighty-nine thousand. ''We thought it would peak a few years back but people just kept pouring in,'' the woman there told me. "Young people, middle-aged people, people who are reengineering their careers." The job market is being flooded with all these high-level thinkers.

The trend is creating an elite group. If you don't have your MBA, you're considerably handicapped. And the people who do have their degrees are honed to the idea, not of loyalty to the corporation, but of being hired guns.

And the fact that these "hired guns" make good managers hasn't escaped the attention of corporate America. Think of all the troubled companies that have pulled in new blood from entirely different industries to resuscitate them. Because they are likely to spend time at two, three, or more companies in the course of their careers, such mobile managers are unlikely to be cowed by the customs and ingrained attitudes they encounter.

There are all sorts of corporate cultures. There are laid-back corporate cultures, aggressive corporate cultures, traditional corporate cultures, lost-in-the-past corporate cultures, and asleep-at-the-switch corporate cultures. When I ran it, ITT had a no-baloney corporate culture. At some companies, the expression should be corporate cutlery. Everybody has a knife in his back.

I've never really liked the term "corporate culture." It's a bit like the phrase "corporate governance." Everybody uses it and nobody knows what the dickens it means. Well, the riddle is solved: Corporate culture is pretty much what the boss says it is. The boss calls the shots, and the troops fire away as instructed.

Chief executives who are hired to turn troubled companies around usually have to transform the cultures they find there. You don't think IBM's culture hasn't transmogrified since Lou Gerstner took over? He's abandoning their headquarters in Armonk, New York, and selling off all their million-dollar European oil paintings. He even opened two IBM country clubs to the public. You can bet his message of dispensing with frills and focusing on winning back market share has trickled down to the rank and file. They're saying, "Boy, he means business."

I quickly moved to change ITT-Europe's "corporate culture." Previously, European managers had been excessively deferential to the American bosses. I changed all that by making it clear that I welcomed their views and that they wouldn't be punished for expressing opinions contrary to my own.

I also tried to break down the excessive formality. You weren't, for example, supposed to call somebody by his first name unless you had gone through an informal yet somehow formal ceremony of drinking with him to the point of locking arms and singing barroom anthems. By tradition, this ritual might not take place until an acquaintanceship had ripened over many years.

To me, that was baloney. Pretty soon, I had everybody calling one another by their first names. And we set up something we called "Strategy Action Boards" to decide policy. It sounds impressive, but the real purpose was to make all these nationalities work together. Over five or six years, we welded them together into a group that had the same spirit. But it took a hell of a lot of hard work on my part.

Albert Dunlap, who was hired in 1994 to rejuvenate Scott Paper Company and who announced its merger with Kimberly Clark Corporation in 1995, made this comment to *Forbes* magazine: "If an executive says, after two years, 'I'm frustrated by the culture,' my answer to that is that your role as chief executive officer is to change the culture. People say, 'We'll get back to you in three weeks with a report.' You say, 'No, it's Wednesday. We'll meet Friday.' 'Oh, is that how we do it.' 'Yeah, that's how you do it.' "

I'll bet if you ask the people at Compaq what their culture is they'll say, "We don't have time to talk about it." They were too busy fighting their way to becoming the number one maker of personal computers, with $14.8 billion in revenues in 1995 (up from $10.9 billion in a single year). At ITT, we didn't write a corporate "mission statement" to inculcate our values into our employees. We simply set the example. People picked up on it quickly. Rewarding their initiative won their loyalty. Encouraging thoughtful risk taking drew out their creativity. After all, we were all part of a team.

Sometimes, a personality cult can build up around a boss with autocratic inclinations. At Jones & Laughlin, when the senior Mr. Laughlin got on the elevator, everybody else got off on the next floor, regardless of their destination. At Bell & Howell, Mr. McNab, founder and ruling potentate, wrote unsigned notes to underlings in blue pencil. No one else in the company was allowed to use a blue pencil, so they needed no signature, and commanded instant attention.

Not so long ago, an investigative journalist for a leading business publication reported that I had required managers at ITT in the 1960s to wear "laced shoes." Not true! They could have come to work barefoot, for all I cared—so long as they did their work.

This is not to say that a company's trademark idiosyncrasies are without significance. I've heard that at the funeral of any of the partners of the renowned law firm of Cravath, Swaine & Moore, the first two rows of the church are always taken by all the surviving partners. It is a pleasant notion, a touching tribute to the deceased and undoubtedly a solace to him in his prior contemplation of the event. You certainly could call this a manifestation of Cravath, Swaine's "culture."

But corporate culture is made up of much more than mere tradition. It is a living, evolving organism. When I was a young man on the New York Stock Exchange in the 1920s, the whole west side of the floor would occasionally burst into a robust rendition of "Wait 'til the Sun Rises Nellie."

Everybody kept working. But all of a sudden we were smiling, whereas a minute earlier we had been grimly slogging along. We knew what was coming next. And sure enough, after a short interval, the east side would respond with a slightly more subdued rendering of "The Wearing of the Green."

I'm grateful to whatever boss encouraged, or at least tolerated, that facet of the stock exchange's 1920s culture. By contrast, some traditions are just as well abandoned. At Jones & Laughlin, every office had a big brass spittoon, polished nightly. Most of the men walked around smoking and chewing poisonous-looking twisted cigars called Pittsburgh Stogies. The air reeked of them. When the company moved to a modern building in Pittsburgh's Gateway Center office complex in the early 1950s, this aspect of the company's culture didn't make the trip. And those big brass spittoons became flowerpots in the homes of many employees. Such is the passing of a custom.

Nobody has to be a corporate drone. Sixty years ago, I took a psychology course at New York University from a Professor Hoopingarner, who moonlighted as a headhunter for the telephone company. Mr. Hoopingarner never tired of repeating his dictum for getting ahead: "Get yourself in the top twenty percent of your group."

This was night school, and most of the students held day jobs, so Mr. Hoopingarner must have viewed us as a fertile field of young minds in which to plant his theory. Indeed, on occasion he recruited kids right out of his classroom. He said the 20–80 rule rarely failed him.

The beauty of it is that even ordinary Joes can make it pay off for them. You don't have to get yourself into the top 5 percent, or even the top 10 percent; you only have to rise to the top 20 percent.

That leaves a little room. Anyone who is willing to work hard can achieve that goal. And if you're in that top 20 percent, you'll keep your job in hard times and get promoted in good times.

But you should demand more of yourself. For me, it goes back to my elementary school days at a Catholic convent. If I misspelled a word, I got my hand whacked with a ruler. It made me want to do better the next time. If that happened in a public school today, the teacher would be fired, the school would be sued, and the incident would become a cause célèbre. The *New York Times* would thunder reprobation from its editorial pages: "Singapore Justice for Our Children?" It didn't hurt that much, though. It was just a little whack.

Of course, young, ambitious men and women have always been impatient to get ahead. I remember interviewing an MBA about to graduate from Harvard when I was at Jones & Laughlin. He wanted to know how long it would be before he was made a vice president. A pretty direct question, I thought.

So I said, "How old are you?"

"Twenty-two."

"Are you willing to work until you're sixty-five?"

"Yes," he replied.

"That's forty-three years," I said. "You know, in that time, the entire management of this company will turn over at least three times. What job is it you would like?"

I couldn't help smiling a little bit at his attitude. He thought his degree came with a coupon that was exchangeable for one vice presidency. He had yet to learn he would have to earn his way to the top. Still, I didn't resent him. After all, he had a goal in mind! I hope he made it.

Remember, though, that the tortoise beat the hare. You don't start off in a company with the idea of taking charge the next day. You start with the goal of advancing to the next position. You can be as ambitious as you want, and think to yourself that someday you'd like to run this company—but keep your eye on that next rung up.

The message I'm trying to convey is simple. There is no real security in the corporate world. The only security can come from within you, and specifically, from your determination to improve and broaden your abilities.

Take a cue from Professor Hoopingarner: Strive to rise to the top 20 percent of your field, and work like hell to stay there. The effort will soon become a habit. There are no rest periods in today's competitive corporate environment.

Competent risk takers are made, not born. They know when to hold back, too; no risk is worth taking if you aren't prepared to live with the consequences. And taking risks is only the beginning. It is after you take them that the real work begins.

If ever there had been a candidate for corporate servitude, it might have been me, back in the days I attended night school at New York University. I studied accounting. The depression, I guess, demoralized almost everybody. It would have been natural enough for me to seek the security of a comfortable job in a respectable firm and stay put. I could easily have gone the way of the corporate servant.

Instead, when the right risk came along, I opted for it. And I've been taking risks ever since, for seventy years and counting. It's a great way of living. I recommend it.

5

The Art of
Goofing Off

You may remember Horatio Alger—the nineteenth-century American hero of uplifting books about youths of humble origin who achieved wealth and social status through hard work, high moral principles, and a cheerful disposition.

I have always preached that Horatio Alger was right. And why not? I myself was a penniless lad of sixteen who rose to a pinnacle of American industry by pushing myself, seizing opportunities, and taking risks.

But that was the Old Harold Geneen. He is still going. But in this brief chapter, the New Harold Geneen will challenge the orthodoxies that have guided me until now. I will even offer advice, based on nearly three quarters of a century of observation, on how to breeze and bluff your way through life with a minimum of exertion.

I am not sure how many people really like work. I have long puzzled over the lack of serious studies into ways of avoiding it. This chapter is aimed at filling that research gap.

Let us assume, then, that Horatio Alger got it wrong. After all, plenty of people have celebrated idleness as a virtue. The poet Wordsworth spoke of "that majestic indolence so dear to native man." Or, as the comedian Edgar Bergen remarked, "Hard work never killed anybody, but why take a chance?" Indeed, through the years I have bumped into endless numbers of people who enjoyed all the accoutrements of wealth—big houses with servants, flashy cars, expensive clothes, summer cottages on the beach—who never seemed to do a lick of work.

Some, of course, inherited their wealth. They didn't walk around wearing signs on their foreheads that read Trust Account, but they might as well have. They often gave themselves monikers that hinted at untold hours of toil behind a desk or in a studio: investor, consultant, artist, freelance photographer. The desk was often real; the toil was invariably imaginary.

Inheriting money is an excellent system for achieving a life of ease. The trouble is, you can't select your parents. I'm working on that problem, but until I solve it, you'll have to look at alternatives.

I am also assuming that the old-fashioned method of marrying a beautiful, rich, and fun-loving widow (or widower) is too gauche for our select clientele. (Come to think of it, you might have to work pretty hard to pull that one off. And we are sworn against work, even work as sublime as that. Our motto is: Inactivity wherever possible, simulations of work wherever necessary, but *no work* under any circumstances.) That leaves only one option: real jobs with make-believe duties.

Here, then, is our list of assignments for those who would pursue the ideal of an honest day's work for an honest month's pay. It is hardly exhaustive, and I encourage others to draw up similar compendiums. It is my fond wish that, someday, mass-circulation magazines will publish guides to the most laid-back occupations as enthusiastically as they currently print guides to the most livable cities in America.

Our professional staff has searched the globe to identify professions that don't require matriculation from the school of hard knocks. And it has selected only those that sound important but that aren't tainted with the knotty demands of crass commerce. Our findings should send out beacons of hope to those who, by accident of birth, are long of wind and short of talent.

Probably the best way to achieve the lofty goal of ne'er doing anything without being classified publicly as a ne'er-do-well is to get elected to Congress. Qualifications for this position include the ability to sit for long periods in wooden armchairs without squirming, a knack for adjusting your convictions to fit the latest opinion polls, a willingness to travel, and a fondness for greasy drumsticks and lumpy mashed potatoes. Pay: good. Fringe benefits: excellent. Extra bonus: You'll get into really serious money after you finally leave the august deliberative body, but everybody will still refer to you as the former congressman.

State legislatures and city councils also offer a refuge from the strain of purposeful activity. Aside from elective office, here are the vocations that are most likely to land you on easy street:

NEWSPAPER COLUMNIST. As best I can make out, all you'll have to do is read the papers, watch the talk shows, hobnob with buddies who hold exactly the same views as you do, and then sound off—just like 98 percent of Americans do. But you'll sound off in print, and get paid for it. Pay: okay. Fringe benefits: okay. Extra bonus: You get to hector thousands or even millions of people with your views of the world but won't have to listen to them tell you what *they* think.

CORPORATE VICE PRESIDENT IN CHARGE OF SPE-CIAL PROJECTS. Often derided as an ignominious, career-stopping demotion, this is actually a ticket to a life of leisurely expense-account lunches, bull sessions with similarly underemployed executives, trips to Europe, and periods of ''working at home.'' The more accomplished special-projects gurus set up desks at various parts of the corporate empire so that their bosses, who don't much care what they're doing, anyway, lose track of where they are and assume they're at the Toledo plant when actually they're on the golf course. Pay: excellent. Fringe benefits: excellent. Special bonus: You might actually come up with a moneymaking innovation and get promoted again. Then you can maneuver to have your former boss assigned to take over your duties on the special-projects front.

BUREAUCRAT. Much manual dexterity is required here. Candidates should be adept at sharpening pencils and shuffling papers. Beyond that, maintaining the right attitude is a key to advancement: You must have a rigid frame of mind and an abhorrence of compromise. You must demonstrate strong character, and not be deterred from enforcing a petty regulation simply because doing so might destroy overnight a small family business that took decades to build. While generally you will be expected to put in long hours—ten to four, minus an hour-and-a-half lunch, for the first four days of the week and 11:20 to 1:50 on Fridays—this disadvantage is compensated to some extent by the opportunities for making long personal phone calls, taking numerous coffee breaks, schmoozing at the water cooler, reading the papers, dozing off when the tedium gets to be too much, and calling in sick every couple of weeks. Pay: low to moderate. Fringe benefits: decent. Extra bonus: You'll have the power to wreak havoc in other people's lives while enjoying ironclad job security and the prospect of an early taxpayer-financed retirement for yourself.

SCHOLAR. Thousands of college professors work their bottoms off for meager salaries because they love learning and enjoy imparting it to young people. Avoid that trap. The trick is to worm your way into a senior position in a large department at a prestige university like Harvard or UCLA and then let the assistant and adjunct professors do all the work for a pittance while you immerse yourself in ''research'' and write obtuse articles that few will read, fewer will understand, and nobody will enjoy. You might well have to travel extensively to the great libraries of Europe, located conveniently in London, Paris, Milan, Prague, and other cities whose charms you will probably be able to squeeze into your schedule—say, from 8 A.M. to 3 P.M. and 5 P.M. to midnight. Pay: good. Fringe benefits: good. Extra bonus: You'll give the same lectures so many times that eventually you'll learn them by heart and be able to wow dinner companions and cocktail party confreres with your erudition by quoting snippets.

ECONOMIST. Remember what Harry Truman once said: He wished he could find a one-armed economist, because all the ones he knew were always saying, ''On the one hand this, on the other hand that.'' Economists have to juggle lots of statistics around in their heads and pepper their statements with fancy-sounding words and phrases like ''macroeconomic'' and ''derivative financial instruments.'' They can use these statistics and phrases to advance any position whatsoever on the economy, provided that they stick in an "on the other hand" caveat somewhere to the effect that it's possible they've got it all wrong. Pay: all over the map, depending on whom you do your cogitating for. Benefits: ditto. Extra bonus: If you master the art of totally baffling the world with abstruse and convoluted commentary, you might get appointed to the Fed.

FINANCIAL PLANNER. A lot of insurance salesmen use this description as a cover, but a true financial planner lives up to the title by planning to get rich on other people's finances. It's fairly simple: You draw up fancy reports of your clients' net worth, urge them to spend less and invest more, and charge them $5,000 for your advice. You should also tell clients to call you anytime, day or night, but make sure you take your cellular phone to the beach and the golf course, your two main workstations. Pay: anywhere from nothing to $1 million a year. Benefits: none, since you're self-employed. Special bonus: Your brother-in-law will think you know what you're talking about when the conversation turns to the stock market.

COMMODITIES TRADER. True, you'll have to work like hell and scream yourself hoarse for four hours a day, but you'll make enough money to retire at forty and play golf for the rest of your life. Pay: fantastic. Fringe benefits: none. Special bonus: You can both confuse and impress your friends by describing complicated deals you orchestrated that netted you hundreds of thousands of dollars. (You won't bore them, of course, with the complicated deals you orchestrated that lost you hundreds of thousands of dollars.)

AUTHOR OF BOOKS LIKE THIS. See newspaper columnist, above. Special bonus: free lunches with your agent and editor.

WELFARE RECIPIENT. The juxtaposition of this category with the previous one is purely coincidental. It will be remarked that this particular dodge has fallen into low repute, but I would argue that those on the dole should try to educate the public to the usefulness of their idleness. Bear in mind that whole troops of bureaucrats are kept employed conceiving and administering welfare plans, while hordes of speechwriters are kept busy concocting reforms to a system that is unfixable. Meanwhile, you can make a modest living by dining at the public trough. Pay: low. Benefits: few. Special bonus: Ample opportunities to conduct advice forums for similarly minded individuals.

LOW-LEVEL UNITED NATIONS DIPLOMAT. This specimen is basically a bureaucrat with a foreign accent, but he gets paid a lot more than the typical American government functionary and does even less. Pay: outrageous. Benefits: ridiculous. Special bonus: You get to park your car in no-parking zones without the risk of being towed away.

PSYCHIATRIST. This does require one skill: You must be able to doodle. You will also have to invest in a couch and some spiral notebooks. A sad but serious face is mandatory; a beard, optional. Pay: generous. Benefits: none, if you're self-employed; extensive, if you work for a corporation. Special bonus: Where else can you make a bundle merely by repeating six short phrases over and over again: "How are you feeling today?"; "Please go on"; "What did you do then?"; "What makes you think that?"; "Is there anything else you want to say about that?"; and "Our time is up."

LAWYER. You will engage in a lot of activity that the world at large might confuse with work. Your main task is to turn small problems into chain reactions of lawsuits. Thus, with a minimum of effort, you will be able to collect a maximum of lucre. The requisites for entering this career are a vivid imagination and a steady, outstretched hand. The only serious drawback is that in court you have to give equal time to the opposing lawyer's blather. Pay: up to five hundred dollars per billable hour (not the same as an hour of work), plus contingency fees that can measure in the hundreds of millions of dollars. Benefits: lovely. Special bonus: You get to run the country, along with all the other lawyers.

Those are the main routes of escape from Adam's curse. Many others exist. Indeed, almost any job can be turned into a sanctuary from the painful struggles of the workaday world, if the jobholder will but put his mind to it. I have known Fortune 500 chief executives who were more adept at napping than at mapping strategy, and investment bankers who were more proficient at mixing cocktails than at merging corporations.

People who just don't want to work can always find a way. Here are some basic techniques to help them along:

Adopt the first principle of warfare: camouflage. Scatter papers on your desk. Write urgent notes to yourself to perform fictional tasks and tape them in prominent spots for passersby to see. Phone the weather number and loudly proclaim to the recording that you're sorry, you're going to have to cancel dinner tonight because you're meeting with an important client. Noisily stuff your briefcase with documents of all sorts before rushing out of the office (to the nearest bar).

Always wear a harried look. Practice in front of the mirror. Make sure your hair is tousled. Develop nervous tics. Gulp down lots of coffee and leave the empty paper cups on your desk. Store a ready supply of crumpled sheets of paper in the back of your drawer, for scattering in and around your wastebasket at crucial moments. If smoking is still permitted in your workplace, keep a coffee can full of cigarette butts within easy reach, for dumping into your ashtray first thing in the morning. (Being a professional goof-off, you will undoubtedly have friends who can collect them for you.)

Create the impression that you spend most of your time in the office. I call this the evocative-imagination approach. Some effective stratagems: Get to your desk fifteen minutes before everybody else and, when they show up, ask, "Is it nine o'clock already?" At five, just as your secretary is getting ready to leave for the day, instruct her to call a restaurant and arrange for a steak dinner to be delivered to your desk at midnight. Because your bizarre request is sure to disrupt her schedule, she will undoubtedly spread news of it to your colleagues the next day. Of course, you will have to stay at your desk looking busy until the last employee has departed. At that point, immediately ring for the night superintendent and ask him when his birthday is. No matter what he replies, congratulate him and tell him you want him to have a nice steak dinner at your expense—and that you'll arrange for it if he'll just come up and get it at around midnight.

You may then proceed home. Go to bed immediately, because you're going to have to get up early the next morning. Don't bother to shave, and put on the previous day's rumpled clothes. Get to work even earlier than usual. As they say, "Come as you are." When the others arrive, mumble apologies for your appearance through extended yawns. At 10 A.M., clutch your heart and stumble to your feet, muttering, "Maybe I overdid it, but I wanted to do the job right." Then go home and play golf.

It is our hope that you don't have a beautiful, buxom secretary. She may be overcome by compassion, in which case you'll never get home by ten.

You may have to go through this routine two or three times before getting a raise. So snoop around and make sure your boss doesn't have a dentist's appointment on the mornings of your dramatic departures.

Do not pass these tips on to too many of your friends. We'd like to keep them fresh for as long as possible.

The whole point is to induce your boss to conclude: I must be working this fellow too hard. You should, of course, be careful not to go overboard, lest you become in management's mind a high-risk hospitalization plan user. Every third or fourth business day, whistle merrily to show your bonhomie.

My purpose in this chapter has been to get you thinking about how you, too, can achieve health, wealth, and good cheer with a minimum exposure to *work*. More broadly, I am hoping to dislodge one of the last taboos to infest our popular culture. America long ago abandoned civility, modesty, discipline, restraint, kindness to strangers, and other quaint Victorian notions. Why must we cling so stubbornly to the idea that to get ahead, you have to work hard?

Sadly, I conclude that my life has been a dreadful mistake. In the early 1930s, when I was scouring the suburbs of New York City for businesses willing to place classified ads in the *World Telegram,* I took an afternoon coffee break with a fellow salesman in a diner along some lonely highway. "Well," he said, "I've had enough. I'm knocking off for the day."

I was stunned. Knocking off—at 4 P.M.? I never saw him again. At the time, I thought he was a slacker. Now I realize that far from being a malingerer, he was the harbinger of a great movement. He took the smart turn; I, in my naïveté, doggedly pursued the false path of struggle and toil.

Nevertheless, now that I have seen the light, I generously share my conclusions with you. Making a lot of money for doing nothing is the wave of the future. For that reason, I propose that our business schools begin offering courses on the topic and allowing their leading lights to fritter away their time and our children's tuition dollars doing research on it.

The Catch-22, of course, is that the students who sign up will almost certainly not bother to pay attention in class or do their homework, though true to the principles laid out in this chapter, they will show up for class and pretend to be interested.

I read an obit recently about a legendary professor at one of the Ivy League schools who told his male students that his purpose in life was to reduce the time they spent thinking of girls to 60 percent from

80 percent of their waking hours. Surely, the young scholars who take these courses will increase the time they spend thinking about the opposite sex to 100 percent.

If asked, I will be glad to teach an introductory class. I will call it Nonwork 101. My only conditions are that I be paid a lot of money and that I don't have to show up in person to deliver the lectures that my assistants will write for me.

SHOWING

LEADERSHIP

6

Memo to Bosses: Motivation Is the Key

I guess I can't write a chapter on management without commenting briefly on all the management theories popping up these days like mushrooms after summer rain.

You know: Total Quality Management; empowerment; reengineering the corporation; the human investment model; cycle-time management (it seems a Canadian consultant was trying to patent this one); the four Rs of reframing, restructuring, revitalization, and renewal; the five skills of breakthrough thinking, open-book management . . . Like mushrooms, they look enticing, but their nutritional value can be suspect. Some are even poisonous.

This barrage of management creeds and screeds is nothing new: Back in my day, we had Theory X and Theory Y and Werner Erhard's Seminars Training. No one remembers much about them today; certainly, I don't. Do you?

Some of the latest manifestos make a certain amount of sense to me. But how new are they, really?

Take reengineering. The book *Reengineering the Corporation* by James Champy and Michael Hammer was published in 1993 and has sold more than 2 million copies worldwide. Its influence on corporate thinking is said to be enormous. The basic idea, as I understand it, is that corporations have to redesign their structures from scratch, using the latest information technology, in order to achieve huge savings and increases in productivity.

It sounds good, if not exactly earthshaking in its originality. And it has a familiar ring. When I was working for steel company Jones & Laughlin in the early 1950s, I took a course in what was then called "operations research" at the Case Institute in Cleveland. Basically, the message was to reexamine things to see how you could do things better.

I remember there was a department store in the area that advertised free delivery of parcels on the day of purchase. It was a time-honored practice and the owner prided himself on it. There was no way that he was going to abandon it.

However, an "operations research" study conducted for him revealed that on days that only one package went out to the farthest point in the delivery area, the "free" delivery cost him up to $165. That was it. End of policy.

Reengineering?

In World War II, there was great concern about the number of our planes that were being shot down by our own antiaircraft fire. It turned out that a lot of pilots simply forgot to turn on their IFF, an electronic system for recognizing friendly aircraft. (The acronym stands for identification, friend or foe.)

The pilots' lives might depend on their turning the device on. Yet many simply forgot. So the air force came up with a brilliant solution. They sent a guy out to the end of the runway, and every time a plane took off, he'd hold up this huge sign that read, "Turn on your IFF." Reengineering? Or common sense?

You should always be on the lookout for ways to improve your operation. And you'll be surprised at how simple they can be, once you get the facts.

Fortune magazine came out with a "Devil's Dictionary" in 1995 of some of the latest management terms. It defined reengineering as "the principal slogan of the '90s, used to describe any and all corporate strategies." The choice of the word "reengineering" was smart. The dictionary defines engineering as planning, constructing, designing, managing, maneuvering, directing, or guiding. Dull, humdrum verbs. If Champy and Hammer had titled their book *Replanning the Corporation* or *Guiding the Corporation along New Paths,* it might never have made the best-seller list. But "reengineering" is a robust verb. It conjures images of driven scientists equipped with high-tech equipment, busily putting things right.

I now read that Mr. Hammer concedes any other buzzword probably would have failed to capture the public's imagination. "If I had used another term, it would have fallen flat," he said. And I notice that each coauthor of *Reengineering the Corporation* has his own sequel out. Mr. Champy has written *Reengineering Management.* It seems a lot of companies were unsuccessful at their reengineering efforts, and he blames management for insufficient attention to the principles of reengineering. Buying *Reengineering Management* would appear to be the ideal correction to this oversight.

Meantime, Mr. Hammer has written *The Reengineering Revolution* as a kind of update to the original book. Maybe we could call their combined writing efforts "reengineering the publisher."

Buzzwords are for the birds. "Reengineering" no doubt takes the number one spot as champion buzzword of the 1990s, but "synergy" isn't far behind, and is gaining fast. "Value-added," though an adjective, is a contender, because you can tack it onto almost anything, including, I suppose, management theories. Which leads us to this question: If you reengineered your synergies, would the process be value-added? Or, if it became a trend, would it signal a paradigm shift for corporate America?

Well, my views on management don't have a name. They don't amount to a theory, either. They're just commonsense observations. But taken together, they might make a reasonable guide to some aspects of being a boss.

The most important point I'd like to make is that you don't build a company with geniuses. There aren't enough of them to go around, and they are not the most reliable foundation, anyway. You build it with just regular people who are motivated.

That's the key: motivation. You motivate your employees with money for work well done, of course. But you also motivate them with trust. It is an old-fashioned concept, perhaps out of style in our "downsizing" era. But it can work wonders. It can even earn you your employees' loyalty. Remember loyalty?

At ITT, we gave everybody lots of leeway to initiate and to show what they could do. Today, I believe they call this empowerment— as if it were some bold new idea. In fact, it's human nature. If you give somebody responsibility to do something, he'll almost always do it. If you do everything in your power to make your workers succeed, they usually will. And the icing on the cake is that they will reciprocate. They will fight like hell to make you succeed, too.

Should a boss be "tough"? It depends on how you define tough. Some people think of toughness as ruthlessness. They are sadly mistaken. Real toughness means being realistic and showing persistence— sticking with a problem until you solve it.

It also means being fair—that is, rewarding hard work and initiative and moving against laziness or insubordination. Happily, if you stick firmly to those principles, you'll spend very little time punishing people and most of your time rewarding them.

Above all, a boss should not be a bully. He sets the tone; if he is perceived as in control of himself and fair-minded, his employees will eagerly pitch in.

In dealing with employees, you should remember where you came from, and how hard it was to get where you are today. Then ask yourself if the employee is working hard and doing his best. If he is, you have to like him. If he isn't, there is no such requirement.

One mark of a good boss is that he probably works harder than anybody else, and does so by choice. I still keep long hours. For me, work is fun. Besides, what else would I do? I could sleep to 10:30 every morning. But then what?

Was I a hard driver? Well, not purposely. But I was determined to keep things moving. And I'll tell you this: ITT was a great training center for candidates to corporate America. A number of future chief executives of major corporations were part of our team, and sat in on our monthly meetings in New York and Brussels. I likened the process to the Harvard case studies. Only ITT was better because it was a continuing case study, and we played for real winnings or losses.

If an employee puts in her best effort but still flounders, you have the obligation to help her, at least up to a reasonable point. If she doesn't make that effort, you have the obligation to put pressure on her. In either case, she might surprise you with a better performance than you thought possible.

Money is a powerful motivator only when the recipient feels he has earned it. It then becomes a realistic confirmation of his progress. At ITT, I figured that anybody in a senior position who joined us by the age of thirty-five should leave the company at least a millionaire at sixty-five. Maybe today we would aim higher.

In hiring people, we went through a grueling selection process. The board had approved my request to pay new hires over the going rate if we could get the right candidates. As a result, we got the best management material in corporate America. It was a very sound investment.

If motivating people is your first duty, melding them together into a team is a close second. Teamwork is as essential to the smooth functioning of a corporation as it is to the smooth functioning of any team.

One thing a leader is able to spot, and which he quickly eliminates, is office politics. The basic feature of office politics is an attempt by somebody to control people or information to make himself look good, or to lead a splinter group. Why do people indulge in office politics? Usually it is because they are insecure or ambitious beyond their abilities. The best way to deal with them is to identify them and get rid of them.

I like to talk about leaders, not leeches. For example, the executive at American Can in New York who was in charge of Amertorp was a Mr. Carl Preiss, a true leader. He'd come out to the Amertorp plant in Chicago once a month, by which time, under the pressures of wartime production, everybody was overworked and on edge.

Mr. Preiss would give a big party, and make a short speech about the importance of our mission and congratulate us on the progress we had made. By then, we'd all had a few drinks, and Mr. Preiss would work the crowd. A bluff and hearty yet astute man who took no nonsense, he made you glad to be on his team. He instilled the warm glow of brotherhood in our hearts.

This would last for some days into the next month before we started snapping at each other again. Even so, Mr. Preiss was a great example of the influence of a strong leader on the spirit of an organization. He earned people's trust, and that says it all. In warfare, a leader used to charge into battle ahead of his troops. They trusted him to lead; he trusted them to follow. And they stood or fell together. No "mission statement" was required.

If people extend you that trust, you have to reciprocate by showing concern for them and their careers. If you demand the best from them, you have to give your best to them. You don't have to spell out your intentions; they'll know. The relationship is one of mutual respect.

At our monthly management meetings at ITT, we encouraged people to speak freely, and we did not put anybody down. You gave an honest answer to any query, even if you thought it was off the track. And sometimes we discovered it was very much on track.

I have somehow gained a reputation as a harsh and impatient taskmaster. I was even accused in a best-selling book in the early seventies (Anthony Sampson's *The Sovereign State of ITT*) of having despotic tendencies. Mr. Sampson put me on the theoretical throne, casting laggards to the lions. I guess you could sell books that way.

But I believe that picture is undeserved. At our corporate meetings, I'd fire questions at the participants, and they were free to fire questions right back! My only interest, and theirs, was to root out the facts. Facts are earned—not given away. That's the theory of advocacy law. There is nothing personal about such give-and-take.

We had a primary operating rule: No surprises. Have you ever noticed that 99 percent of all surprises are unpleasant ones? Problems we expected, but not surprises. We were all in this together. If one guy messed up he was letting the whole group down. If he succeeded, we all succeeded.

Were my managers loyal to me, personally? I would say so. Certainly, they trusted and respected me. But their loyalty was really for the company, including me but also including themselves.

I always wanted to be in charge—but when I achieved my goal, my greatest pleasure was to share my success with everybody else, because they were part of it, too.

Some people try to get ahead by politicking and pulling strings. Remember the guy in the musical *How to Succeed in Business without Really Trying* who showed up for work twenty minutes early every day and dumped cigarette butts into dirty coffee cups to make it seem he had been there for hours? It was a funny scene—but there are plenty of frauds who make a career out of tricks like that. (See the chapter entitled "The Art of Goofing Off.") What they never understand is that most people can see through them right away. I firmly believe you can't be in a company for more than a few weeks before everybody there knows pretty much what kind of a person you are.

The chairman I worked with at Jones & Laughlin, Admiral Ben Moreell, was a good-hearted guy and a natural leader. He ran the Seabees—the combat construction corps during the war. The CEO was Lee Austin, a well-meaning but austere, opinionated man with a short fuse.

Anywhere in the mills, down to the sweeper in our huge plant in Aliquippa thirty miles away from headquarters, if you asked an employee what he thought of the admiral, the answer was always the same: "Great guy. Fair. Honest. Cares about his people."

And Lee Austin?

"———!" (Expletives deleted.)

You have to win your people's respect by standing for certain principles and sticking to them under fire. In my early days as controller at Jones & Laughlin, I kept visiting the manager of our sheet mill to try to persuade him to run the operation on a budget that would help him control his costs. That was anathema to an old steel hand. A budget? You brought in your crew and used your supplies and operated the equipment, and that was it. He didn't want to discuss it. Well, I really wanted to help him.

Have you ever seen one of those big sheet mills? They run for two blocks. At one end, they put in molten slabs of steel which go through the big hot mill and come flying out at forty miles an hour as a red-hot ribbon of steel a quarter mile long. It then goes through still other mills and comes out as a thinner hot sheet, and finally it gets rolled into huge coils.

It's hot and dangerous work. And here I was, a college-educated accountant in a white shirt and tie, trying to tell the guy in charge of all this massive operation that he had to set up a proper budget on paper.

But I succeeded. I returned again and again and hammered home on the same theme: We had to improve his performance. Finally, he realized I was not some college kid, but an honest do-it guy. I wasn't giving him bull. And by the time we got through, he had himself on a variable budget for his crews and expenses. Afterward he became a great apostle of variable budgets. His conversion interested me because we couldn't have been further apart in our backgrounds.

But you couldn't fool him. He knew I wouldn't have asked him to do it if it didn't make sense. But he couldn't help but be surprised that it really did. And people in an office aren't any different. They respond to the same honest determination.

That's the reason I bought my ITT stock instead of just holding my options. Options are a free ride: If the stock price goes up, you can make a bundle. If you make a hash of things, and the stock price goes down, you lose nothing. Anyone could like that deal.

I thought it was important to show publicly that I had confidence in my company by exercising the two hundred thousand ITT stock options that I received when I came in. Yes, I could have just sat on them. But I borrowed $2 million from the bank to buy them. Every year, I paid interest on the debt. There was never any question that it was the right thing to do. I shared my risk with the stockholders as they did with me.

You don't need to go out and buy a book on the art of being a good boss. The formula is simple: Be competent, be human, be fair.

Remember the old days when a father was called a "breadwinner"? It sounds quaint today, doesn't it? His job was to earn enough money to keep a roof over his family's head. He often worked late into the evenings or on weekends. He was absent a lot, and when he was home, he was pretty tough. But you counted on him to take care of you and to pull you out of rough waters. That's what a boss should do. Take care of his people and pull them out of rough waters. He should be demanding, but fair. At ITT I rarely raised my voice. That just made the people around me all the more sensitive to my moods. You can convey your impatience, or your smoldering anger, without using a two-by-four.

I'd try always to help the guy who was falling behind. We'd send in a whole team to help a division chief, if necessary. I'd never fire anybody who was trying to improve his performance. It never occurred to me to fire huge numbers of people to dress up the bottom line. In the big recession of 1973, we lost only 2 percent of our almost four hundred thousand people worldwide.

What is the worst thing that has happened to business in the past thirty-five years? I'll tell you flat out: management's shirking of its responsibility to look after the welfare of employees. That is what many managers have become: shirkers. This is no way to run a business. It's not just morally wrong, it's stupid. It demoralizes employees and destroys teamwork, the foundation of any successful enterprise.

Too many CEOs today invoke the lame excuse of the "harsh economic climate" to justify booting hundreds or thousands of people off the payroll. For a while, mass layoffs became almost a management fad among Fortune 500 companies. It was a bit like the medieval medical practice of bleeding patients to make them get better. And yet nothing is more destructive of a company's culture than these mindless mass layoffs. Some bosses even seem to revel in the carnage, like Albert J. Dunlap, who relishes his nickname "Chainsaw Al" and who slashed one-fifth of Scott Paper Company's workforce before hacking off *half* of Sunbeam Corporation's in November 1996. Whatever the former culture was—whether its core was hard work, or creativity, or social responsibility, or anything else—it is shattered and replaced by a new culture of fear, anger, and looking out for number one. People won't speak up, won't innovate, won't take chances. Oh, maybe a few lone wolves will play the game the way it used to be played, but the teamwork is gone.

In 1994, corporate profits in the United States hit another record. And the reaction of corporations was to cut more than half a million jobs, up from just over three hundred thousand in 1990, a recession year. I even read a while back that the hottest topic at management seminars was how to fire people. And these courses included pointers on everything from how to physically remove the stunned victims from the premises to making sure you had a box of Kleenex ready when you delivered the bad news.

How terribly immature! And to think that people who took those courses counted themselves as leaders. I avoided that route by planning ahead to grow—and making growth, and performance, articles of faith.

The mass layoffs have to raise the question, Have corporations' bottom lines deteriorated that much? Of course not. But the exercise, while unpleasant, was easy to carry out. Announce a onetime hit—write it off, and forget it. Has foreign competition gotten that ferocious? Not really; just the opposite, in fact. Have corporations failed to grow sufficiently? Ah *yes!*

Also: Has top management lost sight of the fact the victims are real people, with real children and real mortgages to pay? And even more important, that they are real people who have made real contributions to the company?

If things are really so bad, who bears the ultimate responsibility? The CEO and his top officers, that's who. What "downsizing" really means is "We just discovered layers of fat that we never knew were there." That's incompetence, all right—top management's. It is a public admission: We have no vision. No ideas. We're stumped.

In a just world, people who insist on cutting so many jobs should at least think of cutting their own pay and perks. They will never do this, though. Instead, they will raise their pay as a reward for getting costs down. And the opportunities that might have been available are missed, and usually not even discerned.

The press has dubbed the policy of mass layoffs "corporate anorexia." Like the starving girl who looks at herself in the mirror and thinks she is overweight, corporations are now examining their downsized selves and still seeing flab.

None of this is to suggest that you should be anything but ruthless in dealing with nonproducers and troublemakers. Most managers tend to let things slide. It is an understandable lapse. After all, confronting such people is an unpleasant chore and nobody will complain to your face if you don't do it.

But everybody—everybody—is only too aware of the problem and silently resentful of management's inaction. The slacker who survives year after year without suffering any penalty mocks his hardworking colleagues. And they have to ask themselves two troublesome questions: Is management blind? And: Why should I continue to push myself if the guy at the next desk loafs the days away?

The manager who does act to expel the deadwood and the malcontents wins the gratitude of the productive workers. They won't say anything, but they'll respect their boss and feel better about the company. Still, to my way of thinking, there are only a few justifications for firing people: insubordination, unacceptable behavior, gross incompetence, and an unwillingness to improve. And insubordination is not just talking back to your boss but also taking any actions that undermine his authority or that go against the interests of the company.

I once reluctantly fired a heavy-drinking controller after giving him several warnings. He told me that everyone had always given him a second chance. I gave him a second chance, but not a third chance. His wife left him. But losing his job was the shock therapy he needed. Somehow, he pulled himself together. He got back with his wife, who called me to thank me for firing him! And then he thanked me for not giving him a third chance.

Having given up the bottle, he wondered if I could find something for him. I gave him a job in personnel, and he performed there admirably. He never drank again. Unfortunately, he came down with throat cancer some time after. He knew he was dying, yet he never took a drink. I have never forgotten his courage at the end of his life.

Sometimes, management fires the wrong people. Two cases come to mind. In my accounting days, I came across a fellow who worked for a dairy. His job was to run a creamery, moving milk from those big milk containers into a milk pipeline for processing into cream. The company allowed a 2 percent loss rate, figuring he'd spill that much or it would cling to surfaces. But he was so efficient, he didn't need the full allowance. So he helped himself to the difference, figuring he deserved it. His reasoning was as sound as his performance. And his motive was pure: He donated these hidden profits to the Boy Scouts!

I found this approach admirable. Better they should have made him president. He was smarter than their system. But they fired him, just the same, for taking that 2 percent profit.

Another time, back in my auditing days, the Thom McAn chain was selling shoes at $5.99 a pair in all its many stores, except one. I came across one where the price was $6.99. It turned out the manager had unilaterally tacked $1 on to all prices and was pocketing the extra buck. And with that extra incentive, he was outselling just about every other store. Another case where they fired him. Again, they should have made him president. His successful idea could have added 50 percent to the company's profits.

Rules, rules and no judgment. You see it time and again. In the mid-1930s, I stayed for a time in a Pennsylvania Dutch town and did accounting work for a Mr. Hantusch, a prosperous local businessman. Now, this Mr. Hantusch indulged himself in a variety of pleasures of the flesh, including spiritous liquids and spirited women. Indeed, he stood accused of molesting a chorus girl on his yacht, a charge that did not seem to upset him overmuch or diminish his standing in the community.

Mr. Hantusch employed as a bookkeeper a nervous-looking middle-aged fellow who worked long hours. In examining the books, I discovered that this employee had over a period of years regularly diverted funds to his own use and then, just as regularly, returned them.

Upon making inquiries into the matter, I determined that the perpetrator was in fact an honest, forthright fellow who didn't fully grasp the gravity of his transgression. His motive was clear: He had children who needed to be fed, clothed, and educated. The extenuating circumstance was not difficult to ascertain: He was underpaid. And there was an inanimate character witness who testified silently on his behalf: the books themselves, which showed that he always repaid his borrowings, even though he must have thought that his malfeasance was unlikely to be detected.

By the letter of the law and the ethics of my profession, I was duty-bound to report the irregularity of the situation to Mr. Hantusch. But I felt obliged to defend the bookkeeper to his employer, emphasizing his economic privations and probity of character and recommending he be given a raise!

"Ah, no," replied Mr. Hantusch, genuinely distressed by my suggestion. He explained that he had no problem with the man's habit of cooking the books, per se. But one thing he could never forgive: "He was living beyond his means."

That was the worst sin of all. In this upright Pennsylvania Dutch town, in 1935, it was acceptable practice to drink yourself into a stupor or commit adultery by romping with a chorus girl on your private pleasure boat. Indeed, such philandering raised a man's esteem in the watering holes of the region.

But you must never, ever live beyond your means! To do so marked you as a profligate. I will never forget the quaver of indignation in Mr. Hantusch's voice as he uttered the anathema: "He was living beyond his means."

Even after they fire employees, some companies continue to misuse them. In 1995, a large pharmaceutical company hired an outplacement firm to counsel a couple of hundred people it had laid off. It turned out that the outplacement firm was apparently steering them away from jobs in the health-care industry—where they might compete with the company. That's unfair.

Other companies will make laid-off employees sign noncompete agreements as a condition of getting their severance pay. That's pretty heavy-handed, and courts are apt to overturn these agreements. But often, these are little guys who don't have the money to hire lawyers. They simply sign away their freedom to take another job in their field.

Companies are naturally worried that their ex-employees will join the competition. But that is the risk they take when they lay them off.

The idea of firing solid, hardworking, loyal people bothers me because it is an unacceptable waste of a rare commodity—proven ability. It violates a great management doctrine: Treat workers as a resource rather than a cost.

I quote from a recent magazine ad by Mercer Management Consulting: "Research has shown that over the long term, most companies that downsize to increase shareholder value are unsuccessful in their quest." Pretty strong stuff.

Or, as one of the most successful CEOs of today, George Fisher of Eastman Kodak Company, put it: "Plans do not make quota or drive the trucks or design the packaging or, finally, make the customers happy. People do."

People do make things work, and a good boss focuses first, last, and foremost on what the people do. And he can gauge his or her success on one criterion: Has he used his leadership to provide them with "successful jobs"—jobs that are successful for the company? If he has, both he and the company—as well as every employee—will grow and succeed. And his people will respect him. And if that is so, he has succeeded. If it is not so, he will have failed.

7

Asleep at the Switch

He rode madly off in all directions.
—Stephen Leacock

Zeus, the god of gods who ruled ancient Greece from the summit of Mount Olympus, would feel right at home in the American Board of Directors Room.

The panoramic view would surely remind the aging deity of his glory days. The Board of Directors Room sits in magnificent isolation atop the corporate headquarters building, scraping against the heavens. Zeus, acceding to the fashions of the twentieth century, might trim his beard and put on a suit and tie and replace his lightning bolt with an attaché case before making an appearance in this citadel of capitalism. But once there, he would observe the hubbub in the streets below with the same imperious gaze that he once cast upon the mortals of Hellas from his throne in the pantheon.

Even without Zeus, the Board of Directors Room is a sacrosanct place. Its thick carpeting and heavy curtains mute the tumult of the world outside. It usually sits empty, like the sanctuary of a church on a weekday morning, or a tomb. Visitors are occasionally led in and allowed to be awed by its hush. Departed chairmen stare down at them with faintly accusing eyes from oil portraits on the walls. Furniture polish infuses the air with the odor of embalming fluid.

A huge mahogany table dominates the room. It is heavy not just with physical mass but with the weight of responsibility and purpose. It is usually oval in shape to afford directors an oblique view of those colleagues who are not in point-blank range.

Once a month, the stillness is replaced by a flurry of activity. Uniformed factotums rush about, placing bound agendas, ashtrays, glasses of water, cups and saucers, samovars of coffee, plates of Danish rolls, and packets of sugar and dried cream before each occupant's place. All this to give strength for the board's journey into the unknown.

Then the ornate double doors, also made of mahogany, are flung open to welcome the seers, who, upon close inspection, resemble the officers of a small-town Rotary Club more than the demigods of American business. Never mind; appearances can be deceiving.

After all, these are business leaders of the highest accomplishment. Their wealth can often be measured in the tens or even hundreds of millions of dollars. And they come to this room with great resolution.

The doors swing shut again; the directors sit in their high-backed leather thrones; the chairman clears his throat; the deliberations begin. The board is in session! I have often wondered why some forward-thinking company didn't install a pipe organ to complete the splendor of the occasion with a triumphant blast of Beethoven or Bach.

As the proceedings unfold, a lone figure scribbles silently away; it is the company lawyer, taking the minutes. His is an exercise in creative writing. For the lawyer is jotting down, not what the participants are saying, but what they *ought* to be saying. However inflammatory their rhetoric, it emerges from his pen as inoffensive fluff. However ignorant their musings, they appear on paper as brilliant insights. No lawsuit material here!

No one will ever know the depths or shallows of these deliberations. The minutes will recite a lot of facts and record an occasional chorus of ''ayes,'' but will hold no secrets or surprises for future historians.

The lawyer—as chaperone!

The board members are pleased to receive whatever honoraria might be disbursed in recognition of their services. Not all are wealthy; indeed, some make careers of sitting at mahogany tables. And they don't come cheap; annual ''fees'' of fifty thousand dollars or more aren't unusual. That is quite a step up from the twenty-dollar gold pieces that once constituted their symbolic reward for minding the store.

And these days, the fees are only the beginning. More and more corporations, in their gratitude, are awarding their directors a broad range of benefits: stock options, life insurance policies, pension plans, junkets, the use of the company jet, and numerous other perks.

Back when I was in charge at ITT, a director would occasionally be seized by an urge to monitor our operations in Paris. And so we'd arrange to fly him over there. He might spend one day talking to our people and four evenings in the nightclubs. He filled in no report card. He would invariably hire a car. And the local president would feel it to be his duty to squire him around and pay for the meals.

None of the corporate largesse, of course, ought to compromise a director's solemn pledge to monitor management and safeguard stockholder assets. Unfortunately, the directors are busy men and women, and so they leave the task of running the corporation to the CEO. What he says, goes. Sure, they might ask some pointed questions from time to time—but the CEO never fails to respond with soothing answers.

Too many boards rely on the CEO's record. Their attitude usually is: Well, he's been right so far. But what if the CEO has had the equivalent of twelve reds in a row on the roulette wheel? It is unlikely he will hit twelve more. Never mind, the board thinks; he seems like a capable guy.

William Agee, the former chief executive of Morrison Knudsen Corporation, a construction company, seemed like a capable guy to its board. True, he had gone through a career crisis at Bendix Corporation in the early 1980s, when he botched an effort to take over Martin Marietta Corporation.

And true, he raised eyebrows by later trying to run Morrison Knudsen, located in Boise, Idaho, from his estate in Pebble Beach,

California, several hundred miles away, as well as by negotiating an ever-increasing compensation package that totaled $2.4 million in 1993 even while the company was sinking. Morrison Knudsen, created in 1912 and an icon of the construction industry, recorded a $350 million loss in 1994, went into default on its loan agreements and eliminated its dividend, and ultimately agreed to merge in 1996 with a little-known company one-tenth its size. He seemed like a capable guy.

In the end, the board got rid of him. It acted with great decisiveness—but only after it was too late. It is the lock-the-door-after-the-horse-is-stolen syndrome. If Morrison Knudsen's board, populated by such luminaries as investment guru Peter Lynch, former national security chief Zbigniew Brzezinski, and former baseball commissioner Peter Ueberroth, got caught napping, what hope is there for run-of-the-mill boards?

Let's face it: About all most directors know is what the CEO tells them, plus what they read in the papers. If there is any discordance between the two, the CEO will be happy to explain why he is right and the papers are wrong. No CEO ever sends out a notice to the board that says: It's all downhill from here.

Directors do have the financial statements at their disposal. But, alas, accountants are only required by law to record what has happened, not what *will* happen.

Directors can, of course, solicit the views of stockholders. But they rarely do. That is a task they leave up to management, which eagerly fulfills it. The chief executive officer and the chief financial officer court the big stockholders—the funds, the banks, the brokerage houses—with a persistence that would do a lovesick teenager proud.

Even when a major stockholder makes a fuss—when the $80 billion California Public Employees' Retirement System says, ''We're going to sell our stock if you don't behave''—I don't think the average board member worries much. Calpers has too much at stake to take drastic action. If they did sell the stock, they'd drive the price down. So they make a ruckus and force a confrontation; the two sides negotiate; each makes some concessions that can be reported to the press; they resolve the matter. Everybody is happy, including the board's lawyers, who have been holding the members' hands throughout the ordeal.

This reluctance to take the initiative is only exacerbated by the fact that at most companies, the CEO also assumes the position of chairman of the board. This chairman-cum-CEO will run the annual meeting, write the annual shareholders' report, oversee publicity, hold the annual stockholders meetings, and make informal contacts with the shareholders themselves. He will choose his own successor, though that, too, is supposed to be the board's prerogative.

Likewise, the board is supposed to set the salary and incentives of the CEO and his top officers. In practice, directors follow the advice of management consultants, who are only too eager to please management. The resulting compensation packages are quite generous.

Lo and behold, motions to introduce, or increase, fees, pension benefits, stock options, and other rewards for board members find their way onto the proxy items for approval by the shareholders. Indeed, they are usually lumped together with the management incentives. Everybody in the company lives for the next round. The stockholders—often an amorphous, disorganized group—barely notice what's going on.

The wall between the board and management, as important for a corporation as the wall between church and state in politics, has come crumbling down. Arms stretch across the rubble and engage in an orgy of mutual back-scratching.

I have painted a perhaps unduly unfavorable portrait of board members as slackers dozing off at the switch. In reality, it is often more complicated than that. There are all kinds of board members. There are, to be sure, high-minded guardians of the stockholders' trust. There are also numerous other breeds: the power players who revel in their access to other power players; the neophytes who happened to be home when the phone rang; the corporate big shots who view the job as just another prize; and the duffers who don't know when to call it quits. They all fulfill an essentially priestly function: to bless the chief executive, waving Cuban cigars instead of censers.

What can spur them to action? One thing: the fear of looking foolish. Most didn't join the board to make money or prove themselves; they joined for the prestige. To see that prestige threatened is their worst nightmare. The dread of humiliation is their one great motivating force. Thus, if a board member's golf partners start making wisecracks about the company that he is supposedly guiding, watch out. He'll get into fighting trim, fast.

Likewise, if another company makes an unsolicited takeover bid, a board is sure to offer stiff resistance. Meekly acquiescing isn't an option. It would be seen as an admission of failure. Similarly, a usually somnolent director will fight tooth and nail against efforts to remove him, even if a quiet exit is promised. He knows that an unscheduled departure, even for ostensibly legitimate reasons, has the smell of failure.

In recent years, boards do seem to have been getting more assertive. John Akers of IBM, Robert Stempel of General Motors, James Robinson of American Express, Paul Lego of Westinghouse, Kay Whitmore of Eastman Kodak, Joseph E. Antonini of Kmart, Maurice Saatchi of Saatchi & Saatchi, Anthony D'Amato of Borden, and G. Kirk Raab at Genentech were all ousted in board revolts.

Even so, by the time most boards realize they might be looking foolish, things have gotten very bad indeed. The problem is their aversion to risk. Board directors are afraid to rock the boat. They don't want to put the CEO on the spot. They don't wish to discombobulate their colleagues. After all, they tell themselves, the company is doing just fine, isn't it? And it will continue to prosper, won't it?

Such complacent thinking has always been dangerous. Today, it is a prescription for disaster. As the world gets more competitive, as CEOs come under fire for laying off workers while enjoying everlusher salaries, as the government and the press and interest groups pick over corporate America's activities for evidence of malfeasance, directors have to be willing to risk confrontation with management and even the opprobrium of their peers to make sure things get done right.

What then can be done? There is no magic solution. But I have some suggestions. Why not, for starters, put the board firmly under the control of outsiders? At most boards nowadays, the insiders hold sway. Of seventeen directors of Archer-Daniels-Midland Company, for example, ten, as of this writing, are corporate executives or former executives or relatives of executives.

In many, perhaps most, American companies, the CEO is chairman. That's a conflict of interest. It means the chairman is saying: ''My job is to discipline the SOB who's the president. By the way, I'm also the president.'' It doesn't add up. The board's responsibility is to oversee the company and take corrective action where needed. That responsibility gets fuzzed over when management and the board overlap.

Remember, it's the chairman who calls the board meetings. If the outside directors decide it's time the CEO goes, they have to call secret meetings in hotel rooms. That's what the board is reduced to when they don't own the chairman.

Inside directors are a strange breed. Theoretically, they represent stockholders. Undeniably, they also represent themselves. Every year, after the stockholders elect the board, the board meets to elect the officers. The inside directors in essence reappoint themselves as the company's senior executives. No individual can vote for himself, but each inside director can vote for all the other inside directors.

The outside directors, who as I have mentioned often get fees of around $50,000, are supposed to be policing the inside directors, who earn salaries of about $750,000. Do the dual loyalties of the inside directors constitute a conflict of interest? Let's call it a divergence of responsibility. Whatever it is, it is a problem that suggests a solution: Eliminate all inside directors except the president. You have to keep him; it's a matter of face. Otherwise, people would say, "Geez, he's the president of the company—and he's not even on the board!" But he is a sufficient representative of management. There is no need to install his coterie.

If that seems too drastic, at the very least the number of inside directors should be reduced to a minority. And only the outside directors should choose the chairman—who should never be the CEO.

A lot of people applauded when John Smale led a boardroom coup by outside directors at General Motors against Robert Stempel and divided his two posts of chairman and chief executive. Mr. Smale, the retired chairman of Procter & Gamble Company, took the chairman's job, while John F. Smith Jr. was named CEO.

Well, not long ago, the same people who had applauded were disappointed when Mr. Smith was given the title of chairman. Back to the status quo, they said. They were wrong, in my opinion. Even as he was promoting Mr. Smith to chairman, Mr. Smale was elevating himself to the head of a new executive committee. What this undoubtedly means is that the executive committee was taking on the role of chairman. In other words, Mr. Smale will still be policing Mr. Smith. I predict that this executive committee will be the last word at General Motors.

The title juggling enabled Mr. Smale to retain power while satisfying Mr. Smith's ego. I applaud him for finding a way to avoid those sneak hotel meetings.

Here is another suggestion for improving the way our corporate boards function: Require the outside directors to hold an executive session every time the board meets, to talk about their responsibilities to stockholders.

Among other things, they should interview the public accountants periodically to make sure they haven't been pressured into withholding important information. I believe directors might be surprised at the points that would be raised at such a closed session. We should give this forum a fancy name to impress upon the world the gravity of the proceedings. We could call it the "fiduciary caucus." If the members have nothing to discuss, they can smoke cigars. Maybe some of the outside board members themselves occasionally need some policing. This certainly can be done more successfully in a closed session, without the presence of management.

Another way to improve the system, in my view, would be to instruct the directors to solicit the views of an outside consultant. This consultant, or better yet, group of consultants, should report to the board—and to no one else.

Is this spying? Hell, no. It's just seeking a second opinion—the same way you'd seek a second opinion if your doctor recommended a triple bypass operation. Or ask around before moving into a community or joining a golf club. Done all the time.

But not by boards. Which, out of a misplaced sense of loyalty, hardly ever make obvious inquiries. In most matters, corporations shop around for the best deals. To get the lowest prices, they negotiate with more than one supplier. To project the best possible image, they're forever switching advertising agencies. Shouldn't boards apply the same principle of diversification of sources in seeking information?

Granted, there are drawbacks to going outside the company. Consulting firms don't come cheap. There will be some resentment in management ranks, at least at first. The consultants might do a rotten job, fail to grasp the way things really work and make dumb recommendations. Or they might be tempted to go too easy on management, for fear of alienating a potential future client.

Even so, it's a risk worth taking. The consultants will produce a report, nothing more. You can file it away if you want to. But it might just alert you to a serious problem or an untapped opportunity. (Keep it confidential, however; airing your dirty laundry could drive your stock down, give aid and comfort to your competitors, and provide ammunition for class-action lawyers.)

The board needs to listen to somebody besides management. If juries only listened to the accused in criminal trials, who would ever go to jail?

Not every corporation is going to rush out to hire an outside consultant. However, short of that, boards should at least try to devise ways of improving the flow of information within the corporation, perhaps by setting up some sort of ombudsman, some critical set of ears and eyes to look over management's shoulders.

Here's another idea: Boards should ask management tougher questions. They should get into a more skeptical frame of mind and push the CEO a little harder.

Let's say your CEO tells you he wants to get a return of 8 percent. The first question you should ask is, "What can we do to make it better than that?" And you know what? If you question him hard enough, he'll come up with lots of ways.

I don't know of anybody who has been fired because he got an 8 percent return instead of a 10 percent return. But why not put some heat on a CEO who falls short of his goals? Demand excellence! Otherwise, why pay those multimillion-dollar compensation packages?

There should be tougher accounting by the boards. I think the public would be a lot more indulgent toward executive compensation packages the size of Zaire's gross national product if more CEOs got axed for merely mediocre performance, rather than for disastrous showings.

Mind you, terminating a CEO should be a last resort. But a good rule might be to never be satisfied with his performance, and keep bugging him on how he's going to improve it.

The board should also routinely interview some of the company's principal officers and department heads, including the controller, the legal counsel, the heads of the subsidiaries, the personnel manager, the sales director, and the new-products director. The conversations would be confidential; the purpose, to get firsthand, unfettered opinions.

Now, assuming that our directors succeed in becoming fully informed about the company's operations, it wouldn't hurt if, periodically, they wrote their own report on the company's future—not just analyzing prospects for growth but also examining potential pitfalls.

Boards should be asking themselves more often: What if? The end of the cold war wreaked havoc on the defense industry. Many defense companies have either gone out of business or merged. Of course, nobody could have foreseen the end of the cold war. But it's too bad boards weren't asking ten years ago: What if the cold war ends? What will we do then?

Here's a proposal that might not win me any popularity contests, but that even so might do wonders to make directors more accountable: Make it easier for stockholders to fire boards. If corporate America can sacrifice millions of blue-collar workers and middle managers and even a scattering of million-dollar chief executives in the name of efficiency and competitiveness, why should the boys at the top be spared?

I can already hear the screams of indignation. "What? Fire the board? One does not fire a board." Well, why not? Here's one way it could be done: In the annual election of directors, add a box in the proxy statement next to the voting section: "None of the above."

The percentage who vote for "None of the above" would be an excellent barometer of shareholder discontent. A 1 percent rejection rate would be bad enough; 5 percent would be a slap in the board's face; and 20 percent would be a public-relations disaster. And some higher threshold figure—say 40 percent—written into the company bylaws would trigger the dismissal of the board and put the selection of a successor in the hands of a special stockholders committee.

Is 40 percent undemocratic? Some might say so. But a board would have to be grossly incompetent to get a 40 percent repudiation and shouldn't be allowed to keep going if it does. After all, a board under fire never fails to send out the corporate shock troops to banks, insurance companies, and investment funds to plead for understanding and to promise better things to come.

And the board won't neglect the little guys, either. They are sure to bombard stockholders with prospectuses one-fourth inch thick, with glowing accounts of past glories and ominous ruminations about the dangers of changing horses in midstream. Under such circumstances, if 40 percent say it's time to go, it's time to go.

Boards are full of people who never open their mouths. They aren't adding anything. Yet directors never volunteer to leave; it would be a black mark against them. They have to be persuaded to go, usually by the chairman or some "director of influence."

It shouldn't have to be done that way. It should be possible to change a board without stigmatizing the individual. There ought to be some simple escape clause. And the reelection process shouldn't be quite so automatic. The sheer fact that there's no way to change the board is the issue. That never comes out in the open.

Stockholders never get to grade the board, much less fire it. The only person who grades the board is the raider who tries to buy the company cheap. But he is usually giving it an F.

Granting greater power to shareholders is a worthy goal, but difficult to achieve, because so many of them are short-term investors with no real commitment to the company beyond the desire to make money as fast as possible. Millions of Americans with money in mutual funds have no idea what actual companies they hold stakes in. With hundreds of millions of shares trading hands daily on the nation's exchanges, corporate ownership becomes a fluid concept.

To help correct that, I propose the creation of a special "loyalty dividend" to all long-term stockholders, equal to 10 percent of the regular dividend for each year they have owned the stock, up to a maximum of 100 percent in the tenth year and all subsequent years.

Thus, a six-year holder of a stock that pays a regular $1 dividend would get an additional 60¢ loyalty dividend, while a holder of ten years or more would get an extra $1. For an added twist, you could defer the loyalty dividends for the first ten years and then pay them in a lump sum—in this case, $5.40. And early sellers would forfeit half of the accumulated total.

Let's say I hold the stock for five years. I will be credited a dime for the first year, 20¢ for the second, 30¢ for the third, 40¢ for the fourth, and 50¢ for the fifth, or an aggregate of $1.50. It would be foolish for me to sell at this stage because I've built up an ever-expanding base for future dividend earnings; it would be doubly foolish because I would be throwing away half of past earnings.

Our loyalty dividends would do the federal government one better. It rewards long-term investment, too, by taxing long-term capital gains at a lower rate than short-term gains. But it has a single threshold: six months. Hold a stock that long or longer, and you will be taxed at a lower rate if you sell it. But we have ten thresholds, and increase the payoff at each one. Note that the government rewards you if you sell; we reward you if you hold. Of course, the government is trying to save the country; we're just trying to save the company.

The loyalty dividend would have the positive result of driving the stock price up, as fewer and fewer people would be willing to part with their shares. It would also decrease the volatility of the market and force a lot of stockbrokers into productive lines of work.

You could come up with all sorts of variations on this proposal. For example, you could simply double the dividend for shares held for more than seven years. Whatever the formula, it would change the nature of investing by adding a new element: time. People would be investing their time as well as their money in a company.

This inspires another idea, with the same purpose as the first, but even more radical: fidelity voting rights. You get one vote for each year you have held a share.

This would, of course, give people concerned with the long-term health of a company a bigger say in its future. A Kirk Kerkorian with a 20 percent stake that he bought last year would have the same voting power as a retired schoolteacher who bought a 1 percent stake in 1975. What's wrong with that?

The loyalty dividend and the fidelity voting rights wouldn't merely reward stockholder faithfulness. They would also induce people to stick with a company for the long haul, instead of jumping in and out of stocks in the hope of making a quick kill. They would make companies less vulnerable to unfriendly takeover bids.

Will all of this stand up under legal challenge? I don't see why not, so long as the board of directors, which represents the stockholders, has approved it. While they're at it, they might want to stipulate that the measures can only be reversed with an 89 percent majority.

By now, we are truly rewarding the long-term investor, making him the beneficiary of ordinary dividends, loyalty dividends, fidelity voting rights, and a lower federal tax on long-term capital gains if he cashes in. Our proposals, if implemented, could change the way people invest and the way companies raise capital in this country.

We're saying: Give the market back to the investors. To hell with the professionals. They're not doing anybody any good. As Warren Buffett has proved, the longer you hold a stock, the more money you make.

I have yet another proposal for making boards more effective: Reduce their size. You might be better off with five, not twelve, bright and competent people. No matter what size the board is, you're going to end up with a disparate collection of individualists. Such groups are more open and more manageable if they're small.

Moreover, in seeking new members, perhaps existing boards ought to consider lesser lights as well as corporate luminaries.

Boards are often afraid to consider anyone but the Big Names of American industry to put at the helm of the corporations they oversee. And with reason. After all, if they choose Gerstner and Gerstner fails, the world will say: Gerstner failed. But if they choose Joe Schmoe and Joe Schmoe fails, the world will say: What a stupid board!

The system is stacked against risk taking. It doesn't pay for a board to look for somebody who's good but cheap. Nobody cares about saving $10 million if the fate of a $20 billion company is at stake.

But I think the risk is worth it. There are huge numbers of smart, energetic unknowns out there who would jump at the opportunity to make a mark at a major corporation. These might be young presidents of midsize companies who are just beginning their careers; middle managers in bigger companies; private consultants; and so on. You could get the Wharton School to select them.

What about directors' pay? This is getting to be a hot topic, as more shareholders groups criticize the lavishness of compensation packages. I'd vote for paying them even more than they get now— but paying them in stock only. No more cash fees, pension benefits, travel expenses, and all the rest. Just stock.

If you reduce the size of the board to five members, you can afford to raise their pay. For Fortune 500 companies, for example, I propose an annual award of stock valued at five hundred thousand dollars or ten times today's standard fifty-thousand-dollar salary. Five hundred thousand dollars—that's real money. To earn it, the directors might feel compelled to exert themselves. To stick to the old, leisurely pace would smack of laggardness. And that would damage their precious reputations.

The chairman, especially, should redouble his efforts. He should start acting like a chairman. Right now, his title is mostly honorary. Everybody sits and says what he pleases. It's a very clublike atmosphere.

The chairman should take charge. He should lead. He should assign responsibilities. He shouldn't try to impose his will so much as to pull together the rest of the board. He'd have no luck trying to impose his will in any case; these are independent people. But under the current system, there's no way he could get the directors to do all that extra work.

After Albert Dunlap took over Scott Paper Company in April 1994, he started paying directors entirely in stock and told them they had an obligation to buy stock. He himself bought $4 million worth.

At smaller companies, the directors usually have money tied up in the corporation. It makes them more inquisitive. Directors at big companies will walk through the plant as a courtesy. At small companies, they do it because they damn well want to know what's going on.

As my next-to-the-last proposal, I'd like to put in a word for the little guy: Why not assign one director to represent small shareholders?

As stock ownership becomes more and more concentrated in mutual funds and institutions, the independent investor is being neglected. And yet he is probably the most loyal investor of all. So one director would be responsible for looking out for the interests of people owning fewer than, say, ten thousand shares.

Finally, I'd like to suggest that we change the corporate governance terminology. Let's do away with the phrases ''inside directors'' and ''outside directors'' and replace them with ''management directors'' and ''independent directors.''

Window dressing? Perhaps. But the new designations would be a constant reminder of where the loyalties of the title holders lie: the management directors' with themselves as well as with the shareholders; the independent directors' with the shareholders alone.

So there you have it: a few thoughts on ways to make boardrooms function more smoothly.

I'm quite aware that there has been a recent groundswell to overhaul the current system. Nearly 20 percent of shareholders voted against the reelection of the Archer-Daniels-Midland Company board after the company came under a federal antitrust investigation. And more companies are making stock a bigger part of their compensation. Asarco eliminated a pension plan for directors; Campbell Soup Company dropped cash payments, pensions, and other benefits and switched to mostly stock and stock options.

Even so, more needs to be done. I'm a firm believer in the principal that if it ain't broke, don't fix it. But a lot of boards are broke. So let's fix 'em.

Not that I have a low opinion of boards. Far from it. I've sat on quite a few, and so I know from experience that the vast majority of directors are serious, smart, high-minded, and hardworking.

To paraphrase Winston Churchill's observation about democracy, I would say that boards are a flawed institution—with the one advantage that they are the best form of governing corporations so far invented.

Addendum: How to Pick a Chief Executive

Here are three ways for boards to pick a new chief executive:

First, the auction method. It works this way. The auctioneer reminds the assembled applicants and audience that contrary to the usual practice, the *lowest* bid wins.

However, he adds, his fee will be based on the spread between the proposed opening bid and the final bid. The lower he takes the compensation package, the more money he makes.

Then the action begins:

"Do I hear five million dollars? Five million? Yes, I hear five million, from the man with the bowler hat. Do I hear four million eight?"

Then—"Four million eight hundred thousand, four million eight. Do I hear four million? Do I hear four million? Four million it is. Do I hear three-five? Three-five . . . Three-three . . . three-two . . . three million. I hear three million dollars! Do I hear two million three? Two-three it is. Do I hear two-three? Do I hear two-one? Two-three going, two-three going . . . Two-one. I hear two-one. Do I hear . . . I hear two million from the lady in the pink dress. Do I hear one million five? Then it's two million dollars, going, going . . . *gone!*

What's that? You think that's unrealistic? Doesn't happen that way, you say? Okay, maybe this is what you want: method number two: the power breakfast.

Two "influential directors" of the Virtual Washing Machine Company are having coffee and croissants in the birthplace of the power breakfast, the Regency Hotel dining room.

FIRST INFLUENTIAL DIRECTOR: Well, we gotta do something about our president.

SECOND INFLUENTIAL DIRECTOR: Yeah—I don't like that piece in the *Journal*—it depreciates us.

1ST I.D.: Never mind the technical jargon—it doesn't make us look good. Well, have we got any candidates?

2ND I.D.: Yeah, that fellow from Iridescent Hardware—Jefferson Tobias.

1ST I.D.: He look good to you? (*After a pause*) Who else we got?

2ND I.D.: Well, there's that guy Homer Crinkle from Detachable Vanues.

1ST I.D.: Well, what's he want?

2ND I.D.: He said he'd come for a signing bonus of four million dollars.

1ST I.D.: That's a lot.

2ND I.D.: Well, he must be worth it to ask that much.

1ST I.D.: This other fellow—he want that much?

2ND I.D.: Nah—he comes cheap—one million dollars.

1ST I.D.: Let's take the other—what was his name?

2ND I.D.: Homer Crinkle.

1ST I.D.: I believe you get what you pay for—let's take him.

2ND I.D.: Want to call the other directors?

1ST I.D.: Nah—call the *Journal*—and tell 'em—Homer Crinkle is our new president. (*Under his breath*) That'll give 'em something to chew on—calling us nitwits.

2ND I.D.: Okay—we got ten minutes before the meeting—to let the others know. But what about Silas? You know—he's still our president.

1ST I.D.: Well, tell him to skip the meeting and pick up his severance check in the treasurer's office.

2ND I.D.: Okay. I'll catch 'im before the meeting.

1ST I.D.: Well, we better get going.

2ND I.D.: Well, Joe, you really are a man of decision.

1ST I.D.: Well, something got me this far—didn't it?

2ND I.D.: Yeah. It couldn't have been your old man who founded the place—could it?

1ST I.D.: What a kidder you are!

They leave.

Maybe you like that one better.

But if all else fails there is always method number three, the headhunter approach.

This script would go like this:

The scene is the plush offices of Straight, Arm, and Jack, the holding company for the Mountain Moving Machinery Company.

Mr. Straight is leaning back in his office chair looking out the window and suddenly he has a thought.

MR. STRAIGHT: Miss Bloomfield—get me Anchor Watt.

MISS B.: Who's he?

MR. STRAIGHT: He's president of the We Break Walls Executive Search Company. We had a letter from him last week.

MISS B.: Oh.
His phone rings.

MISS B.: I have Mr. Watt for you.

MR. STRAIGHT: That you, Watt?

WATT: Yeah—and have I got the guy for you.

MR. STRAIGHT: You have—that's great—who did we steal him from?

WATT: From Consolidated Freight Cars—that's from whom.

MR. STRAIGHT: Hmm. What does he know about Mountain Moving?

WATT: Everything—trust me.

MR. STRAIGHT: So what's he want?

WATT: My fee for this one is going to be high—but it's worth it. You see—

MR. STRAIGHT (*breaking in*): I'm not interested in your damn fee—what's he want?

WATT: That what I'm trying to tell you—three times our fee.

MR. STRAIGHT (*exasperated*): Three times what?

WATT: Three times our fee.

MR. STRAIGHT (*his voice rising*): Well, Watt—what are you trying to tell me?

WATT: Our fee is two point four million dollars—and cheap, if I do say so.

MR. STRAIGHT: Damn it, Want, what does he watt? I mean, what does he want, Watt?

WATT: Well I don't know how many times I hafta say it—it's gotta be three times our fee of two point four million. That comes to seven point two million, and there also is a signing bonus of five point eight million.

MR. STRAIGHT: Well, he better be good. But it's a deal, if you can knock that two hundred thousand off and make it an even seven million dollars.

WATT: Can't do that unless I add the two hundred thousand on his signing bonus and make it an even six million dollars. But then I'll have to increase my percentage to thirty-four two from thirty-three three. The fee stays the same, though—just two point four million dollars.

MR. STRAIGHT: Ah, come on. We've given you a lot of other business.

WATT: Well, seeing you're an old customer—okay, okay. But let's see, thirty-three point three percent of seven million dollars is two million three hundred thirty thousand. But I want you to know I got two other takers. And I haven't mentioned any fee on the signing bonus of six million dollars. We'll talk about that later.

MR. STRAIGHT: ''Well, okay, he better be good; I'm in a kind of hurry to make an announcement. The stock went down over two points yesterday.''

WATT: He'll give notice right after he finishes his lunch. I'll send my bill over.

MR. STRAIGHT: By the way—what's his name? Hello? Hello!

MISS B.: He hung up, Mr. Straight.

MR. STRAIGHT (*addressing no one*): Some things seem endless. (*Pause*) Miss Bloomfield, isn't it time for my Maalox?

He leans back in his chair and resumes staring out the window.

Well, there you have it. Agreed, no matter how you go about it, the process is tedious. But somebody has to do it. And in the old days people even insisted on a handshake. Now, it's done by phone and fax. Well, that's progress.

8

Dear Shareholder: About That $203 Million Paycheck

You have to ask, What are corporations paying those mega-millions for? The solemn answer comes back from the board of directors: "Demonstrated capability."

But if the company is doing well, surely the CEO's predecessors deserve some credit. I propose breaking up Fortune 500 chief executives' pay, giving one half to the incumbents and splitting the other half among his demonstrably capable predecessors and their heirs.

Absurd? Of course. That's the point. At the moment, there is no logic in these things. The size of the pay package is dictated by habit. To be sure, most companies will hire consultants to advise them on an "appropriate level" of compensation, but all they do is tote up what everybody else in the industry is making and recommend that their clients pay roughly the same. They are, after all, eager to please their clients' bosses. As I said, it's a matter of habit.

This also leads to a steady escalation in the size of compensation packages. Look at the trends:

In 1995, the average compensation package for CEOs of major corporations surveyed by *Business Week* rose 30 percent to $3.7 million, ten times the 2.9 percent increase in wages and benefits for American blue-collar workers. Lawrence Coss of Green Tree Financial was number one with $65.6 million.

That was nothing compared with the famous $203.1 million that Michael Eisner reaped the year before at Walt Disney Company, mostly from exercising options; or for that matter with the $127 million that Thomas Frist Jr. got in 1992 at Hospital Corporation of America. For the five years ended in 1995, Mr. Eisner pulled in $233 million; Stephen Hilbert, chief executive of Conseco, nailed down $232 million; and Sanford Weill, head of Travelers, was paid $200 million. And Mr. Eisner had $318 million of unexercised stock options.

These figures are getting up to the stratosphere. Lou Gerstner seems to be doing a great job of turning IBM around. But he's going to make $20 million even if he does nothing but make mistakes.

How do you motivate somebody who makes $40 million in one year? The answer seems to be: "With even more money." Inevitably, some people work themselves up into a high-minded lather about these corporate pay packages. The word they most often use to describe them is "obscene."

"The amount of money that some of these people are making is just too obscene," says business author Milton Moscowitz. None other than CBS Incorporated chief executive Laurence Tisch says, "Even in well-run companies, chief executives' pay is too high. There is a certain obscenity in some of the greed taking place in corporate America." Compensation consultant Alan Johnson adds: "I'm shocked at some of the levels of pay out there." Even *Business Week* wonders, "Is anybody worth this much?"

Well, what is the truth? Are CEOs worth their paychecks? If so, by what standards? Who sets the standards? Who enforces them? To what extent does dumb luck decide the total?

All good questions—and ones that can't be answered by outbursts of moral indignation. To say that "no man is worth $203 million'' isn't a reasoned argument. It is a value judgment. It fails to account for accidents of circumstance. And once we let our gut reaction to supposed excesses guide our social policy, we will be well on the way to socialism.

It would be easy to ask, With millions of Americans plagued by poverty and drug addiction, is anybody worth a salary of $1 million? But that is a purposely loaded question. There is no logical connection between the two points.

You might as well ask, Is anybody worth $100,000? How do you put a number on a man's, or a woman's, performance?

I have a suggestion: Why not just use logic? To start off, why not ask: What is excessive? There should be some measure of reasonableness. You have to set some objective standards for measuring worth. Otherwise, all you get is hot air. One critic says, ''This is unfair. Who can be worth that much?'' And the CEO's defenders retort, ''That's the price of genius.''

If I had to choose, I would err on the side of paying too much for proven performance. It's a risk, but it's a smart *risk*. However, I would ask a lot of questions: Was the performance really as extraordinary as everybody seems to think? Against what odds did he achieve it? How did the company's profits and stock price stack up against others in the same industry?

Unfortunately, most boards don't delve too deeply into the methodology of calculating the true worth of performance. Doing so might ruffle feathers.

Much easier to follow the practice of posing two simple questions to the CEO: What did you make last year? And what should your increase be this year? (I'm oversimplifying, of course. Boards deliberate the question of the CEO's pay with great solemnity. Then, nine times out of ten, they approve a double-digit raise.)

Only when a company is desperately seeking a *new* chief to put its house in order does the question become: What are you worth? Unfortunately, in such a crisis, the rigorous analysis that would make sense in ordinary times becomes irrelevant. All the probing of the candidate's strengths and weaknesses boils down to a single question: Can he save the company? If the answer is ''no,'' he is worth nothing. If the answer is ''probably not,'' he is worth nothing. If the answer is ''maybe,'' he is worth nothing. If the answer is ''probably,'' he is worth nothing. Only if the answer is ''yes'' is he worth even a penny. But in that case, he is worth pretty much whatever he asks.

Consider: In 1993, George Fisher was paid $25 million to leave Motorola and run Kodak and Lou Gerstner was paid $15 million to leave RJR and run IBM. Both packages included $5 million signing bonuses. Were they worth it? Of course! But if boards had exercised a bit more due diligence in assessing their predecessors, things might never have come to such a pass.

Another reasonable approach for constraining a CEO's pay, aside from its link with performance, would be to set ratios to lower levels of compensation. One rule of thumb used to be that the number two guy should get about 80 percent of the number one guy's pay. Adopting that criterion would make a lot of CEOs poorer—or a lot of second-in-commands richer.

Another interesting comparison that has captured the attention of compensation specialists for years is between the highest- and lowest-paid people within an organization. To be sure, there is no realistic connection. From a purely business point of view, it makes no sense to base a chief executive's pay on multiples of the janitor's. But the notion appeals to social thinkers.

The ancient Greek philosopher Plato, for example, recommended that nobody should earn more than 5 times the lowest-paid worker. The turn-of-the-century American financier J. P. Morgan proposed a more flexible limit of 20 times. Management guru Peter Drucker once said that makes sense. I don't know what Peter was thinking that day, but such a formula would certainly put a ceiling on pay even before performance is judged.

In any case, it hardly corresponds to reality. In the mid-1970s, the average American CEO earned 40 times the pay of the average factory worker. Today, he earns *149 times* more. The highest-paid might earn 500 or 1,000 times more.

Some are worth every penny. It all goes back to "true performance." The board of directors' problem is to identify the who, the how, and the why.

While it would be a mistake to assume that the number of prodigies capable of running a big corporation is so small that boards have no choice but to pay them $5 million or more, it would also be a mistake to shrink from paying *whatever it costs* to get the best. After all, it is the most important investment a company ever makes.

So important, in fact, that the question shouldn't be: How much does he, or she, cost? The main question is: How do we know he really is the best?

Of course, financial reality always places an upper limit on what any company can pay. Gerstner couldn't have demanded a salary of $100 million. A $10 million maker of organic baby food can't pay some Harvard-educated whiz kid $2 million to turn it around. But as a general rule, I'd argue that boards should focus on how, not how much.

That's what we did at ITT, and it paid rich dividends. In addition to going through the obvious motions—looking at the candidate's record, talking to his previous employers and their directors, seeking out the opinions of his old high-school and college teachers, and of course, interviewing him—we put him through a rigorous psychological review, using standardized tests.

When I say rigorous, that is what I mean. We had a small department of trained industrial psychologists who conducted the tests and drew up profiles of the job seeker based on the results. Then we brought him in for yet more interviews, using our knowledge of his psychological makeup to probe even deeper into his character and motivation.

Tough? Sure. But it worked. It was our secret weapon. It enabled us to identify the cream of the crop. At a conglomerate that was growing as fast as ITT was, we needed the best of the best. And we got them by offering salaries that were 10 percent above the industry average. That motivated them to join us instead of somebody else, and to work harder than they otherwise might. Money well spent. It gave us a real competitive advantage.

Other curbs on CEO remuneration have been suggested. For example, boards could decide that in no given year should the chief executive be able to collect more than three times his combined salary and bonus in stock-option gains. But the boards still must decide what he is worth—and pay him that and a little bit more.

In other words, it may make sense to set guidelines, but not to dictate ceilings. There has always been a rule of thumb that a company shouldn't have more than 10 percent of its shares outstanding represented by options, for example. And 10 percent is high. Yet, more and more companies are breaking the 10 percent threshold.

In fact, 10 percent is now the national average, three times the level of the 1970s, and almost all of the options often go to a dozen or so people at the very top. As of 1995, Time Warner had set aside 20 percent of its stock outstanding for option plans. Upon acquiring Turner Broadcasting System, Time Warner said it would award Ted

Turner 2.2 million options over four years. Ultimately, that could reap Mr. Turner tens of millions of dollars. His risk? Zero. Also in 1995, H. J. Heinz's Anthony O'Reilly received 4 million stock options, in addition to the 750,000 he got in 1994, all priced *below* the market. (His contract did state his eventual take couldn't exceed $125 million.)

There is nothing wrong per se with breaking the 10 percent rule of thumb. There is nothing wrong with paying an executive whatever it takes to hire him and keep him. I'm not even sure I'd approve of the limit on Mr. O'Reilly's compensation. The goal should always be reward for performance, and mathematical formulas would obstruct that.

Compensation consultants tell corporate boards: "You're not out of line with other companies in your industry." But this thing just keeps drifting higher and higher. You can collectively get to the moon and still not be "out of line." Being in line or out of line is relative. So it isn't so much how much the CEO is earning as whether or not his compensation is out of kilter with the company's performance.

And, yes, it's legitimate to consider the impact on company morale if the top guy is getting $20 million and blue-collar workers are struggling by at $7.30 an hour and worried about the next round of layoffs. The workforce feels disconnected from the 0.2 percent who run the show. They don't think the higher-ups are in the same world.

They can do some math of their own—like figuring out if only ten of them, out of ten thousand, earned the same kind of money, the company would go bust. In reality, they are thinking mostly in their own terms—what do I think I am entitled to? Am I getting it? Is my pay better than last year? Is my job secure? Can I expect a promotion? Pretty simple. It's when the answers to these questions come out "no!" that employees start looking for somebody else to blame. Again it's a matter of the company's performance.

In bad years, CEOs might find it hard to justify enormous pay packages for themselves at the same time they are laying off thousands of people. Even if the guys before them caused the problems, they ought to be aware of the discrepancy and consider ways to share the pain. Perhaps by taking a pay cut.

Otherwise, loyalty becomes a lost cause. Workers begin to lose faith in the system. In their minds, the company becomes "the damn fool company."

Options were designed to avoid such situations, because they aren't supposed to be worth much unless the company really is doing well. While I support the idea of rewarding performance, I think the current system should be reformed so options don't reward the fluctuations of the business cycles, or chance economic disturbances, or the momentum created by the CEO's predecessors.

Right now, they often reward mediocrity or worse. And I feel compelled to note a minority viewpoint that is anathema to many: Maybe all those options don't spur people on to better performance, as is widely believed.

Consider the view of Graef Crystal, the much quoted critic of executive-compensation packages that he considers excessive: "Will the promise of more money motivate a CEO to perform better over the long term when that CEO is already working as hard and as smartly as he can? And when he is already earning, say, $5 million? The Japanese and the French and the Germans and the British all say no. And so do all my studies."

While I believe Mr. Crystal makes a positive contribution to the debate by forcing boards of directors to question their assumptions, I disagree with his conclusion. I myself have conducted numerous studies on the subject, and found that linking pay to performance increases long-term shareholder return. But it is not the only factor; it is not even necessarily the main factor.

Moreover, the linkage must be designed effectively. Performance must be measured *in profit per share over an extended period*. Options must be linked to that performance. If you do that, there is no way that they won't affect performance.

As for what the Japanese, the French, the Germans, and the British think—don't waste your time. Their governments have traditionally shown such intense hostility to options and other performance incentives that they can hardly have an open mind on the subject.

I discovered firsthand the universal appeal of pay for performance when I was restructuring some previously Communist-run plants in the former East Germany after its breakaway from Soviet rule. The managers showed intense interest in options and stock ownership, all the more so because they had never been allowed to own anything under the socialist theory that the means of production belonged solely to the state. If you want to know the power of options to motivate people, you should have seen how they picked up on the idea. And, of course, the Communist system illuminated more starkly than any argument I know the disastrous consequences of eliminating risk from the business equation. Managers of the state-owned enterprises in the Soviet bloc never dared overstep the dictates of the Party apparatchiks. The result was the greatest experiment in mismanagement that the world has ever seen.

At ITT, we tried to structure incentive programs for our European and Asian managers that didn't run afoul of local laws. The interest that those managers took in our efforts belies the contention that foreigners "all say no" to the concept; perhaps they never had an offer to accept. Our options went pretty far down the ranks, all the way to plant supervisors.

To the uninitiated, options might seem complicated. Here is how they work. The compensation committee informs the CEO: "You've done such a wonderful job that we've decided to award you two hundred thousand options." A dozen or so other senior officers get lesser grants. An exercise price is set, usually at the stock's market price on the day of issue. And an exercise period is set, typically ten years.

Every time the stock goes up a buck, the CEO's two hundred thousand options in the safe-deposit box gain $200,000 in value. If they go up by $20 over ten years, his paper profit is $4 million.

Let's say a high-level guy accumulates five hundred thousand options over a dozen years. Presumably, he wouldn't get them unless he was performing. Let's say he cashes them in regularly at an average profit of $25 per share. He does this by buying them at the low exercise price with money he borrows from his broker, then reselling them at the market price, repaying the loan and pocketing what's left. Don't forget, for each option he gets, he has ten years to aim for the maximum hit. His total profits at even $25 will be $12.2 million. A nice chunk of change, even in this day and age. And, of course, in some cases, top CEOs may get more than that. James Barksdale got 4 million options to buy Netscape Communications shares at about 11¢ each when he took over at the beginning of 1995; after it went public later in the year, the share price shot up to $174 at one point, before falling somewhat, giving him a paper profit at the peak of $696 million. That, of course, was an unusual case involving extraordinarily lucky timing. High tech was hot, the Internet was hot, and the stock market was hot, all at once.

And here is the advantage for the company: Options don't cost it anything! The profit that the executives make is essentially skimmed off the top of grateful shareholders' stock gains because the newly created shares dilute their holdings. (Few understand this, of course.)

And there is no downside. If the stock price languishes, or sinks, the paper in the bank is worthless. But even a CEO who bumbles the job loses nothing.

In some cases, the board will feel sorry for the guy and actually *reset* the exercise price downward for him and all.

Will they reset the price if the stock goes way up? Never.

There's a discrepancy there, even though the purpose is to get the job done. If a company's stock tanks along with the broader indexes, you can bet the CEO will point out that "it's the market." But when the broader indexes go up, you won't hear him say, "It has nothing to do with me. It's the market."

The corporate CEO likes things the way they are. If the market goes down, he often gets more stock options, plus an alibi for his stock's poor performance. If the market goes up, he gets credit for his stock's surge, and maybe a great cash payout. That is, if he has done everything else right.

A proposal by the Financial Accounting Standards Board to require companies to take a charge against earnings when they award stock options highlights a little understood side of executive compensation: It comes at the expense of shareholders. Few would object to paying the price in the form of slightly lower dividends—if the CEO's performance gets the stock price up. It is only when his payout reaches stratospheric proportions that they are likely to ask the question we are posing: Is he worth it?

The Securities and Exchange Commission now requires companies to spell out what their top managers earn in the proxy statements that they send to stockholders every year. That's an improvement. Trying to find these facts buried in the verbiage used to be quite a chore.

Now, at least, it is spelled out and people can say: "Wow!" And, one hopes, they add: "But he's worth it."

I myself made some money on options. It was nothing like some of the modern-day bonanzas. I actually exercised the ones I received on joining ITT at an early date and financed the purchase myself. Even though I had ten years to cash them in, I felt that as CEO I had the responsibility to shareholders to take the same risk they were taking. I also believed in ITT, and believed in the way I was running it.

So I borrowed $2 million from several banks to pay up front for those shares because I wanted to be a stockholder, not an option holder.

Unfortunately, when I left ITT in 1977, sky-high interest rates of over 20 percent and rising oil prices weighed down all stocks. By the time I paid off my debt to the bank, I was ahead only $2 million. That was my payback for eighteen years of building ITT into one of the great companies in the world. It was just bad luck—and one reason why I think option prices should be related to stock market trends.

But on the bright side: If I had gotten $12 million instead of $2 million, maybe I wouldn't have worked so hard after leaving. With $12 million in the bank—$36 million in today's dollars—even a workaholic might get a little lazy.

But I would do the same thing again, and exercise my options early, and for the same reason. A leader has to share risks. A leader has to lead. Besides, I didn't need a huge retirement nest egg because I had no intention of retiring.

How could we make the current system work better? Here are some ideas:

Relate the option's exercise price to the broader swings of the market, which the company cannot control.

A chief executive should be rewarded for outperforming the market, not coasting on it. If the Dow Jones Industrial Average doubles and his stock goes up by only 50 percent, he is clearly lagging. There is no reason why he should get a large unearned windfall.

Similarly, if the Dow tumbles by 50 percent and his stock only slips 25 percent, he has excelled. He should get a compensatory adjustment in the price.

Perhaps the exercise price should be readjusted every three months in tandem with the broader market. Thus, if the Standard & Poor's 500 index, say, gains 10 percent, the exercise price of $20 should go up to $22. If the index falls 10 percent, the exercise price should go down to $18. The real progress of the company would easily be measured by its cumulative gain from the adjusted award-cost amount.

This is a commonsense proposal. The board's attitude would be: We're here to pay you bonuses on performance, not bonuses based on the Fed's interest-rate policy or the twists and turns of the business cycle.

In the five years ended in 1994, H. J. Heinz's stock fell behind the S&P 500. Yet Mr. O'Reilly, the chairman, made $37 million from exercising his options in the same period.

A few companies take a tougher approach. Colgate Palmolive, for example, gave its CEO, Reuben Mark, 1 million shares of stock in 1993, exercisable at 10 percent *above* the market price at the time but then at higher and higher levels in future years. In 1996, Monsanto created four sets of options, with varying exercise prices. Devised when the stock was trading at $116, the plan allowed executives to purchase shares at $150, $175, $200, and $225, with the cheapest options expiring earliest and the most expensive ones expiring after only six years, instead of the usual ten. In addition, the top executives had to buy stock at market value with money borrowed from the company at full interest.

Spread the options payoffs over a longer period.

One of the flaws of the current system seems to be that options are leveraged off short-term results. That encourages the CEO to do all sorts of things to pump the stock price up, even if the long-term impact will be negative. This is especially a risk if he has to retire before his ten-year exercise period is cut short.

For example, he might act to raise dividends excessively. It'll hurt the company's long-term health by funneling profits to shareholders that might otherwise go into research, equipment, or just a cash cushion against emergencies or downturns in the business cycle. But the stock will go up near term.

Or he might spin off divisions or split the company up, both dramatic moves, and both irreversible. Will that increase the company's worth? Or will it merely jack up the stock price—for a short period?

The average CEO's stint is about five years. And the company has a whole bunch of guys lined up to replace him. I would say that he should get some grace period of, say, four years beyond his retirement date to cash in his options. That would motivate him to strive to improve long-term results.

It would also encourage him to seek out a talented successor—even one who might outshine him.

Otherwise, you couldn't blame him for thinking, ''I'm going to run this show damn careful, boy. We're not going to take any unneeded risks. I have a million dollars coming to me. I can lose it by doing something magnificent for the company that might also be detrimental to my short-term option gain.'' The board might even want to stipulate that only two-thirds of the CEO's options can be exercised during his tenure, and the final third after his retirement.

Introduce penalties for poor performance as well as rewards for sterling performance.

Currently, stock options are a one-way street. There's no downside, only an upside. But if the current system pays out one dollar per option for every dollar gain in the market price of the stock, one could require the recipient of such largess to pay a more modest sum, say fifty cents on the dollar, for stock-price declines.

We could call this the "exercising price" of the option to reflect the fact that a lot of corporate honchos would get pretty exercised if it were implemented.

While options represent the most obvious target of reform because they can create the instant pots of gold that some pundits have found so "obscene," other parts of the compensation package are also ripe for critical scrutiny.

Bonuses, for example. Many boards pay hefty bonuses, and if they are tied to performance, they are earned. But perhaps they should be scrutinized more closely to make sure they don't reward mediocrity. Take a look at the prospectuses of any ten companies whose performance was average last year for their industry. You'll find that most or all of them paid their top people very respectable bonuses. It sort of resembles the tipping habits of some restaurant goers: They automatically give their waiters 15 percent, and only withhold the extra money for extraordinarily bad service, though they add a few percentage points if they are treated like royalty.

Boards must show more gumption in scrutinizing their CEOs' compensation packages. Yes, this might create tensions, even upset stockholders. So be it. The risk is worth it for the very reason that a tougher stance introduces a healthy element of risk into the CEO's calculations. He'll know that he must work harder and show more imagination or else run the danger of forfeiting a pay increase, forgoing a bonus, even losing his job.

In sum: Tinker with the system, but don't fault it. Above all, the government shouldn't shoulder in with social-engineering solutions. David Ricardo, the nineteenth-century economist, got it right in 1817: "Wages should be left to the fair and free competition of the market, and should never be controlled by the interference of the legislatures."

The system works well so long as the board of directors does its job and management does its job. Options can be a powerful incentive to performance and reward shareholders at the same time. But they must be an incentive for performance, not a substitute for it.

9

A Salute to Some Business Leaders

Strong CEOs come in all forms, from bold and risk-taking to cautious and methodical.

Their mission can range from making a profitable company even more profitable to saving a floundering company from bankruptcy.

Their average tenure is about six years.

There is only one true test of a CEO: You must be successful. And success is measured in quarters. You might get four quarters, or even eight—one or two years—to prove yourself. You won't get much more.

Today's corporate superstar can become tomorrow's fallen idol if his performance slips. It is amazing how quickly once-adoring stockholders, Wall Street analysts, and financial journalists will turn on him if they catch the tiniest whiff of failure.

A company's success depends on one thing: the CEO's leadership. It depends on his ability to think straight, show guts and vision, and stay the course. In a sense, so long as he holds the job, the CEO *is* the company.

Here are some key attributes of a successful CEO:

HE IS A RISK TAKER. He sticks his neck out. He's careful, not cautious. He never takes ill-considered risks. But he isn't afraid to take big ones. Announcing an ambitious goal is a big risk. It's also a wonderful motivator. Now you have an assignment, not just a good intention.

When I took over at ITT, a good friend, Jerry Tsai, said, "You'll have to tell the people there what you intend to do." I said, "I'll tell them I'll work damn hard." He said, "No, that's not good enough. Tell them something concrete." So I told them I would double earnings in five years.

A gamble? Sure, but I doubled the earnings in five years. I had put myself in a vulnerable position, and now I had to rescue myself. Nobody else was going to.

A GOOD CEO PROMOTES GOOD PEOPLE. I loved a line in a recent magazine article about how Lou Gerstner made a surprise promotion of a computer scientist at IBM nobody had ever heard of while simultaneously pushing two high-profile executives out the door.

This guy wore jeans and a sweater to work. I myself usually don a white shirt and tie, but mode of dress is irrelevant. What matters is performance, and this fellow had performed. He had built an IBM unit around parallel machines to deliver mainframe power. And he was getting 58 percent gross margins on them as compared with the 40 percent that IBM was getting with mainframes.

Best of all, he was filling a big gap. We've all read about how IBM's mainframe business is inexorably declining. Those lost revenues have to be recouped somewhere. And sales of the new parallel machines are expected to quintuple to $1 billion by the end of 1996. So Gerstner made this guy's unit a full-blown division.

Promote good people. Reward talent. Make sure everybody knows it.

A GOOD CEO IS A TEAM PLAYER. That doesn't mean, necessarily, that he's a nice guy. But he encourages full and frank discussions, as the diplomats say. He rewards people for their performance. He helps his managers and expects his managers to help him. It's a two-way street.

A GOOD CEO CHASES OPPORTUNITY, NOT MONEY. The truly driven CEO would *pay* for her job if she had to. My starting salary at ITT was less than $150,000, on the low side even in those days. I didn't care. Hell, this was the opportunity I had been waiting a lifetime for. I went for it. The money came later.

A GOOD CEO ANALYZES EVERY ASPECT OF THE COMPANY. At Jones & Laughlin, I was astounded at how many maintenance people they had, so I conducted a full-scale review. I found out there was even one guy who reported to work every morning and headed off with his toolbox—for home! He didn't do a lick of work for sixteen years. I reformed the system, finding meaningful assignments for productive workers and eliminating deadwood. It saved the company several million dollars in the first year.

Here are some ruminations about various CEOs and other corporate luminaries.

Michael Jordan, Westinghouse

Some people view his early performance as a disappointment. He is one of the management gurus brought in by boards after shareholder revolts. But whereas Lou Gerstner of IBM and George Fisher of Kodak got quick results, he has been slower to have an impact.

Some blame the huge debt he inherited; some Westinghouse's complex organizational structure; some the difficulty of revving up a staid corporate culture; some Mr. Jordan's own easygoing nature and reluctance to take drastic actions like mass layoffs.

To me, his problem is Pittsburgh.

I spent six years in Pittsburgh as financial vice president of old Jones & Laughlin Steel. Westinghouse occupied the upper floor of Gateway Center No. 2, and we occupied the lower floors. Often, we

invited their top brass to our executive dining room, and they recip-
rocated.

At every symphony concert or charity event held in Pittsburgh,
we commingled with executives from

- Westinghouse

- U.S. Steel, then in its prime

- Gulf Oil

- the Aluminum Company of America

- the Mellon Bank

- and other steel and chemical companies and fabricators, as well
  as a couple of railroads.

And all of this corporate activity was taking place in a small
peninsula bordered by the Allegheny and Monongahela Rivers that
converge at the "Golden Triangle" to form the Ohio River.

The corporate executives all made the Duquesne Club their social headquarters. Since, in those days, decent restaurants were few in
number, we all saw a lot of one another.

And our camaraderie was intensified by a shared exposure to the
elements, in this case man-made: the choking smoke that required us
to change our shirts at noon and that, at times, literally blotted out
the sun, creating a midday twilight.

Today, the smoke has been abated and the Golden Triangle has
been rebuilt. The blast furnaces and the coke ovens and the open
hearths that built Pittsburgh are gone. So, too, are Jones & Laughlin's
Bessemer converters across that river that lighted the sky when they
blew sparks and fire into the air.

Michael Jordan is up against tradition.

Westinghouse had been in motors, power generation, consumer
goods, defense electronics, nuclear businesses, real estate, locomotives, lightbulbs, TV broadcasting. . . . I'm sure I've left out some
other interests. Its factories were outside town in an area called Turtle
Creek; the highway there suddenly shot up into the hills and you could
look down and see a huge hollow filled with Westinghouse plants.

But its crown jewel was the Westinghouse Credit Company.
Westinghouse Credit became a lending powerhouse, offsetting grow-

ing problems in its other areas. The TV stations were sold, the light-bulbs faced competition from General Electric and the generators and motors from abroad; the consumer lines were sold; the defense business was all but wiped out with the end of the cold war.

Morale suffered.

Then the credit company hit the skids.

Morale suffered a lot more.

This is what Michael Jordan stepped into.

If a building is tottering, you knock it down and rebuild it.

But you can't do that with a company, not a big, traditional company in a traditional town like Pittsburgh.

Neither Fisher nor Gerstner had to face this kind of problem.

I understand Jordan is a builder, not a downsizer, a long-term consolidator, not a quick-fix specialist. He didn't take over an IBM or an Eastman Kodak; he took over Westinghouse.

The tourniquet should have been applied years ago.

He agonized for three years before deciding to spin off Westinghouse's industrial and energy units. To old-timers like me, the split-up was a bit of a shock. But it seems to have made stockholders happy. Better yet, he saved most of the jobs in the old-line businesses. In the long term, it looks like workers will benefit.

Lou Gerstner, IBM

Maybe somebody ought to charge him with grave robbing for snatching IBM from the jaws of death.

He's done everything the textbooks call for: laying off thousands, launching new products, hoarding cash ($11 billion at last count), buying back IBM stock (it's up), buying a product (Lotus Notes) that gives him a crack at breaking Microsoft's domination of the operating software market and moving aggressively into the emerging technology of network computing.

But the most important thing he has done is to attack the old corporate culture of arrogance and aversion to risk. He hasn't destroyed it quite yet; it's like poison ivy—you have to know how to root it out or it'll infect you, and even if you think you've rooted it out it tends to grow back in unexpected places.

Lou, don't be lulled into a false sense of security by the warm words of Wall Street. They can turn cold pretty fast.

IBM is a great company. Think about its products, its people, its size, its complexity. Sure, Compaq is growing faster—for now. But still, Compaq has, what? One-fourth of IBM's revenues?

And IBM has a huge number of machines out there. It'll be a long time before the IBM mainframes disappear.

Gerstner has come under some criticism for moving too slowly, being too timid, being a "technocrat" who lacks grand vision.

I don't buy that. IBM is all over the world. It has subsidiaries in the United Kingdom, Japan, France. And it isn't all that easy to control foreign subsidiaries.

Given IBM's hugeness and complexity, Gerstner is doing the right thing. He's indicating in broad terms where the company's going but he's being very prudent for now. That's smart.

Because he's built up his cash reserves, he can spend his energies worrying about growth instead of money. And that means he has to remind himself: We're not in this business just to turn out products. The products have to make money. Seems pretty basic—but a lot of CEOs miss that basic point.

If it is any inspiration, Lou: It took awhile, but Hercules ultimately cleaned out the Augean stables. Rome got built, if not on a Sunday afternoon. And elephants can be trained to perform, if not with a wet noodle.

Best of luck.

Kirk Kerkorian

In the spring of 1994, Mr. Kerkorian, who owns 13.6 percent of Chrysler, made a bid for the automaker that was so badly organized some people thought it was a hoax.

But he came back with a more serious effort. This time, he had disgruntled former employee Lee Iococca on board. He also recruited Chrysler's former chief financial officer, Jerome York, and was demanding a board seat for him.

What did Mr. Kerkorian want? More money, apparently. He wanted Chrysler to return some of its $6 billion-plus "cash hoard" to shareholders in the form of higher dividends. People say he also hoped to get the share price up so he could sell out at a profit.

It would be unfair to invoke the Wall Street saw that bulls ultimately make money, and bears ultimately make money, but hogs get nothing.

After all, Mr. Kerkorian has been doing deals all his life, and was recently worth $3.4 billion by *Forbes* magazine's estimate. In any case, he finally reached a settlement with Chrysler in 1996. It was a complicated agreement, and I'm not sure how much he actually gained. But I noted his stock holding had doubled in value since he acquired it.

But Chrysler's chairman, Robert Eaton, has done a superlative job of turning Chrysler around. He very wisely wants to hold on to the cash kitty to ease the company through future cyclical downturns.

For heaven's sakes, he's not going to abscond with it.

Kirk couldn't run Chrysler if he tried.

Anytime a CEO is doing as good a job as Bob Eaton is, my vote is with him.

Still, you have to applaud Kirk's persistence. After buying and selling Metro Goldwyn Mayer twice over the years, he bought it again in 1996 for $1.3 billion.

Michael Eisner, Walt Disney

I've never met Mr. Eisner and, I must confess, I think I would be out of my element trying to run the Walt Disney Company. I wouldn't be able to figure out how much Mickey Mouse is worth.

By most accounts, Mr. Eisner has done a brilliant job of reviving Disney since he took it over in 1984. He has built up the company's movie and resort businesses and expanded its overseas operations. He has got revenues, profits, and the stock price way up. On the other hand, some people say he is slipping. He alienated and lost the genius who ran Walt Disney Studios, Jeffrey Katzenberg. And he angered a lot of Americans with his attempt to build a theme park near the Civil War battlefield of Manassas.

I don't think you can argue with success. But what intrigues me about Eisner is his purchase of Capital Cities/ABC in 1995 for $19 billion.

That is because, almost exactly thirty years earlier, I agreed to buy ABC—for $400 million! As part of the deal, I promised to sink enough money in the network to pull it from its third-place berth, behind CBS and NBC, in the number of its TV stations.

However, the Justice Department blocked the transaction for reasons I have never understood. Its pretext was that ITT still had a few cable companies, though our cable holdings weren't enough to alter the competitive balance.

After all, how could number three ABC pose a monopoly threat? I fought the Justice Department for two years, then threw in the towel. To think that we almost acquired the network at a little more than 2 percent of what Mr. Eisner is paying.

Carl Icahn, Investor

One of America's savviest investors, he early bought a large railroad leasing company that provided him a steady flow of cash.

His forays to buy Phillips Petroleum Company and TWA made headlines, as did his tendency to back his views with ferocity in the press and in the courts. More recently, along with his fellow investor and former archfoe Bennett LeBow, he was putting pressure on RJR Nabisco to spin off its food business.

He seems ageless and, more to the point, he is certainly tireless. I've sat at the same dinner table with him a number of times and was struck by his sense of humor. I have never met anyone who exuded such a sense of pressing forward, even when he was sitting perfectly still.

He always turned up at Drexel's fabulous weeklong annual bashes that assembled all the big power players of the country, maybe a thousand in all. And he always showed up at the cocktail splash at bungalow 4 of the Beverly Hills Hotel, hosted by Don Engel, and limited to about 150 of the biggest, most active financial movers. Michael Milken ran the banquet.

I never thought to add up the assets represented in that one room. Perhaps $100 billion would hit the mark.

Carl is bigger than life and, incidentally, taller. He is still going strong, lately buying into oil for the next world shortage.

They say you can't teach an old dog new tricks. In his case, who would want to try?

Gerry Levin, Time Warner

The market views him with a big question mark. Two big headlines in early 1995 tell the story. The *New York Times:* "Battling for Hearts and Minds at Time Warner." The *Wall Street Journal:* "Out of Time? Frustrated Investors Ratchet up Pressure on Time Warner Chief."

He was still around in the fall, though, when he bought the Turner Broadcasting System to make Time Warner the world's biggest media company. The critics were still carping that he hadn't managed to get the stock price up or solve all of the company's many problems, including huge debt, management infighting, and cultural clashes.

He was still around early this year. Something tells me he'll be around for a long time.

I like him because he says he hates the word "synergy" and because he preaches the gospel of teamwork. Quote: "Anyone who isn't on the team is out." I wish him luck.

Warren Buffet, Berkshire Hathaway

If you become America's richest man—and he was number one on the *Forbes* list in 1993, with a net worth of $8.3 billion, though he subsequently slipped to number two, worth, however, $15 billion in 1996—you must be doing something right.

His methods don't seem all that magical. He's a modest man, unlike so many Wall Street sophisticates. But he does his homework, delving deep for the fundamentals. He doesn't scatter his shots; he limits his big investments to a dozen or so companies. Coke is his biggest bet. He doesn't get greedy and take a quick profit; he's in it for the long haul. He has always conducted himself honorably. He even warned investors in 1996 that Berkshire Hathaway might be overpriced. (Not that many people could afford it; it was trading at around $36,000 a share at the time.)

It is remarkable that his choices of risks worth taking have been 98 percent on the mark. That's a bit like shooting two under par for six holes straight on a golf course.

George Fisher, Eastman Kodak

Fisher likes to talk about the importance of taking risks. Since he took over Eastman Kodak Company in 1993, he has put himself on the spot by announcing ambitious sales-growth goals.

The problem with Kodak before Fisher came was its dominant position. It lost its sense of urgency—what I call "tension thinking." I get the term from "tension mountain climbing," where a climber never rests his entire weight in one spot. His continuous momentum saves him from falling and propels him forward.

Fisher improved quality and morale at Kodak and invested in new products like a digital camera. By mid-1996, he had gotten the stock price up to the mid-seventies from the low forties two years earlier. I especially like Fisher's tenacity in challenging Japan's protectionist ways. He fought to open Japan's markets to pagers and cellular phones when he ran Motorola, and he is fighting to open them to film today.

Jack Welch, General Electric

He certainly fulfills the first duty of a CEO: to succeed. He does it by identifying and promoting talent.

GE's loan group is a conglomerate in itself. They're in everything you can think of. They're making partial acquisitions by their loan structure. They study companies and their management before investing in them. They advance money in return for stock; if you look at their portfolio, you'll see they have an operating interest in a lot of them.

I guess the one thing Welch has got to be worrying about is the fact that his credit company got to be such a big part of his earnings. It's a lot to have in one basket.

But GE is a true conglomerate, in everything from medical-imaging equipment to light bulbs. Toward the end of 1996, it was the most valuable company in the world, worth more than $150 billion, and still growing fast. And it is highly profitable. Jack Welch is probably America's most revered chief executive, and deservedly so.

Armand Hammer, Occidental Petroleum Corporation

A genial man, the late financier and art collector obviously had his own agenda, as recent revelations about his Kremlin connections make clear.

He knew oil, he understood the capriciousness of the stock market, he bought and sold the jewels of Russia's fallen nobility, and he even made a bid for the Chesapeake & Ohio Railroad. Whatever his politics, he got around.

He was generous toward his pet causes. When I joined the board of the Salk Institute, I was surprised to see that he was one of the biggest supporters.

My good friend Zoltan Merszei, who gained a reputation as a whiz kid for taking Dow Chemical to the heights, took on the job as vice chairman and chief operating officer at Mr. Hammer's company, Occidental Petroleum Corporation. But he eventually left, reasoning that he would never get the number one spot so long as Mr. Hammer was alive, and concluding from long observation that Mr. Hammer might be immortal.

He was wrong; Mr. Hammer died, and, as I recall, Occidental's stock price rose several points on the news.

William Gates, Microsoft

This guy's fast on his feet. In a matter of a couple years he wins, then loses his bid for financial-software maker Intuit. He wins, then loses, then wins an antitrust battle with the Justice Department. He launches Windows 95. He spends $30 million for a Leonardo da Vinci manuscript. He acquires the rights to Ansel Adams photographs. He gets married. He writes a best-seller. He becomes the father of a baby girl.

Microsoft turned twenty years old in 1996. Though he was only forty, Mr. Gates had by then become the world's richest man and his company supplied the software for the vast majority of the world's personal computers.

Mr. Gates: Don't look out those "windows," or, as baseball legend Satchel Paige once said, you might see what's gaining on you. If you do look out, and it's the Justice Department in hot pursuit, run like hell. Justice at the Justice Department is often in short supply.

Martin Davis, Investor and Former Paramount Chairman

I grew to know Martin fairly well. We had several lunches in his office overlooking Central Park in the old Gulf & Western Building. (Gulf & Western became Paramount Communications in 1989.)

He was considered a tough businessman, but I found him to be a very warm guy and a good listener who was willing to help on any deal. After making about $10 million in the sale of the Leslie Fay clothing company, I was considering bidding on a company that Gulf & Western had just put on the market. It didn't work out, but I was impressed with the scope of Gulf & Western's operations, which ranged from a California swimsuit maker to sugar holdings in the Dominican Republic to a big American loan company and Paramount Pictures.

Martin was overburdened with work, I could tell that; yet, he never lost his enthusiasm. And he was a great conglomerateur, having assembled his empire from modest beginnings. Perhaps that is why we got along so well.

I remember him especially for one kind gesture. After I stepped down from ITT, I was feeling an inner emptiness. For some reason, I gave a dinner at the 21 Club. When the king is drowning, the waters tend to close over him pretty quickly, unless he learns to swim a different stroke.

I had invited a fair number of CEOs to the affair, yet fewer than a dozen showed up. But Marty was one of them. It was a very busy time for him, and I am sure he had more important things to do, but he was there.

Barry Diller, Silver King Communications

Few people have been involved in as many major deals as Barry Diller. A refugee from Gulf & Western, where he ran Paramount, he created the Fox network, built up QVC, the home-shopping service, and recently started another television network, Silver King Communications, which then acquired the Home Shopping Network and Savoy Pictures Entertainment.

All this activity isn't going to stop him from gunning for other targets. I'll have to predict he'll get some bull's-eyes. He always searches for deals—big deals—worth doing.

It occurs to me that the Bronfmans, Martin Davis, and Barry Diller all have a streak of the conglomerateur in them. Is it because they like doing deals? Is it because they like to spread their risk? I would contend it is both.

Eckhard Pfeiffer, Compaq Computer

He turned around Compaq Computer. Sales and profits were eroding and the stock price was dropping when he was called in in 1992. Within two years, he doubled sales, to almost $11 billion, and quadrupled profits, to almost $900 million. Revenue rose to $4.2 billion in just the first quarter of 1996.

Like George Fisher, he puts himself on the spot. He announces an ambitious sales goal—and then has to meet it. He said Compaq would be number one in personal computer sales by 1997, and then beat the target by two years. Last I heard, he had declared the company would triple sales by the year 2000. It probably will.

Lewis Platt, Hewlett-Packard

He certainly meets the main criterion for success: growth. HP's earnings per share were up more than 50 percent in 1995, the share price was up 90 percent, and revenues up more than 25 percent, to $31.5 billion.

But unlike so many other big corporations, HP achieved those astounding gains without resorting to massive layoffs.

That's a tribute to Lewis Platt and, to my mind, it is an affirmation of the principle that growth and teamwork go together.

Andrew Grove, Intel

If a cat has nine lives, Andy Grove must have twenty. He keeps taking risks—and keeps pushing Intel to the limit.

He made a $5 billion gamble on the Pentium chip and as a result captured 75 percent of the microprocessor market. It looks like he's making an equally huge wager on the next chip generation. Some analysts predict sales could triple by the end of the decade to $50 billion and profits could approach $10 billion.

And Intel is already the world's biggest and most profitable chip maker. He just wrote a book called *Only the Paranoid Survive*. Well, Andy Grove is much more than a survivor.

You know, a straight line extended could reach the moon. But you can't put a number on proven vision.

Carl Preiss, Amertorp

I'm saving the best for last.

Few people have heard of Mr. Preiss. He was my boss at Amertorp, the American Can subsidiary set up during World War II to make torpedoes. Actually, he never made it to the top; he was "only" an American Can vice president, but he had all the key characteristics of a leader, in spades.

He was physically rugged and mentally quick. He was decisive and demanding. He always got to the root cause of any failure and figured out how to make it a success.

In less than a year, he got two wartime naval ordnance plants— one thrown together on a Chicago golf course and the other in a St.

Louis clay pit—up and running and churning out intricately designed aerial and deck torpedoes.

I have never met a man who could drill so unerringly to the root of any problem. He had the knack of sizing up the human elements and then moving expeditiously to overcome them, by quiet persuasion if possible, by force if necessary. He acted so quickly that people hardly noticed how he did it. All they knew was that delays were ended, feuds settled, distractions removed, crises averted, logjams cleared, and broken machinery repaired.

And he did this in wartime, when access to materials and manpower was problematic and when the lines of authority within corporations, and between corporations and the federal government, were often a bewildering maze.

To recruit and train twelve thousand people from scratch and then turn out a weapon of incredible technological complexity, a self-propelled explosive metal projectile that raced under water at sixty miles per hour and kept its course for several miles within one degree of its target—and this in the days before computers—was an enormous feat. Without a doubt, Mr. Preiss contributed to America's victory in the war.

He was the man, in every sense of the word, for the hour.

And the twelve thousand people in those two plants gave everything they had because of the kind of leader, and the kind of man, he was.

Yes, the conditions under which he worked were unusual. And the full measure of his accomplishments couldn't be found in the financial statements. Nor are they found in the history books today.

But I have never seen a performance that could equal his.

I remember Mr. Preiss with deep respect as a model of what a CEO's responsibility really is.

He was an inspiration.

10

The Myth
of Long-Range
Planning

If somebody starts talking about ''long-range planning,'' run. Fast. There's no such thing as long-range planning. That's right: It is a fiction.

Sure, you can sit around and ponder the distant future. ''Where do we want to be five years from now? Ten years from now?'' Those sorts of questions can presumably lead to deep ruminations about the purpose, scope, and *destiny* of the organization. But what they can't do is pay the current bills, or win new customers.

In my early days at ITT, everyone in top management started laying out great long-range plans, from new product development five years hence to European partnerships ten years down the road. Wonderful dreams. But when it became apparent after a couple of months that all of our great future victories were theoretical, but our less-than-satisfactory earnings were only too real, I put out a real all points bulletin to top management: "There will be no more long-range planning."

The message was unambiguous. It was followed by a longer but equally emphatic tract on the importance of "short-term performance," which, over time, would produce long-range results.

That's when we began our real plans. We went on to build a large company, and a sound one. We focused on this year's profits, products, management methods, costs, and market penetrations. All the elements that go into running a company in the present. They inevitably led to the next year's plans. But that was about as far out as we needed to go. Of course, we did consider the long-term implications of our actions. But that was not a plan.

Our system worked, year after year. We got to the point of working out our business plans for the following year in detail by May of the current year. You could call that "short-short-range planning." We set the May deadline to give us time to work in the changes we needed before the end of the year to reach the "goals" for next year. In other words, we worked to meet short-term goals. That was our plan.

Most companies have five-year plans. They draw them up every year, then file them away. Nobody pays any attention to them, except perhaps to scan the numbers. They are really meaningless. You can't plan the operation of a company five years ahead. Too many things change. You can, at best, plan ahead one year at a time.

But corporations still do long-range planning. It makes the top executives feel secure, and it reassures everybody since long-range plans almost always make rosy projections.

Think about the Boy Scouts. Their motto is "Be prepared." But they aren't talking about five-year plans. They mean: Bring the insect repellent along on the hike or else get eaten alive by the mosquitoes. They mean: Pack bandages, matches, and a Swiss army knife to deal with emergencies as they arise!

They also mean: Learn lots of skills, such as tying knots, locating mountain springs, building lean-tos, and reading the stars for directions. In other words, be prepared for contingencies.

What good is long-range planning if you make short-term blunders? The fact is, the troops in the field often have trouble planning five minutes ahead, much less five years. Back when I was selling ads at the *World Telegram* in the early 1930s, I read a book, *How to Win a Sales Argument,* by Richard Borden and Alvin Busse, two professors who had sat in on thousands of job interviews. You'll never guess the biggest single reason for failure to complete a sale. After the talking was done, and the sale was made, it was forgetting to ask for the order!

The book set down some basic principles of selling. One was never to interrupt a customer—not because it was rude, but because he would be impatient for you to shut up so he could finish what he was saying. Therefore, he wouldn't listen to you. Another was to repeat the customer's complaints or objections *more forcefully than he voiced them.* This would make you seem both smart and sympathetic in his eyes, would make him feel more at ease, and would therefore allow you to steer the conversation to your point of view. The wisdom of that book was greater than any argument I have ever heard on the need for long-range planning, yet it can be summarized in twelve words: Listen to the customer, agree with him—and take the damn order! Those were my biblical commands.

A lot of long-range planning is retrospective. That is, people will sit back and say that where they are today was the result of long-range planning. But is it? Isn't it more apt to be the cumulative result of a lot of smaller planned steps? Realistic ones, too—that you can build the next step on.

Yet the lure of long-range planning has long endured at corporations. It starts as a road to El Dorado, clothed in rainbows, with streams of cool water gushing on every side. It is usually only after it is too late to turn back that hidden mountain crags and fog-swathed gulches come into view. And, suddenly, the objective changes to: How do we get out of here?

Sadly, many a doughty party of would-be business planners departed in high hopes and spirits, never to return, getting lost in the sinkholes of their region never meant to be penetrated by man: the mystic future.

A few lucky survivors over the ages have emerged after all hope for them had been given up. Their scattered and incoherent reports tell much about their privations, but little about what they met out there.

So my advice is: Leave that track alone. Follow, instead, the path of the experienced woodsman. He decides his course according to *what he can see ahead.* He heads north, or south, or east, or west, with a compass to guide him, but takes numerous detours and retreats to meet the demands of the moment.

His purpose at all times is to face what is *real,* and think from there. This sort of person always comes back home, maybe a little late, but in one piece.

And one step at a time.

Step by step. You may achieve an objective, but it will be the result, not of a long-range operating plan, but of many short-term reconnaissance missions and goals. And along the way, your objective may change.

At Amertorp, where I worked during the war, at Bell & Howell, at Jones & Laughlin, at ITT, and at a dozen medium-sized companies I've been involved with since leaving ITT, we always spent endless hours every week solving current problems to keep things on track. You can't anticipate problems two years ahead, much less five years, and solve them now.

We always had long-term *goals.* They could be stated quite succinctly: Grow and make shorter-term goals. To do even this you had to do many things, primary among them:

- Spend a lot of money on research and development,

- Make acquisitions,

- Expand markets,

- Get adequate financing,

- Hire top talent,

- Maintain and increase your market share in each product line.

Some people say that the most important man in the business world today is Alan Greenspan, the chairman of the Federal Reserve System. Do you suppose he said, in 1990: "Let's start planning for the financial collapse of Mexico; Orange County, California; and the British investment bank Barings PLC five years from now, and perhaps while we're at it decide what restrictions to place on derivatives trading"?

If he had, most people at the time would have asked: "What on earth are derivatives?"

Of course, Mr. Greenspan undoubtedly engages in a great deal of contingency planning, contemplating his reaction to innumerable what-ifs. But those aren't his primary goals; they're his strategies, just in case.

What the Fed really does is take short-term measures—raising interest rates, or intervening on the foreign-exchange market to shore up the dollar—and then sit back and see what happens.

Its long-range *objective* is more ambitious. It might want to keep the dollar as strong as possible. Or, in a booming economy, it might want to engineer a so-called soft landing, slowing growth just enough to avoid both recession and inflation.

The big budget debate between the Republicans in Congress and the White House at times got a little ridiculous. Both sides were making projections seven years into the future about economic growth, inflation, tax revenues, and so forth when nobody really knows from one month to the next what's going to happen. The business press routinely interviews economists at the end of the year for their prognostications for the coming year, and the economists just as routinely get it all wrong, sometimes missing the mark by a mile. And that's just their guesswork for one year ahead!

Consider the conflicting views of Gail D. Fosler, chief economist of the Conference Board business group, and John Mueller, chief economist for Lehrman Bell Mueller Cannon Incorporated, looking ahead a mere twelve months at the beginning of 1996, as reported by the *New York Times*.

Ms. Fosler projected economic growth for the year of 3.1 percent; Mr. Mueller of –1.1 percent; Ms. Fosler foresaw unemployment at the end of the year at 5.3 percent, Mr. Mueller at 6.9 percent; and Ms. Fosler guessed the Federal funds interest rate would be 6.8 percent, while Mr. Mueller predicted 3.25 percent. Forecasters missed some of the biggest economic phenomena of the past quarter century, including the oil shock of 1973, the stagflation that followed, and the quick economic turnaround of the early 1980s. All those computerized models that promised so much back in the 1960s lost their luster. One reason why corporations indulge in so much risk management these days (buying all those derivatives and the like) is to protect themselves against unforeseeable events.

With such disparities rampant in assessing short-term trends, why should anybody's views about economic fundamentals two years hence, or five years, or ten years be taken seriously?

People with political axes to grind, whether of the Left or the Right, will make assumptions that may or may not be true, then draw conclusions that may or may not follow from their premises, then draw further conclusions, all as though they were dishing out irrefutable proofs that they are right and everyone else is wrong. I read an essay by some liberal the other day who said cutting the budget deficit would obviously strengthen the dollar, which would obviously worsen our trade balance, which would obviously lead to massive layoffs in American industry, which would obviously create a national crisis.

Could happen. Who knows? Nobody. Does anybody want to bet me a hundred dollars that the budget really will be in balance in the year 2002?

If you diagrammed a long-range plan you'd come up with a straight line. In the real world, there is no such thing. Short-range planning is a zigzagging path that retreats before unforeseen setbacks and leaps at unanticipated opportunities.

And yet you have the authors of a book about corporate planning (*Competing for the Future* by Gary Hamel and C. K. Pahalad) lamenting that senior executives only spend 2.4 percent of their time "peering three or more years into the future" with the aim of "building a collective view of the future." They urge top managers to increase that figure sharply in order to gain "deep insights into the trends in technology, demographics, regulation, and lifestyles that can be harnessed to rewrite industry rules and create new competitive space."

I'd recommend a better course of action: Get out and talk to the workers in your plants and to your customers wherever they are and figure out what you can do today to make things work better tomorrow. I read about a little company in Illinois that was the biggest maker of plastic knobs in the country. To what extent they planned ahead I don't know, but they got hit with a collapse in demand in the early 1980s after microprocessors and digital technology made most knobs obsolete.

The company went on to prosper—probably, I would guess, because it was fast on its feet, not because it followed a master ten-year plan that it kept hidden away in some drawer for a rainy day.

Consider a cross-country car trip. Your *objective* is to spend a relaxing vacation somewhere. Your long-range plan is to drive to San

Francisco from New York in five days. Your short-term plan is to get to Akron on the first day. But it turns out there is heavy construction work in eastern Pennsylvania, so you swing south and hook up with the Pennsylvania Turnpike. You drive for a while but hear on the radio that there is flooding a few miles ahead. So you take a detour onto Interstate 70 and end up in Columbus instead of Akron.

As you drive along, you keep running into obstacles and taking detours. But you still make pretty good progress, and on day four you're racing along Interstate 40 in Arizona when you hear the news: There has been another earthquake in San Francisco. So you take the turnoff for Highway 93 and head for Las Vegas instead. You check into a hotel with a big swimming pool and tennis courts and a golf course, and you spend five relaxing days there. In short, your long-range plan fell through—but at least you've met your objective. Now you ask yourself where you will be driving five years from now. It gets pretty conjectural.

An example of long-range planning is the restaurant business. I'm on the board of a restaurant chain and I know a lot of people in the trade. And nobody ever knows if a particular restaurant or its theme will succeed. It helps to find a good location and hire a motivated staff, of course. But even then, a restaurant can fail. You can summarize the industry in four words: Some work, some don't.

Likewise, Blockbuster can have a long-range plan to build fifty stores in Cleveland. But if a new competitor unexpectedly opens a hundred stores in Cleveland, it has a new problem.

You can hardly open the paper without reading about some company that planned its way into a corner. Microsoft figured its new on-line service would overwhelm America On-line, Prodigy, and CompuServe, but some say it didn't grasp until late in the game how potent a force the Internet server group had become as a potential rival. Not long ago, I read that one Pentium PC has one thousand times more computing power "per dollar" than a mainframe of a decade earlier and that a network of four PCs can do as much as a quarter-million-dollar mainframe. Who could have foreseen that in 1985 or even 1990?

I know a fellow who put his life savings in South Dakota farmland in the late 1970s. The price of the land had been soaring, but everything he read, everybody he talked to, and pure logic itself all told him the same thing: It could only go higher. Why? Simple. First, land is finite. There is only so much of it in the world. Only a fraction of it is fertile. And some of the most fertile is in South Dakota. Second, the population of the world is increasing by leaps and bounds, and most countries can't grow enough food to feed themselves. Third, the world is getting richer: Formerly impoverished lands such as India and Indonesia are industrializing and exporting and earning huge treasure troves of foreign exchange—with which they can buy, among other things, grain.

Thus, my friend reasoned, a huge and growing market existed for South Dakota corn and grain. He bought more than a thousand acres. Not long after, the market crashed. My friend is now an absentee farmer and a convert to the belief that long-range planning can have serious flaws.

Go back and read the comments goldbugs were making in 1979 and 1980. Gold had shot up to more than eight hundred dollars an ounce from two hundred dollars in a fairly short time, but it still had nowhere to go but up, they said. Why? Well, gold had always been a refuge from inflation, and inflation was getting worse in all four corners of the globe. And using the same argument that trapped my friend, they insisted that the growing hordes in Third World countries with nearly worthless currencies would have nowhere else to park their savings. Yet, gold fell back below four hundred dollars fairly quickly and languished in the upper three hundreds for many years, well into 1996.

A company that relies on any sort of long-term economic or political prognostication makes itself vulnerable to the unexpected. Better to be prepared and flexible enough to spin on a dime and confront the new conditions instead of dying with the old.

So are companies vulnerable that ignore new realities. My steel company, Jones & Laughlin, built some very expensive open-hearth furnaces. But the steel industry has since gone to continuous casting; they don't need those open hearths anymore.

Jones & Laughlin also once spent big money to buy bigger hot-metal ladles. They could handle more tons per lift. These ladles have since become largely obsolete, but the guys in charge had grown up in the mills and they stuck to what they knew. They didn't look ahead to what might be coming.

That isn't to say you can't make certain obvious time assumptions. You can say, "This warehouse will last five years," or, "The cost of paying off this loan over five years will total two point six million dollars." But that isn't planning; that is mathematics.

And you can set a timetable for coming up with new products and services. A biotechnology company, for example, can allot three or five or ten years for the development of a drug to fight cancer or Alzheimer's disease. But again, that isn't planning; it's an overhead expense. Why? Because only when you've got the drug approved can you create an operating plan.

If every year you do everything you need to do to keep your business running and you contemplate whatever you're going to have to do for the next year, that's the most productive planning. You have time to change—and you aren't caught with a lot of half-completed plans. The problem is, people have dreams. They get enmeshed in those dreams instead of making a dollar today.

Contingency planning is another thing. That means preparing for the possible—fire, flood, lawsuits, oil crisis, trade war, recession, SEC investigation, or a stock market crash—that could happen tomorrow, or in the year 2020, or never. Contingency planning is a must, for both the individual and the corporation.

None of this is to suggest that you shouldn't try to make an educated guess about how things will develop over the next few years, using logic, common sense, intuition, and, of course, an examination of the facts. If you make baby carriages, and the birthrate in the country has slowly declined to 1.7 births per woman today from 3.5 in 1955, and actual births have leveled off at around 4 million, you can make a fairly accurate estimate of your market over the next five years.

I'd be willing to hazard a guess—even bet a hundred dollars—that gambling in this country isn't going to be the hot industry that it is today, for example. Why? A simple examination of some elementary facts suggests tough times ahead.

First of all, there is bound to be oversaturation. What do you have to have to start a gambling business? A location and a law to let you open it for gambling. What do you have to know? The odds on cards. What do you have to do? Form a company and sell some stock. This is not exactly a complicated endeavor.

You can't just "go into" the chemical business or the insurance business or the automotive business or even the cigarette business. But you *can* just "go into" gambling. Anybody can set up a casino. It's the adult equivalent of a sidewalk lemonade stand.

It's already a crowded field. Five years from now, it's going to be as jammed as Times Square on New Year's Eve. You can hardly pick up the paper these days without reading about some state legislature approving gambling or some Indian tribe opening a casino or some down-at-the-heels resort area trying to revive itself by setting up a casino. Gambling riverboats ply the nation's waterways. (Funny how the gambling industry always takes the middle two letters out of the word, as though to disinfect it.)

The danger signs for the gambling industry are proliferating. I was amused to read in 1995 that real-estate tycoon Donald Trump had filed suit to block a new New York State lottery game. In the old days, outraged religious moralists might thunder against the evils of wagering, but here was Donald Trump, high priest of the Temples of Chance, railing against the corrupting influence of Quick Draw. "It's the most highly addicting form of gambling," he declared. His concern for the victims was touching: "People won't be paying rent," he said. "Welfare rolls will go up."

But while Donald Trump battles to protect his turf, real people really are becoming addicted to gambling—and not just to Quick Draw. While the novelty wears off for most, it enraptures and entraps others—and I fear the nation will spend a huge amount of money and energy repairing the damage that these abusers do to themselves and their families. And that is where the second danger for the industry arises: A public backlash is building. And all the more so because gambling adds nothing to the economy; most of the money is tourist dollars that would have gone to other forms of entertainment if the casino wasn't there. That's why Disney spent so much fighting a gambling initiative in Florida.

For the businessman, there's another problem. Indian gambling has a built-in competitive advantage: It generally doesn't pay any state or federal taxes. So I guess you'd have to seek Indian partners. In the end, the real competition might be for the Indian tribes. The question might become: How much do we have to pay the Sioux and can we get a better deal from the Seminoles?

Finally, there is the ever-present threat of criminal corruption. They say they've chased the Mafia out, but I don't believe it. And the Mafia doesn't think in business terms. I knew a fellow out West who had an oil-exploration company and got some Mafia money to do some drilling. In oil exploration, you get rich if you hit oil, and you lose your shirt if you don't. It seems obvious, but the Mafia only understands the first part. When my friend came up dry, the Mafia sent him a picture of his family. He got the message, and repaid the "loan."

That's my analysis. But it's not long-range planning; it's common sense. Don't count on long-range planning. Make long-range goals, yes, and take the steps—one by one—that get you there. You've heard the phrase "a shot in the dark." Try to solve today's problems, and next week's, and next month's, and maybe even next year's, and the long-term future will take care of itself. But don't lose sleep at night worrying about what might happen in the year 2001 or 2010.

Remember the gag sign that reads "PLAN AHEAd" in huge letters, with a scrawny little *d* squished in at the end because the artist forgot to allot enough space for it? That kind of encapsulates the problem at many corporations today. They have a bold vision but neglect the nuts-and-bolts steps required to achieve it.

There is a poem by Percy Bysshe Shelley called "Ozymandias" that captures the folly of trying to peer too far into the future. It is about the arrogance of an ancient king, who boasted of his power.

"I met a traveler from an antique land
Who said: Two vast and trunkless legs of stone
Stand in the desert . . . Near them, on the sand,
Half sunk, a shattered visage lies, whose frown,
And wrinkled lip, and sneer of cold command,
Tell that its sculptor well those passions read
Which yet survive, stamped on these lifeless things,
The hand that mocked them, and the heart that fed:
And on the pedestal these words appear:
"My name is Ozymandias, king of kings:
Look on my works, ye mighty, and despair!"
Nothing beside remains. Round the decay
Of that colossal wreck, boundless and bare
The lone and level sands stretch far away.

So beware of too much unrealistic long-range planning, or you'll end up like Ozymandias. Better to follow the advice of the ancient Chinese sage: "A journey of a thousand miles begins with a single step."

A successful company sets long-range objectives but engages in extremely focused realistic short-range planning; it learns to react to setbacks and seize opportunities as they arise. And, by the way, it can do this best if it is a conglomerate.

11

A Pitch for Old-Style Worker Empowerment

It sounds so obvious as to be banal: People want to get ahead. But it is the strongest force in management. Learn how to channel it, and you can accomplish marvelous things.

It is the Force in industry.

Odd as it may seem, many companies try to stifle that urge. The message that too often comes from management is: Slow down. Don't go out on a limb. Don't take risks. Play by the rules.

In the old days, General Motors was one of the most stratified companies in the world. They had dossiers on all their people and made entries all the time on their performance. Nobody, but nobody, wanted to stick his neck out for fear of getting in that dossier. It was a system that stifled decision making.

Even today, it must be hard to shake that legacy. For the strongest car company in the world—perhaps the greatest car company of all time—to be struggling for market share with Chrysler tells you something.

It tells me that GM had too many layers of management. There's nothing wrong with bigness. The bigger the better! But watch out for bureaucracy. You know what happened at GM? The facts got lost in all those layers. The company bred a kind of reticent management.

It is remarkably easy to subdue the ambitious, to turn a fired-up go-getter into a burned-out clock-watcher. And there is a simple reason for this. Ambitious people are natural risk takers, but they can also be cautious. They do not want to throw away their careers.

The first rule for a manager, then, is: Reward your subordinates for their risk taking, and they will blossom. Penalize them, and they will shrink into themselves.

And the first rule for ambitious people is to make sure their boss deserves their confidence. They should be asking: Does my boss reward people for taking risks? For showing initiative? For working hard?

If you lose confidence in your boss, leave. That's what I did, time and time again. It's an excellent guideline.

Think back on your career. Count the number of bosses you worked for who were inept, or otherwise fatally flawed. Did you stick around too long, hoping that, somehow, things would change—that the boss would somehow mend his ways, or that you would figure out how to manage him better, or that your talents would be recognized by somebody else, somewhere else in the company?

Futile hopes, weren't they? Not worth wasting your career on.

By definition, the ambitious person wants to be in charge someday. If you didn't have that urge, you'd quit whenever you thought you had enough money to be comfortable. So don't let an incompetent boss hold you back.

No matter what position you hold in a company, if you have the Force you are always striving to go one step higher. If you lack the background, you will do something about the background.

If the urge is strong, you'll do what it takes. If you lack education or training, you'll find a way. You'll go to night school, change your focus, find a new job, switch careers—you'll do what you need to do to get there. You've got to keep bumping your head on the ceiling.

A lot of career women these days complain about being kept back by a male-dominated culture—the so-called glass ceiling. Instead of complaining, they would be better off fighting even harder. That's what every truly successful man or woman I ever met does.

Some of the ceilings I rammed my head against felt more like concrete than glass. But you kept banging away. If you have that Force—ambition—the concrete ceiling will eventually crumble, and a glass ceiling will shatter. Your head may get a bump, of course, but it'll be worth it. You will gain confidence from achieving your goals, and that self-assurance becomes a force in itself.

Is the Force a special gift, reserved for the chosen few? Not a bit. It is truly universal. Everybody has within himself or herself an ambition to get ahead, and ultimately, to be in charge. This urge begins young and knows no boundaries of race, sex, or social station. Even a motorcycle-gang member wants to be the leader of the pack.

But then, one by one, most people eliminate themselves from the competition. And most always for the same reason: They don't want to put in the effort or to make the sacrifices that their goal requires.

The winners share certain qualities. And believe it or not, one of those qualities the psychologists tell us is often an inferiority complex. Most successful people are driven by a sense of inferiority. They are "running scared." Getting ahead for them is a therapy for their self-doubt. They, therefore, force themselves to be superior.

Odd as it might sound, the lack of an inferiority complex can be a terrible handicap in the world of business. People who think they are terrific often don't amount to much. They believe they are entitled to life's rewards, so they tend not to work too hard to get them. People who are running scared, by contrast, feel they have to accomplish great things to prove their competence. They drown their doubts in their successes.

Think of George Soros, one of the most successful investors of modern times. "I am not a professional security analyst," he said. "I would rather call myself a professional insecurity analyst—I recognize that I may be wrong. This insecurity keeps me alert, always ready to correct my errors."

This recognition of his fallibility helped George Soros make $1 billion in a single huge foreign-exchange bet against the British pound recently.

Another paradox, akin to the benefits of an inferiority complex, is the advantage that lies in growing up poor. Kids who grow up poor have to prove themselves again and again, both to others and to themselves. They've got to fight like hell to get ahead. Along the way, they get knocked down a lot, but they learn to bounce right back up. They get fire in the belly. Bit by bit, they gain confidence in themselves and control over their lives.

If you grew up poor, the memory of how hard it was climbing up the ladder of success will make a difference between you and everybody you talk to or meet for the rest of your life. You're a little bit more independent. You're a little bit more able to think about life as you want to cast it, as you want to be seen in it, as you want to go through it.

I've known successful people who never knew poverty or self-doubt, but they tend to fall apart when unexpected adversity strikes.

Another quality that winners often exhibit is a fear of failure. It is a great motivator. It forces you to work, work, work. Remember what Thomas Edison said: Genius is 1 percent inspiration and 99 percent perspiration. I'd add that there isn't all that great a difference between ordinary people and geniuses. Geniuses are a little bit smarter, sure. But an ordinary person who works his duff off will win out over a genius who sits on his duff—100 percent of the time.

But don't go so far as to let fear paralyze you or deter you from taking risks.

As the Force carries you forward, you can't look back. The past, so familiar and comfortable, will always tug at you. It says: Why take a risk? You have already achieved a house, a family, you are known in the community. Stay where you are—why do you need this?

I remember the night that I left my Bell & Howell office for the last time to go off to the steel mills after five years. It was winter. As I walked to my car in the parking lot, I turned back for a moment to look at my office among the darkened windows. And I thought, gee, I don't know if this really makes sense, to waste all that experience, all those years of building the company. Maybe I should reconsider.

I could have stayed there and been quite comfortable. My future was assured. I thought about it for a long moment. But, finally, I told myself, no, you know damn well it's time to move on.

One of the greatest threats to anyone's career is contentment.

People who get too comfortable tend to avoid risk and stress. Such false contentment is like the sirens of Greek mythology who lured the sailors to their deaths on the rocky shores. After struggling for so long to get to a certain level in your company, it's a great temptation to let down your guard and say, "Well, here I am." There are a couple of answers to that. How long do you think you'll be here with that attitude? And is this where you really want to be?

Never be content. It's much healthier to worry. Yes, worry. It's a nuisance, an aggravation, and a stimulant to action. It can wake you up faster than a double espresso with two lumps of sugar. It forces you to pay attention, inspires you to work harder, and can even spur you to stay in the office past five.

The caveman had to worry about wild beasts lurking behind the next bush. Modern man worries about the irritants lurking in the next office memo.

We have a whole class of professionals—psychologists, psycho-analysts, therapists—who, for a fee, will instruct you on the proper way to worry. We have medical columnists who will inform you of new health hazards to worry about. (So you thought margarine was good for you and caffeine was bad for you, did you? Hah!)

As we get older, we worry mostly about our bodies, or rather their failings and misfunctionings. Who cares about the Fed's interest-rate policy, the White House's trade policy, or even your town's garbage-collection policy when your hip joints scream at you for sitting down and your knee joints scream at you for getting up and you can't remember if you're supposed to take one blue pill and two green ones at 9 A.M. and one red one and two blue ones at 3 P.M., or the other way around?

Well, I guess this is as good a way as any to wind up your earthly journey. So, my word of advice is: Don't worry so much about worrying so much. Worry is a positive force; if early man had been deprived of it, the saber-toothed tiger would now rule the earth. Alas for the saber-toothed tiger, it never fretted much about the possibility a man might be lurking behind the next bush.

Worry rouses you from your lethargy, alerts you to danger, quickens your pulse, stirs you to action, forces you to do useful things you might not otherwise do, and reminds you you're part of this world. It keeps you alive. Happy worrying!

If you stop taking risks—if you stop beating your head against the ceiling—then slowly, without realizing it, you will take on the posture of a man or woman who is going nowhere. I've seen it happen. And then what?

That's the real reason why you should always be looking for the next risk. In the long run, it's *less* risky. If you keep moving—up—you will never be a target.

Life is full of ironies, and the Force—or ambition—is no exception. The Force is guided by a paradox: Avoidance of risk is risky and undue reliance on safety is risky; you just have to keep moving—up.

It's a fact of life that at around the age of fifty many people abandon their dreams of setting the world on fire and worry more about keeping warm. They become preoccupied with holding on to what they've got.

Yet the dreams die hard. Some people adjust by transferring them to their children. Others reformulate them: They plan one day to write a book, run a country inn in New England, start a fish-and-tackle business on a lake. I hope they really do.

Eventually, of course, we may all have to scale down our ambitions. But first why not try to achieve them? It's one of life's great satisfactions. And you won't be doomed to living out your last years asking, ''What if?''

At my age, I would hardly expect to now be asked to run a Fortune 500 company. Maybe I could, but I'm not sure I'd want to. But even at eighty-seven, I don't have to quit. I'm going to continue to take risks, though perhaps more moderate ones. But I still have the urge to improve myself. Does that make sense? I know I can manage a company like ITT, because I've done it. But turning around a little company in Connecticut is a new challenge. So I'm trying to do just that.

And if I succeed, maybe people will say: ''Harold Geneen? Isn't he the former ITT chairman who is still running companies in his late eighties? He must be nuts!'' But what they say isn't important. I think of the New Testament parable of the talents, about the guy who had a gift and didn't use it. I think that would be a terrible fate, to have a talent and have to bury it. Even in your late eighties, and for all I know, into your late nineties, you've got to try.

To be sure, the possibilities of life narrow considerably when you're old. You accept the fact that you'll never be a golf champion. You accept the fact you can't drive a car long distances, if at all. You get tired more easily. You slow down. But you don't quit, you can't quit, you mustn't quit. The passive approach deserves what it sounds like—reproach.

Keeping young is a matter of attitude—of determination. You've got to hang on to your competitive urge. If I had to place this urge somewhere, I'd locate it at the base of your neck, between your shoulder blades. It's the spot that a lineman in a football team tightens up as he hunches down and pushes forward. It's the space where your hair stands up when there is danger.

This competitive urge can have a magically countervailing influence on the brain's corrosive logic. As you get older, the brain keeps telling you that you have passed the zenith of your career, but the competitive urge has a different message. Forget about that, it says; push ahead.

That competitive urge allowed the caveman to stand up to the saber-toothed tiger and allowed you to stand up to adversity in your younger days. And it will enable you to stand up to the final tests of life. Believe me.

The competitive urge is a force that enables some people literally to refuse to die. A doctor will tell them they have an incurable disease, and they'll say, no, I'm going to lick this thing. Such sheer stubbornness doesn't confer immortality, of course. But it works better than listless resignation.

To be sure, you can't walk around all day with your shoulders all hunched up and punching your fists in the air. But you can talk yourself into that hunched-up-shoulder feeling. You can say, "By golly, I'm going to enjoy going forward. I'm going to enjoy handling this problem. I'm going to be in charge."

You may have liked Richard Nixon or you may have hated him. I consider it my good fortune to have known him, albeit only casually. He knew me well enough to wave to me in the street once. His impact on history was enormous. His accomplishments were many. But of all the things he did, his final moment impressed me the most.

A photograph captured the scene: He grinned that familiar grin that seemed to say, "You haven't beat me yet." From his deathbed, he held an arm upright and spread his forefinger and middle finger into a V for victory. What an exit! Say what you want; to the end, he was a fighter.

I'm not ready to exit yet, but I'm still ready for a fight. And I will fight to the end. It's just that now I realize that whether I succeed is immaterial. It is the seeking that turns out to be the meaning of life.

I recently wrote this note to a friend on his eightieth birthday:

Dear ———,

Shakespeare wrote something called the Seven Ages of Man.

But, of course, he was a confused young man himself, more interested in making a shilling than in the scientific facts.

So, after exhaustive research, I have reduced life to the essentials:

0–80 years—stripling

80–100 years—youth.

So, many congratulations, and enjoy your youth.

Glad to hear you're still shaking the dice.

Warm memories and best regards

Hal

Retirement—what a word! The first dictionary definition of retire is "to withdraw to a sheltered or secluded place." The second definition is "to go to bed." The third is "to give ground, to retreat, to withdraw." It is only the fourth definition that refers to the practice of quitting your job at sixty-five and living off a pension.

Consider those first three meanings: hiding, sleeping, retreating. Not activities that stir the imagination, are they? Yet they are lumped together with the supposed great adventure of cutting yourself loose from your career.

People who sell their homes and head for Florida remind me of those elephants of African lore who suddenly stop what they're doing and trek a thousand miles to a jungle burial ground, where they sink to their knees, roll over, and die. They haven't been struck by crippling disease, obviously, or they would never be able to cover all that territory. Rather, they have simply decided to give up. And while the elephant burial ground may be mythical, there is nothing fictional about the descent of millions of Americans into a pointless idleness that hastens their end.

Am I being too gloomy? I don't think so. I *am* saying that life can continue to hold wonderful adventures for all those who will seek them.

I don't think there's such a thing as doing nothing. Do nothing, and you become nothing. The way I see it, some people are obsolete at fifty-five or even thirty-five, whereas others are full of vim and vigor at eighty-five or even ninety-five. Yes, that includes me.

I quote Richard Cumberland elsewhere in this book as saying he would rather wear out than rust out. I feel the same way. It's probably the secret of healthy old age. Look around you—most of the people who are still going strong in their eighties and nineties are all energetic *doers,* aren't they? Whether they're organizing church rummage sales or bird-watching in Alaska, they keep busy pursuing *purposeful* activities. They retain their zest for life.

I was talking the other day with some people who were well advanced in age and extremely well fixed. You would recognize their names, but the point is that they were still working hard. All had started their careers in the depression, driving trucks, loading ships, doing anything in order to eat. And they hadn't forgotten those hard times; indeed, they laugh about them now. But they had tapped into their primal urge early. And today, though in their late seventies and early eighties and with plenty of money, they are still pushing themselves. The Force is still pushing them on. You think that's a mistake? They don't. They are still doing things. They are alive in the full sense of the word and enjoying themselves.

I've known people who seemed to be driven from one romance to another, year after year, even into their old age. Same primal urge, different objective.

I've known teachers who devote their lives to helping their students. They are paid a low salary; their sacrifice is hardly acknowledged by society, let alone rewarded. But they are driven by that same basic urge, not for material success, but for purpose.

It's more than just drive. It's deeper than that. And it's not the desire to get money. Money is only a scorecard. The Force is really the desire to build something. It is the most fundamental human urge, the urge to create.

May the Force be with you.

SLICING THE BALONEY

12

The Information
Superhype Way

New Utopia? Horrifying Sham!
—From a list published in *Business Week* of anagrams made
by rearranging the letters in the phrase "Information
Superhighway."

Everybody has books. Everybody buys books. Everybody has
stacks of books. Everybody tries to give away books. Everybody does
everything with books except read them.

Will the information superhighway inspire us all to read books?

Books are the repository of practically all the wisdom of hu-
manity from the beginning of history. Long before I was born, they
awaited readers in the great libraries of the world. They still await
them.

But few people seek them out. Now, millions of books will be instantly accessible on the Internet. But will that availability turn us overnight into a nation of scholars?

There's a book on your shelf that you have always wanted to read. It contains profound truths, or so you have been told; it brims with facts and quivers with insights. The book's binding is thick; its title is intimidating. Each time you walk by, it reproaches you for neglecting it. Someday you will open it, you tell yourself. Someday you will have the time. But not right now.

Will you magically find the time to read it—if it goes on-line?

Furthermore, if you finally do find time to read that book, will you, given the choice, read it on your computer screen? Or, instead, will you read it on the beach, or in a hammock, or nestled in a beat-up old armchair in front of a crackling fire?

I have a suggestion. It will be my contribution to the electronic revolution: Let's ban the phrase "the information superhighway." It's a terrible metaphor, conveying a false impression of smooth, effortless travel to a prearranged destination. Worse yet, it was coined by Vice President Al Gore. Thus, it already has more than its share of political implications. Will we need a passport to go overseas on it? Where will they set up the tollbooths? Highway?

Nonsense! What we're really talking about is a lot of hatching birds. Some grow into strutting peacocks, others into noisy blue jays, and yet others into soaring eagles. Some, unfortunately, will turn out to be turkeys. Then, of course, there will be chickens that come home to roost. Based on this, how about a new name: "the information aviary?"

The information aviary is like a graduating high-school senior. Some day he'll amount to something; he might become a rocket scientist or a world-famous surgeon or maybe even the president of the United States. But for the moment, he's just a kid, full of energy and bubbling with hormones, but not quite sure what he wants to do with his life. We shouldn't be overawed by the information superhighway; we shouldn't feel duty-bound to embrace it. It's just another choice. And those most extravagant in its praises are often just parading their knowledge.

Now, let's try to get past the hype and examine what the information aviary really has to offer. There is no question that it gives us quicker access to information than we ever had at our command before. But will it end by burying us under an information avalanche? People with common interests—from archery to laser surgery—can share ideas and information on bulletin boards and "Web sites." If restricted to a very small number of specialists with valuable ideas to offer, these information exchanges can be useful tools.

But enforcing restrictions on access may be difficult. And if there are no restrictions—if every Tom, Dick, and Harry can have his say—then meaningful discourse will be drowned in a sea of blather. There's nothing so boring as listening to a speaker who hasn't condensed what he has to say to the essentials. The information superhighway risks becoming the electronic equivalent of that windbag preacher whose sermon meanders into every conceivable digression and never ends.

They say that the fifteen thousand discussion groups on the Internet's Usenet service pump the equivalent of four thousand novels into the system every two weeks. Or to return to my aviary metaphor, Net surfers who are after kernels of information will be like those cowbirds that pick through cattle droppings for kernels of corn.

Sure, the Internet can facilitate communication among large groups of people. Investor Paul Kazarian made a big to-do about his plan to launch a bid for an unspecified high-tech company from the World Wide Web. He was using his Web site to store information on potential targets and ultimately to communicate with the targets' shareholders and officers, potential investment partners, and other interested parties. Well and good, but a takeover attempt is a takeover attempt, and I can't see that use of the Internet will alter the outcome.

For many Americans, the information superhighway mostly means buying a lot of expensive equipment and trying to figure out how to use it. If most of us have trouble programming our VCRs, how can we be expected to move this boldly into the information age? To do it right, we'd probably have to neglect important job duties, or worse, give up golf.

Some critics fear that cyberspace fanatics will become so addicted to on-line relationships that they will lose interest in real people, and will become so enamored of virtual reality that they will forget the problems of the planet they live on. Well, maybe.

Wait! others will say. With our PCs tapped into data banks, the information aviary will enable us to browse through vast libraries with the press of buttons. There's some truth to that, of course. But again, the danger of too much information arises. I guess if you're adept at narrowing your search for information down to something very specific, you might be okay. But if your question is general, you might have to choose from thousands of entries. The *Wall Street Journal* coined a word for this: "cyber-dreck." And columnist William Buckley says two Internet experts tried on two separate occasions to find for him a simple piece of information—the years that Thomas Jefferson spent in Paris as ambassador—and both failed, one devoting a full hour to the search, the other giving up after half an hour.

And will we really prefer to sit at home, scrunched over our PCs and "surfing" through databases, to wandering through the hushed rooms of our local libraries? In just a matter of years, there will no longer be a need for these literary storehouses with their redbrick exteriors, their enormous windows looking out on green lawns and cherry trees, their musty bookshelves and their eccentric amateur scholars fussing over the card catalogs. But do we really want to shut them down?

There are other downsides to the ready availability of so much information. In the business world, many managers are already having to put a lid on Net surfing by bored office workers. You can understand the temptation that an eight-dollar-an-hour data-processing clerk might feel for sending an E-mail message to her boyfriend, or for doing a comparison study of holiday package tours to Florida, or even for going job hunting through the electronic classified ads! Especially if, to the casual observer, she seems to be toiling away, fingers flying.

And don't forget, the current anonymity of the Net enables terrorists, racists, child pornographers, and all sorts of degenerates to set up their own Web sites and push their agendas. The federal firearms bureau says random bombings are on the rise, like the booby trap that killed a man walking along a street in Miami early in 1996, because so many computer bulletin boards give information about how to make explosives and rig them with trip wires. About the same time, three thirteen-year-old boys in Mineola, New York, were arrested on a tip. They had built a fertilizer-and-fuel-oil bomb working from plans obtained from the Internet. They planned to blow up the school on the weekend when it was empty. This was no crime of passion; just a request for some time off. It was real, all right. A test bomb had worked well in an orchard.

And there is the additional problem of scams. Apparently, penny-stock con artists are already crawling all over the Internet. Even well-meaning but misguided folks—say, those who preach vitamin C as a cure for cancer or denounce fluoridated water as a Communist plot—have a new, efficient mechanism for trumpeting their causes. Sophisticated advertisers and propagandists will dress up their messages as ''news'' and probably fool more people in cyberspace than they could on TV or in print. How do you sue or hold for accountability a mysterious billboard poster from outer space?

But there are some great positive visions for the information superhighway. Enthusiasts say we'll be able to order anything, anywhere, anytime, by typing into a computer instead of making a phone call and talking with a human. But will we want to? When we buy something that's important to us, don't we want to be able to feel the cloth, kick the tires, or look the salesman in the eye? Americans aren't going to buy a pork roast over the Internet. They want the option of complaining to the butcher that there's too much fat on it. And what fishing nut will order a rod on the Internet? He'll want to walk into a store, feel the grip of a half dozen models, and strike up a conversation with the salesman.

The *New York Times* gives an example of the benefits awaiting consumers. ''More than a dozen insurance companies have agreed to offer information and services at a central site on the Internet's World Wide Web. The agreement, which was announced yesterday, raises the possibility that a central Internet site may evolve where consumers can get information and shop for a wide range of policies, without having to communicate with each company separately.''

Be prepared to hold the line indefinitely on this one. In fact, I'd call that free advertising. In my view, if you decide to buy insurance, you call a broker. You want advice independent of the seller. As I said, you want to go kick the tires.

Another great vision for the information superhighway is its power to provide entertainment to the masses. It will be possible to punch a code into a computer and get the movie of your choice on your TV screen within seconds, it is said. Wonderful. The average American already watches 10 zillion hours of television and/or movies every year. Now, he will be able to watch 20 zillion hours. In addition, a broad range of violent and sexually explicit films will be made accessible to our young people and our growing population of psychopaths.

In time, presumably, ''virtual reality'' will come to cyberspace. People will put on helmets and goggles and park themselves in front of their screens and enter a world of such vivid sound and imagery that it will seem almost real. But the fact is, it will be make-believe. You can't take your kid fishing on the information superhighway. You can't go out for drinks with your friends on the information super-highway. You certainly can't make love on the information super-highway.

Besides, humans have had their own parallel world of virtual reality ever since they began walking upright 2 million years ago. It's known as imagination. When I was a kid, I read every fairy tale ever written. The moral was always the same: The villain got his just deserts and the hero got his one true love. But each story was different, and magical. Talk about virtual reality: The written word can create a strange and wonderful world in the imagination of a child.

I'll never forget the mysterious lost civilizations of Africa depicted by the nineteenth-century English author H. Rider Haggard in such fables as *King Solomon's Mines* and *She* (the latter about the quest for the "Flame of Eternal Life"). It was pure enchantment. If somebody puts *King Solomon's Mines* in a database on the information superhighway, I might call it up just to relive a small part of my childhood. But will the boys and girls of today call it up? Or would they rather play Mortal Kombat II and Sonic & Knuckles (in which a hedgehog defeats Dr. Robot) on their computer screens instead?

True, electronic mail speeds up communications in the global economy. But it's just one more way to say hi. We also have speech, the mail, phones, sign language, faxes, Federal Express, smoke signals, ham radio, body language, telex messages, and bottles with notes inside tossed into the deep. The Internet just naturally attracts people who like to twist dials. And, I say, let them have their fun. New technologies have always fascinated the young and curious—not because of what they could do to improve the world but because they were *fun*.

In the early days of radio, I built a crystal set. I toiled long into the night assembling and testing it. Every so often—paydirt!—I'd receive a new station. The big thrill wasn't the content of the program. It was capturing hitherto undetected waves of electromagnetic radiation in the crystal before me. "Mom! I got KDKA in Pittsburgh!" As soon as I achieved that feat, I'd look for something else. It was a game.

Isn't the information aviary something like that crystal radio?

Exclude the entertainment value, the electronic games, and the thrill of chatting with people you don't know, and what do you have? I'm trying to be helpful. I really want the information superhighway to succeed. There's got to be an excuse for it: Otherwise, the whole damn electronics industry will come crashing down.

I'm struggling. Please help me! The information superhighway is . . . Why am I waiting for somebody to explain to me in words of one or two syllables why it is the greatest thing since Mom's apple pie? Please, throw me a life preserver. I feel I'm sinking in a sea of hyperbole.

I'm not alone in harboring a measure of skepticism, of course. It has become almost fashionable to mock the overblown rhetoric of the digital diehards. Listen to some skeptics. *Ron Erickson,* former chairman of Egghead software and now a technology consultant: ''Here's my admonition to consumers: Don't get the new version of the old one is working O.K.'' *John Malone,* CEO of Tele-Communications Incorporated: ''Market research shows that there are very few services the public has any interest in on any scale. I think we pretty much know what the locomotives have to be to carry these investments. Video-on-demand is a revenue generator, but not nearly as big as they think. I wish I had kept a file, but at one time [Bell Atlantic Corporation CEO Ray Smith] had video generating something like $10,000 of revenue per household in New Jersey. Even the Mafia doesn't have that kind of disposable income for communications. It was getting to an extreme point.''

Clifford Stoll, an early Internet enthusiast, in his 1995 book, *Silicon Snake Oil:* ''Data isn't information any more than 50 tons of cement is a skyscraper. Simply by turning to a computer when confronted with a problem, you limit your ability to recognize other solutions.'' *Rupert Murdoch,* head of the News Corporation media empire: ''I think it [interactive media] will happen. I'm just very cautious about when. . . . It's proving more difficult and more expensive, and you have to start with what people will pay for. Right now, they'll pay for electronic games.''

Meantime, newspapers and magazines are pouring tens of millions of dollars into electronic editions for which the demand is less than vibrant. Some are now scaling back their investments. Knight-Ridder, owner of twenty-eight newspapers, closed its electronic newspaper, called the *Tablet,* in 1995. ''The *Tablet* is significantly further into the future than we thought,'' the company said. One of the most felicitously phrased mea culpas I have heard.

Other much-trumpeted information-age innovations are slower in materializing than people first thought would be the case. Remember electronic banking? Remember interactive TV and movies-on-demand? Their day may come, but not as quickly as their boosters predicted. I don't want to push my skepticism too far. I recognize the potential of the information superhighway to change our lives and advance knowledge. It can select, tabulate, and relay information quickly and efficiently. It is becoming an indispensable research tool for scientists, economists, historians, and sociologists. It promises to enhance the quality of our medical care. For example, one day health-care providers may be linked together in one vast communications network that will allow a specialist in California to observe the ultrasound image of a surgical operation in New York City and to offer his opinion to the surgeon. Assuming he wants it.

And one doesn't want to be accused of being a modern-day Luddite. (They were the English handicraftsmen who destroyed the textile machines that were displacing them in the early nineteenth century.) Still, when you add up all the benefits, can you really say the information superhighway is going to educate mankind and liberate us from the ancient curses of poverty, sickness, greed, criminality, racism, and sloth; in short, from ourselves? Does anybody really believe that it is a magic potion that will usher in peace and understanding among all peoples?

What you do with the information that you get through this vast network of computers and databases doesn't change, either.

It's kind of like paving an old dirt road. Afterward, you can get to where you're going faster, but it still takes you from point A to point B. Much of the information-superhighway hoopla has a familiar ring to historians. It's part of the age-old hope that new technology will solve mankind's ills. In our country, it has happened time and again. If anything, futurists and editorial writers at the turn of the century rhapsodized more about the potential of the telephone for uniting the world than Internet fanatics today claim for cyberspace. People made an enormous fuss over plastic around the time of World War I. Then, after World War II, we heard all about television's imminent elevation of mankind to new levels of culture and learning.

In the 1950s, atomic power was seen as the elixir of human

progress. The chairman of the Radio Corporation of America predicted in 1955 that atomic energy would soon be fueling "ships, aircraft, locomotives and even automobiles" and confidently asserted that "atomic batteries will be commonplace long before 1980."

In the 1960s, the space race promised a great leap into a high-tech and, of course, more peaceful future. In the 1970s, people were declaring that CB radio would revolutionize human communications. When was the last time you talked into one—or even heard somebody else use one?

To be sure, all of these things—the telephone, plastic, television, atomic power, space technology, even the CB radio—have been breakthroughs with enormous impact on human affairs. But neither they nor any other human invention has ever ushered in Utopia, nor will any future innovation. Like it or not, the human race will always be the human race.

Sometimes, of course, the skeptics get it wrong, providing cheap laughs for future generations. President Rutherford B. Hayes was impressed by a demonstration of the telephone in 1876 but asked, "Who would ever want to use one?" And *Harper's Weekly* prophesied in 1902 that "the actual building of roads devoted to motor cars is not for the near future."

All in all, though, the American tradition of refusing to swallow all the ballyhoo surrounding less-than-apocalyptic technological advances is healthy. Even if doubters err on the side of caution, they provide a much needed antidote to the gushing wonderment at the new and modern that is in itself a national pastime. "We are in great haste to construct a magnetic telegraph from Maine to Texas," Henry David Thoreau declared a century and a half ago, "but Maine and Texas, it may be, have nothing to communicate. . . . We are eager to tunnel under the Atlantic. . . . But perchance the first news that will leak through the broad, flapping American ear will be that the Princess Adelaide has the whooping cough."

Let me put in a good word for the information superhighway. It is indeed a major step forward for civilization, just as the wheel was a million years ago, as the printing press was five hundred years ago, and, yes, as the telephone, the television, and the rocket ship have been in our own age. The information superhighway really will bring the people of the world closer together. It really will advance human knowledge. It will do many other things.

But, believe me, twenty years from now some new grand break-through will be on everybody's lips. And some essayist will write, "Remember when everybody got so excited about the information superhighway?"

13

Mother Earth and Other Business Blather

President Calvin Coolidge said in a speech in 1926 that the chief business of the American people is business. I'd add this seemingly obvious corollary: The business of *business* is business. But a lot of people don't understand that simple concept. Business, they say, should be "socially responsible." What blather.

Management's first duty is to satisfy shareholders. That means increasing profits and getting the share price up. And to do that, the company has to make useful products and treat its workers well. That's all the social responsibility they want.

What about supporting worthy causes, like protecting the rain forests and their inhabitants from the depredations of miners and loggers? It sounds like the right thing to do—until you ask yourself whose worthy cause you are promoting. The shareholders own this business, after all. Did you ask *them* how they feel?

If management decides to give out small amounts of money to this charity or that, the stockholders will go along. But it shouldn't take a position on the controversial social and moral issues of the day without the consent of its owners.

Note that the causes companies do embrace are rarely controversial. It helps if the charity has the word "children" in its name. Think of McDonald's and its Ronald McDonald Children's Charities, Ben & Jerry's Homemade Incorporated and its Children's Defense Fund to Leave No Child Behind, and Seagram's Tropicana and its support for the Children's Miracle Network. Other favorites seem to be saving the rain forests (always, to be sure, on some faraway continent), protecting endangered species (preferably cuddly mammals), providing medical care to people with AIDS and shelter to battered women. Oh, yes, and world peace and feeding the hungry. Who but the coldest-hearted misanthrope could find fault with those noble impulses?

I have no problem with direct cash donations by corporations to worthy causes. Almost all companies do that. They're tax deductible. But they should remain separate from business. The big to-do that many companies make, often around Christmastime, about giving a portion of their sales or profits to charity is so much humbug. They're doing no such thing. What they're doing is a cute kind of advertising: When you buy this, you're giving something to the poor. Well, for crying out loud. The *product* is what the consumer is buying, not a chance to drop a few cents into the poor box. She can do that at the Salvation Army stand outside the store.

American Express went on an advertising blitz over the Christmas holiday season in 1995 to trumpet its "charge against hunger" campaign. It said it would donate up to $5 million to charity, based on three cents for every card purchase during a two-month period. The theme was "take the time out to love someone." At about the same time, Chemical Bank was taking ads out to publicize its sponsorship of the Radio City Christmas Spectacular for ten thousand poor kids.

It was all very touching. And very phony. You can hardly walk into a shop these days without getting hit over the head with corporate

America's civic-mindedness. I was looking at some neckties in Macy's the other day and, lo and behold, a bunch of them had big paper tags urging, "Support Mothers Against Drunk Driving."

At a nearby cosmetics boutique, a package of body-care ointments had a $25 price tag that announced in big letters, "$5 from each purchase goes directly to CARE." A big sign up on the wall (right over the cash register, so customers would be sure to feel good about their purchases) declared its dedication to six grand principles:

Natural Ingredients

Quality Products

Outstanding Value

Environmental Responsibility

Minimal Packaging

Cruelty-free Products

To my way of thinking, only the first three objectives merit management's preoccupation. But my favorite commandment is the last. What a breakthrough! Across America, other companies must be selling products bristling with cruelty, plotting Heaven knows what mischief. But not this boutique. Its wares are "cruelty-free."

I didn't buy the vanilla-scented candle that day because it had natural ingredients or because it was "cruelty-free." I bought it because I thought my wife would like it.

Similarly, I use the American Express card when it suits me, not because they're going to give one penny for every ten dollars I spend to the poor, or whatever their formula is. If I want to give something to the poor, I'll write my own check. And I'll keep quiet about it. If they give something to the poor, I wish they'd keep quiet about it, too. Instead, they're trying to buy the public's goodwill by giving nickels and dimes in this curious way.

I'm sure if you approached any of these corporations, they'd reply, "Oh, no, we really mean it. We really do care about the rain forests." But you can bet that if their contributions were significant enough to put them at a cost disadvantage to their competitors—if sending a nickel to the Rain Forest Fund for every can of shoe polish they sold reduced Shoe-Brite Incorporated's sales by 10 percent— they'd cut the program in a second.

In other words, making charitable contributions is an act of magnanimity only so long as it increases sales. If it hurts profits, though, it becomes simply a stupid business move, and is discontinued.

What if a company were to send a letter to its stockholders saying, ''We have decided to cut the dividend in half. You'll be pleased to know that we are giving the savings to a fund for the protection of the endangered Indonesian spotted leopard.'' There would be a stockholder revolt.

So why isn't there a stockholder revolt when an orange-juice company or fast-food restaurant chain promises to devote a ''portion of all sales'' to feed the homeless or shelter battered women? After all, somebody's paying the price—the stockholders, the consumers, or both.

The answer is that the money involved, as a portion of the company's total revenues and earnings, is a pittance, and the recipients' activities seem benign enough. But you won't see the Remington Arms Company donating a portion of its sales to the People for the Ethical Treatment of Animals. It is equally doubtful that the Canadian Sealers Association will ask its members to contribute money to the International Fund for Animal Welfare.

Ironically, corporations' charitable contributions are way down, to $5.92 billion in 1993 from $7.33 billion in 1987. Only now, they are trying to get more public-relations mileage out of their donations.

The press made a small fuss in 1995 when Proctor & Gamble said it would take a $13 million charge to support relief efforts for 2,600 of its employees affected by the earthquake in Kobe, Japan. Some Wall Street analyst was quoted as saying it was a ''classy move.''

It was a business expense. The Japanese value loyalty above all else. Proctor & Gamble would have lost a lot of face if it hadn't pledged financial support for its workers. But reporters should have asked how it treated laid-off blue-collar workers in, say, Ashland, Kentucky.

Proctor & Gamble has always put a premium on results. If you perform, you're rewarded; if not, you're out the door. If you go to work at Proctor & Gamble, they'll put you through a training course, then put you in charge of ten milk cans. If you do well, they'll put you in charge of one hundred milk cans, then one thousand milk cans. They're very systematic about raising you up the chain of responsibility. But if you falter, watch out. They don't put up with deadwood.

Another marketing play that every company seems to be making these days is the "green" feint to the left. It's getting ridiculous. Here's a notice on a children's game made by Little Harbor Corporation: "Little Harbor cares about the environment. We use recycled materials wherever possible, and all of our packaging is recyclable." Ignoring the fact that the qualifier "wherever possible" is a loophole big enough to drive a gas-guzzling truck through, may I point out that most packaging, from paper and cardboard to plastic and aluminum, is recyclable?

But it's the big companies, especially those in industries like oil, chemicals, logging, and mining, that shout the loudest about their love of pure air, water, and soil. To hear them tell it, the environmentalists might as well pack up and go home. The job of nursing Mother Earth back to health is done.

Johnson & Johnson, McDonald's, Prudential Insurance, and Time Warner all declared recently that they were going to put pressure on their paper suppliers to be more environmentally responsible. The announcement got them good press, until you got down to a reality check in the ninth paragraph of a *New York Times* article:

"Analysts said that the report itself would have little broad impact on the paper and forest products industry, largely because the industry was already investing heavily in recycling equipment and managing its forests carefully."

But that sort of thing doesn't bother me so much as the notion that corporate America has the duty to be "environmentally friendly."

Companies shouldn't use the most "environmentally friendly" materials for their products. They should use the *best* materials allowed by law. And I am sure they do. And I am also sure they abide by a lot of other laws. So do others without a sandwich board. It is up to the American people and their democratically elected representatives to set the standards for clean air and water. By setting the standards, the government is also creating a level playing field. That can to a point offset imports from countries that aren't worrying about level playing fields.

I'm also a big believer in worker "empowerment," for example, another supposedly socially responsible goal. Only I think "empowerment" is a misnomer. What companies are really talking about is worker accommodation.

And the reason you accommodate workers is not because you're some armchair socialist who thinks it might be a good thing to give the working class a better deal. It's because you think that by accommodating them, you're going to get better performance out of them.

A working mother who worries about the kids falling out of the window isn't going to be terribly productive.

Increasingly, companies are offering workers the right to work at home at least part of the time, the option to set their own work schedules, subsidized day care (sometimes right in the office), longer maternity leave, and leaves to deal with family emergencies like caring for aging parents. In return, they are getting worker loyalty. What greater reward could there be?

Naturally, they can't give everybody carte blanche to work when and where she pleases. Let's say my job is to check out ten thousand invoices every week to see if they conform to some kind of a master pattern. I can come into the office at midnight and work until dawn with nobody around if I prefer. I don't need a lot of verbal interchange.

On the other hand, a manager who has to sit down at a dozen meetings a day, some of them impromptu, obviously has to go to the office during the traditional workday. That is where the action and interaction is. You can't make important decisions if some needed people stay at home and the others set their own office hours.

Most concessions to workers make sense. Of course, you have to keep them within reason. The very generous benefits that some European countries offer their workers can have an impact on their competitive position.

But stockholders don't go into any depth of analysis about the drain on productivity of undue worker "empowerment." They don't write angry letters to the chairman. What they will do, though, if they sense that the company is getting flabby, is sell the stock.

There are lots more hot buttons to push in the world of social responsibility. Take diversity in the workplace. In the long run, corporate America can and will hire more blacks, Hispanics, and women. But a good first step ought to be to give minorities who might need it more and better training so it is clear that they can compete with everybody else on an even playing field. I guess we are trying to get there.

But better training means better schools. It would be a costly but sound investment. It should be an investment the *nation* makes. But since industry benefits, it can and should use its efforts to see that it happens.

I also think all people of goodwill want to end discrimination against minorities and to work for a society that offers equal opportunity for everybody. But that is going to take adjustment on all sides and continued progress.

Some women also complain that an "old boys' network" of males keeps them down. They talk about the so-called glass ceiling, an invisible barrier that keeps them from rising above a certain level. Shareholder activists are getting in the act on this one. The $142 billion teachers' investment fund made a policy statement recently that boards should "reflect diversity of experience, gender, race and age," and it forced a shareholder vote on the issue at Nucor Corporation. Alas, the whole idea is wrongheaded. Boards should reflect "competence"—the rest is incidental. But the disease is spreading. Wisconsin recently decided there weren't enough women and minorities on corporate boards in that state and set up a "Glass Ceiling Commission" to create a database of candidates.

New York's Interfaith Center on Corporate Responsibility has made a similar demand; it wants companies to set a timetable for putting women and blacks on their boards. I've dealt with this same kind of well-meaning suggestion in many annual meetings. But the test always has to be, who is capable? It takes time to make changes. You can't rush it.

I revisited my old prep school in Connecticut recently. Since my time it has become coed. What struck me was how easily the girls fit in with the boys. They all acted as if they were "one of the guys." They weren't asking any quarter, or giving any quarter. In the physical way they carried themselves, too, it seemed to me, they weren't so frail as the girls at school were in my boyhood.

I don't think the "glass ceiling" will hold those girls back.

Here are some other hot buttons:

ANIMAL TESTING. Cosmetics companies must have some sort of contest going to see which can put on the greatest show of indignation on this issue. The thought of causing pain to an animal in the interests of science is too much for them to bear.

How deep is their commitment? What if you gave them a secret formula for eliminating wrinkles from human skin? And what if the Food and Drug Administration said, yes, it really does seem to eliminate wrinkles, but we want to be sure it doesn't cause skin cancer? We'll approve it if you can show it doesn't harm rhesus monkeys.

ANGER AT THE SUPPOSED GOVERNMENT UNDER-FUNDING OF THE FIGHT ON AIDS. The Italian garment maker Benetton ran an ad showing President Reagan with AIDS lesions on his face. Its way of accusing him of refusing to increase AIDS research fast enough, I suppose.

This is scare politicking. It only adds to the confusion. If the president of that company wants to take that stand, he ought to do it in his own name. There's a whole bunch of his stockholders that may think entirely differently. Why should he pledge their names, indirectly, to his pet cause?

Even if the stockholders should approve a resolution favoring such advertising by 60 percent to 40 percent, I would still question the action, because it has nothing to do with the business, and there are 40 percent who don't approve, for the good reason that it is clearly outside the scope of business. There are other groups perfectly capable of taking a stand that is 100 percent for or against.

MULTINATIONALS WHOSE OPERATIONS IN DEVELOPING COUNTRIES FALL SHORT OF MEETING THE ENVIRONMENTAL STANDARDS OF THE RICH INDUSTRIALIZED NATIONS. Environmentalists accused Southern Peru Copper, which operates a smelter in Ilo, Peru, of spewing enormous amounts of sulfur dioxide into the air, jeopardizing the health of the locals.

First of all, Southern Peru Copper is abiding by the law of the land. It is probably maintaining much higher standards than Peruvian companies do.

And what about the people who buy its copper? It would be difficult for a copper user to decide to pay ten cents a pound more for copper produced by an environmentally sound smelter. That immediately exceeds the CEO's trust. There are groups he can join for that purpose.

In the unlikely event that a CEO should decide to pay more for another, more "environmentally friendly" source, he would have the obligation to tell his stockholders: "Our earnings were reduced by four million dollars last year because we paid ten percent above the market rate for one of our key raw materials, copper, in order to avoid dealing with a Third World producer that pollutes the environment and harms the health of the local peasants." Better to work constructively for a solution than apply a strategy that defies the basic laws of economics.

When it gets out on the market, a copper saucepan is a copper saucepan. There's nothing engraved on it that says, "This pan was made from copper whose production destroyed thousands of trees and caused breathing problems for hundreds of children." And even if there *were* such an engraving, would it make the pan any better?

ANOTHER HOT BUTTON IS MULTINATIONAL COLLUSION WITH THIRD WORLD DICTATORS. The rap is that big corporations from the United States, Europe, and Japan will sometimes do business with despots to make a profit.

Sometimes the United States will restrict imports from a country whose government is suspected of human-rights abuses or links to terrorism. Thus, it has banned Iranian oil. But making such decisions is what our government is for. There is no way a private citizen can, and no reason he should, try to make these decisions himself.

And consider this: Almost every Third World country either is run, or recently was run, by a dictator.

Doing business with dictatorships doesn't mean you approve of them. And it really is unfair to demand that a U.S. company that has invested years of its time and huge amounts of its capital in a developing country voluntarily engage in high-stakes diplomacy every time that government does something objectionable.

Not long ago, Royal Dutch/Shell came under some pretty harsh criticism for not doing more in Nigeria after the government hanged nine human-rights activists. What could Shell have done? It might well have pointed out to officials that hanging the nine would get them a lot of unfavorable publicity. But they presumably knew that already. You need a more potent weapon than that. And leaning on a sovereign government can at the best be ineffective. At worst, it might have the undesired effect of stiffening its resolve.

Could Shell have threatened to leave the country? The government might have said: "Go ahead, we'll sell your equipment and your oil rights to somebody else." If Nigeria is a cheap source of oil, somebody would buy it no matter how repressive the regime is.

Shell's calculation had to be: What is least harmful to the company, the public-relations fallout from the hangings or the economic loss of pulling out? What it ended up doing was to try to mitigate the situation without walking away.

AND THEN WE HAVE "SOCIALLY RESPONSIBLE INVESTING." There are dozens of "socially responsible" or "ethical" or "ecological" mutual funds out there just waiting to take your money. Most of them perform below the industry average.

I think if it makes you feel good to invest your money in socially responsible funds, go ahead and do it. It's the same gambit as the companies that announce they are contributing a percentage of sales to the Amazon Indians. It's a play on the emotions of susceptible people.

So what should business do to deal with the mounting pressure to act with greater social responsibility? Do what it can within its responsibility to the shareholders. If it's a law—no alternative. If it's a crazy law—oppose it.

Going too far down the social-responsibility road would be irresponsible. Consider this scenario: You let all your employees work at home and then convert your office to a shelter for homeless battered women. It would make good PR. Picture the television commercial. The camera pans dozens of threadbare figures dining in the company cafeteria as a voice intones, "We at General Chemicals and Plastics Incorporated *really care* about society's most vulnerable people. And every time you buy a drum of our nitric acid, one of these people will get a free lunch."

That sponsor should drink some of his own product!

One of the most socially responsible things corporations could do would be to put more truth into their advertising and marketing. Ever notice how traditional measurements can get distorted if it means squeezing a few extra dollars out of the consumer? In my day, a can of coffee weighed a pound. Look at the supermarket shelves today. The cans are the same size but their contents have shrunk to 13 ounces, 11.5 ounces, or even (so I noticed recently) 10 ounces.

The calendar still contains only twelve months in a year, but the Book-of-the-Month Club has discovered a fifteen-month year is more profitable. And, while most people retire at sixty-five, the American Association of Retired People invites you to join a few weeks before your fiftieth birthday. It must be one of the more depressing moments of middle age. You've spent months preparing yourself mentally for the half-century mark, telling yourself that fifty isn't so old, thinking of all the hale and hearty people you know in their seventies and eighties when, boom, that letter from AARP arrives. And you're still only forty-nine.

Well, why not? If you made coffee, wouldn't you rather sell eight 10-ounce cans than five 16-ounce cans? If you marketed books, wouldn't you rather mail out fifteen a year to your customers than just twelve? And if you lobbied on behalf of the elderly, wouldn't you rather collect fees from everybody over forty-nine than everybody over sixty-five?

Another common subterfuge is the claim that products are being given away "free." Read your junk mail. You'll find offers for "free" trials, "free" premiums (must be purchased promptly!), "free" frequent-flier miles, "free" tips, free gasoline, free books, free subscriptions, free hotel rooms, free phone calls, free consultations.

But there's no such thing as a free lunch and none of that other stuff is free, either. John Hertz, who founded the Hertz car-rental empire, understood this. Operating out of Chicago, he was once asked how he built his business without falling into the hands of the then powerful Chicago mob. His answer was revealing. "I never accepted a favor," he said.

Favors are supposed to be free. But unless they come from family or friends, they aren't. John Hertz charged by the mile. He wouldn't have understood the concept of "unlimited free mileage." Come to think of it, I don't, either; whenever I drive a rental car with "free mileage," I still have to pull my wallet out of my back pocket when I get to the checkout counter. There's no such thing as a free ride.

Buy a sofabed and love seat and get a free recliner. Baloney! Buy three shirts and get a fourth shirt free. Baloney! Buy a thirty-two-ounce box of cereal and get eight extra ounces free. Baloney!

All right, you may say. Dreams are free, aren't they? Sure—until you decide to make them come true. Then they cost a lot: in money, in time, in energy, and in commitment.

Everybody wants something for nothing. Everybody wants to win the lottery. Everybody wants a free ride and a free lunch. But there ain't no such thing.

14

Enough Red Tape,
Already!

Fighting regulations is the greatest American tradition of them all. Our country was founded on it.

The Declaration of Independence justified the rebellion against the British Crown by invoking the "repeated injuries and usurpations" of King George III. "He has erected a multitude of New Offices, and sent hither swarms of Officers to harass our people, and eat out their substance," it complained.

Sounds pretty much like what a lot of folks are saying about the government in Washington today.

Fast-forward a century and a half from 1776 and read what

Forbes magazine had to say in 1925: "Among American citizens is a rising tide of revolt against the further multiplication of laws and regulations and restrictions imposed by Washington or by state bodies."

And today? Well, pick up any newspaper. As the French say: The more things change, the more they stay the same.

Any time the government tries to solve a business problem, the problem gets worse.

Even if there is no problem, some bureaucrat will still try to solve it, ignoring the advice of Bert Lance, the budget director of former President Jimmy Carter: "If it ain't broke, don't break it." I would add: If it is broke, don't break it some more.

When the Great Depression hit, the government tightened credit and raised tariffs, thereby guaranteeing that things would get worse. In 1933, one in every four workers was unemployed. For Congress, the solution was obvious: *We need another law.* And we got one: the National Recovery Act, passed in 1933, which made cutting prices illegal. Imagine it: Millions upon millions of Americans unemployed, millions going hungry, millions unable to pay their bills—and Congress decides to ban lower prices.

It installed a minor tyrant known as "Old Iron Pants" Johnson to pursue anybody who broke this law. I remember a little Chinese laundry that got fined. You could even get put in jail.

The Supreme Court ultimately invalidated the law in the famous "sick chicken" case in 1935 by ruling that Congress had no right to give lawmaking powers to the National Recovery Administration. (The case involved a Brooklyn poultry business that sold bad meat.)

Regulations, passed with the best of intentions, make sense in some circumstances and nonsense in others. It must be admitted, too, that we do need *some* regulations; without them, society would collapse into a chaos of lawsuits and counterclaims.

It is the inflexibility of the regulators more than the regulations themselves that so often drives businesspeople nuts—and sometimes out of business.

Take the regulation, enforced by the Occupational Safety and Health Administration, requiring separate rest-room facilities for men and women in the workplace. A great idea for any place where large numbers of men and women congregate. Perhaps it ought to be applied in our increasingly unisex universities and their dormitories. But it seems a little ridiculous to have to create two bathrooms in a small plant—one for the sole male employee and the other for the two females—as a business I know of in New Hampshire had to do. A friend of mine tells me an even better story: He knows a business that had to install separate bathrooms for its sole two employees—a husband and wife. This two-sizes-fit-all mentality is giving some of us headaches.

Did you hear about the time the Environmental Protection Agency threatened to fine a beauty shop owner in Colorado for washing her hair products down her sink? Or how about the California dry cleaner who was fined $250 for failing to post the names of injured employees over the previous twelve months, even though nobody had been injured? Or how Atlanta showed a soft spot for the hometown boys by charging $30 per vehicle for limousine companies based in the city and $600 each for companies based in the suburbs?

Sometimes you have to use a little creative imagination to deal with resultant paperwork. At the torpedo plant where I worked during the war, the naval cost inspector had to fill out endless forms and was obliged by "regulations" to file them according to more than one thousand categories, from orders for metal parts to reports of lost silverware. Confronted by this nightmare, he made a bold decision. "You have to look at the big picture," he told me. And he filed them all under a single category: "Torpedo plant." He had hundreds of files stacked in file cabinets and each exhibit was carefully labeled, "Torpedo plant."

His line of reasoning was simple. When the war was over, millions of such files would be cursorily examined and then shipped to a warehouse for storage or else burned. Nobody would have the slightest desire to know anything more about them than that they originated in a "torpedo plant," and it was doubtful that anybody would want to know even that.

Events proved him right.

Nobody had given him a definition of compliance, so he formed his own. He got away with it, too; his superiors never complained. His approach struck me then, and today, as a rare display of a quality known as common sense.

And besides, we had a war going on.

At bottom, the problem with bureaucrats is their aversion to risk. Laws are often vague, but the regulations written to implement them are much more specific. The regulators play it by the book to avoid any responsibility. Showing flexibility or just being reasonable isn't in the table of contents.

So what if from time to time they drive businesses and ordinary citizens into impossible corners? Rules are rules. They aren't allowed to take any chances.

Let me summarize the findings of various published surveys and studies to show you the extent of this country's regulatory overload:

- Government mandates and regulations have driven 64 percent of U.S. manufacturers to delay hiring new workers, 80 percent to use overtime or temps rather than new hires, and 55 percent to shift resources to legal affairs and compliance, according to the National Association of Manufacturers.

- Business spends *$500 billion* annually to comply with federal regulations! Give that another read. It's worth it. That's more than the government collects in corporate income taxes, by a long shot.

Does that get your attention?

- An estimated 50 percent to 70 percent of all spending under the federal Superfund program for cleaning up toxic-waste dumps has gone to legal and consulting fees.

- The cost to U.S. business of compliance with federal tax law in 1991 was $116 billion—within shouting distance of the $149 billion raised by the corporate income tax.

And what about this:

- The private sector spent 5 billion man-hours in 1988 just dealing with government paperwork, according to the Office of Management and Budget. And that was nearly a decade ago. It's probably up to 8 billion by now. At $30 an hour (my estimate), the cost to business would be $240 billion.

- A 1988 study by the Environmental Protection Agency showed that clean-air rules added as much as $138,000 to the cost of opening a dry-cleaning shop and $218,000 to the cost of starting a wood-preserving business. And that, too, was nearly a decade ago.

- A typical forty-person firm with facilities in five California cities would have to file papers with 101 agencies—12 federal, 15 state, 35 regional, and 39 local.

- A small, light manufacturing plant in Los Angeles could need as many as 150 permits, reviews, and licenses.

- The number of federal regulators rose to 131,000 in 1995 from 102,000 in 1985, according to a study conducted at Washington University.

- Happily, the number of pages in the Federal Register is off its 1980 peak of 87,000, at about 70,000 in 1995, but the long-term trend is still up from the range of 10,000 to 20,000 in the fifties and sixties. As Steve Forbes pointed out in his 1996 presidential bid, the U.S. tax code is ten times longer than the Bible. I would add that it is a great deal less inspirational.

The $500 billion figure is staggering. It dwarfs our $166 billion trade deficit, to which so much oratory is devoted.

What's the solution? Business has adopted the only possible one: Pass the extra costs on to the consumer. That includes foreign consumers, making American products less competitive.

You find red tape at all levels of government. There are millions of bureaucrats in the towns and cities of America, enforcing just as many cockeyed rules as can be found in federal texts.

Right now, for example, I'm fighting for the right to put an awning in the driveway of my home in Florida to protect my car from the baking sun. A lot of people have them. Some guy down the street, though, apparently didn't like the looks of mine.

The odd thing about this tempest in a teapot is that the county I live in says you can't have awnings but doesn't enforce the ban, while my town has no ordinance on awnings but won't let you put them up.

Local governments are constantly coming up with new fees. My town in Massachusetts, which already charges a fee on my boat, recently started charging a fee on the boat's anchor as well.

An acquaintance tells me his New Jersey village instituted a five-dollar annual fee five years ago for the right to park on streets near the train station. The authorities claimed the purpose was not to raise revenue but to keep out commuters from nearby towns; the five dollars covered "processing costs."

Today, my friend reports, the fee is up to forty dollars. The "processing" takes one minute: The car owner shows the town clerk his registration card, writes a check for forty dollars, and gets a parking sticker. That's not processing papers; it's processing people's wallets.

Banks are also going fee-crazy. Some even charge an extra fee for customers who go up to the teller's window instead of using the automated equipment. Who asked for this?

The trouble with fees is they're too small to bother contesting in court. They should be called *fleas*. One or two are pesky; a lot of them can drive you nuts.

The private sector isn't immune to the bureaucratic disease. But there is this difference: Business has to make itself "meaner and leaner" by the hour to survive. Thus, it must endlessly review its bureaucratic procedures and eliminate inefficiencies. Governments, at whatever level, don't feel that constant pressure.

Time and again throughout our history, politicians have assaulted the immense bureaucratic mountain, only to pull back. It is manned by hordes of civil service employees who may be slow to act and refrain from making independent judgments in the course of their official duties, but who are fearsome combatants in defense of their territory. Their numbers are great.

It's the elections, stupid.

Philip K. Howard, who wrote the 1995 best-seller *The Death of Common Sense* on government regulations, says the government-procurement system "almost seems designed to avoid sensible commercial decisions." He gives many examples, including the story of how a sawmill owner in San Francisco offered to pay forty thousand dollars for the dead trees in Golden Gate Park that the city had been paying somebody else fifty thousand dollars to cart out. But it didn't work out that way. The city initiated such a long, tortuous bidding system that the sawmill owner canceled his offer and things went on as before.

The General Accounting Office is supposed to monitor government bureaucracy and audit its efficiency. They're the watchdog of big government. The problem is, they're bureaucrats, too. And they report to Congress, which doesn't really want to cut bureaucracy.

There is no mechanism to control bureaucracies and increase their productivity.

Red tape is like an amoeba, reproducing itself out of sight of human eyes. It has no particular objective except to survive and to resist change. It goes through the motions of promoting change, but it never makes change. It feeds on a single nutrient, paper, in a variety of forms: consultants' reports, studies, memorandums, protocols, and minutes of meetings.

It grows in every organization: federal government, state government, city government, schools, corporations, churches, volunteer fire departments.

The duke of Wellington wrote one of history's more famous putdowns of the bureaucratic mentality when in the course of a campaign against Napoleon's forces in Spain he replied to London's demand for a fuller accounting of supplies:

> Whilst marching to Portugal to a position which commands the approach to Madrid and the French forces, my officers have been diligently complying with your request. . . . We have enumerated our saddles, bridles, tents and tent poles, and all manner of sundry items for which His Majesty's Government holds me accountable. I have dispatched reports on the character, wit and spleen of every officer. Each item and every farthing has been accounted for, with two regrettable exceptions for which I beg your indulgence.
>
> Unfortunately, the sum of one shilling and ninepence remains unaccounted for in one infantry battalion's petty cash and there has been a hideous confusion as to the number of jars of raspberry jam issued to one cavalry regiment during a sandstorm in western Spain. This reprehensible carelessness may be related to the pressure of circumstance, since we are at war with France.

Someone else once compared bureaucracies with the bond market. As the price of a bond goes up, the yield goes down. Likewise, as the size and cost of our bureaucracies go up, their benefit to society declines.

The 1957 classic ''Parkinson's Law,'' by the British scholar C. Northcote Parkinson, enunciated a simple law of bureaucracy: ''Work expands so as to fill the time available for its completion.''

Mr. Parkinson noted some interesting British navy statistics for the period 1914–28: In those years, the number of ships in commission dropped to twenty from sixty-two and the number of officers and men in the navy fell to 100,000 from 146,000. And yet, the number of "Admiralty officials"—the bureaucrats in London—nearly doubled, to 3,569 from 2,000.

It gets worse. The Admiralty staff grew to 11,270 by 1938, as the number of officers and men shrank to 89,500. Subsequently, it shot up to 33,574 in 1967 as the fighting forces declined to 83,900.

In summary:

YEAR	NAVAL FORCE	SIZE OF BUREAUCRACY TO SUPPORT THE NAVAL FORCE
1914	146,000	2,000
1967	83,900	33,574

Food for thought, no?

Mr. Parkinson notes some other interesting data. In 1935, at the height of the British Empire, the British Colonial Office numbered 372. In 1954, as the empire was being dismantled, it totaled . . . 1,661.

With tongue in cheek, the author then states:

"It now becomes possible to state Parkinson's Law in mathematical form: In any public administrative department not actually at war, the staff increase may be expected to follow this formula:

$$X = \frac{2k\ (m)\ +\ 1}{n}$$

k is the number of staff seeking promotion through the appointment of subordinates; 1 represents the difference between the ages of appointment and retirement; m is the number of man-hours devoted to answering minutes within the department; and n is the number of effective units being administered; x will be the number of new staff required each year. Mathematicians will, of course, realize that to find the percentage increase they must multiply x by 100 and divide the total of the previous year (y), thus:

$$\frac{100\ (2k\ [m]\ +\ 1)}{yn}\%$$

And this figure will invariably prove to be between 5.17 percent and 6.56 percent, irrespective of any variation in the amount of work (if any) to be done.

Today, we see Parkinson's Law at work at the Central Intelligence Agency. The CIA, created to combat the Red Menace, has a budget of $3 billion. The Red Menace, if not quite dead, is in its death throes. The Soviet Empire is extinct. Castro has turned his attention away from exporting revolution to Africa and toward cajoling Western European tourists to visit his impoverished land. The Chinese Communists hang on to power as they join the rest of the nation in scrambling after capitalist riches.

So have we dissolved the CIA? Far from it. It has discovered other threats to the national interest to justify its billions.

Save us from bureaucracy! If you have a thick hide and a loud voice you can fight back; you can shout about the danger. But you probably won't get thanked because few people have the time or energy to solve an almost insoluble problem.

And the bureaucrats—they survive. They are the meek who inherit the earth, merely by sitting. They don't make many mistakes because they don't do much work.

A friend of mine who dealt with the Russians under the old Soviet regime told me hundreds of thousands of bureaucrats were exiled to labor camps in Siberia for saying yes to people's requests, but nobody ever went for saying no. Eventually, they all said no. That is the bureaucratic mentality in its purest form.

What to do? We can't just shut down all our bureaucracies. If the immense American army of bureaucrats, their secretaries and support staffs, and all the lawyers, judges, clerks, corporate compliance officers, editorial writers, and others who pick over, interpret, monitor, study, and comment on the laws and regulations of the land were suddenly thrown out of work, unemployment would skyrocket to depression levels. We'd have to set up another bureaucracy—a Job Recovery Program for out-of-work bureaucrats.

There would be millions, maybe tens of millions of them, milling about on the streets, selling apples treated with pesticides approved by the Food and Drug Administration and calling out to passersby a plea that meets the gender-free criteria laid down by federal civil-rights statutes; "Sibling, can you spare a dime?" Private industry is getting rid of its own, so it wouldn't take them. What would you do with them?

My reference book for the federal bureaucracy alone lists twelve executive agencies, ranging from the Central Intelligence Agency to the Domestic Policy Council; twelve presidential advisory organizations, ranging from the Advisory Board for Cuba Broadcasting to the President's Council of Integrity and Efficiency; seventeen executive departments, from Agriculture to Defense; ninety-one independent agencies, from the Environmental Protection Agency to the Commission on the Roles and Capabilities of the U.S. Intelligence Community in the Post Cold War Environment; and ninety-one "quasi-official, international and non-governmental organizations," from the American Red Cross to the Great Lakes Fishery Commission.

Mind you, any single agency has its own brood of subagencies, administrations, boards, bureaus, centers, commissions, directorates, and divisions.

The Department of Labor, for example, is made up of:

The Board of Service Contract Appeals

- The Wage Appeals Board

- The Women's Bureau

- The Commission on Leave

- The Office of Small Business and Minority Affairs

- The Office of Administrative Appeals

- The Office of Administrative Law Judges

- The Employees Compensation Appeals Board

- The Benefits Review Board

- The Office of Public Affairs

- The Office of the Assistant Secretary for Congressional and Intergovernmental Affairs

- The Office of the Inspector General

- The Office of the Assistant Secretary for Policy

- The Office of the Assistant Secretary for Administration and Management

- The Office of the American Workplace
- The Employment Standards Administration
- The Employment and Training Administration
- The Bureau of International Labor Affairs
- The Office of the Secretary of Pension and Welfare Administration
- The Bureau of Labor Statistics
- The Mine Safety and Health Administration
- The Occupational Safety and Health Administration
- The Office of the Solicitor
- The Office of Veterans' Employment and Training Service
- The National Commission for Employment Policy
- The Presidents' Committee on Employment of People with Disabilities

Okay, that's a lot. But this spawn has its own offspring. Take the Office of the Assistant Secretary for Administration and Management. It has:

- The Financial Office
- The Directorate of Administrative and Procurement Programs
- The Directorate of Civil Rights
- The Office of Human Resources
- The National Capital Service Center
- The Directorate of Information Resources Management
- The Office of Safety and Health

It just keeps going. The National Capital Service Center, above, is divided into the Office of Financial Management, the Office of Management Support Services, and the Office of Personnel Management Services.

And going. The Office of Financial Management has the Budget and Resource Management Division, the Financial Policy Division, and the Accounting and Control Division.

Thus: A person by the name of Adele Paskowski is the chief of the Financial Policy Division of the Office of Financial Management of the National Capital Services Center of the Office of the Assistant Secretary for Administration and Management of the Department of Labor.

Impressive. It sure is. If each of the 12 executive agencies were like the Department of Labor, we would have 51,372 separate boards or agencies. Not to mention the employees involved, each with his or her own cocoon of predatory control.

It would take an encyclopedic index to know which building to go to and which floor to get off. But if you have a letter from any one of the 51,372 agencies, subagencies, or sub-subagencies, hold on to it. Somebody has a copy. What does this letter have to do with the functioning of government? Neither the sender nor the recipient knows or, perhaps, cares. The recipient, you, doesn't understand it. The official who composed it probably doesn't, either. So you write back, requesting clarifications. Your best bet is that somebody gets off on the wrong floor, wanders into the wrong office, picks up the letter, thinks it is addressed to him, and acts.

The new Republican Congress insists that it is different. It actually shut down an agency in 1995, the Office of Technology Assessment. "Look what we've done," the members proclaimed. Of course, there were no special interests clamoring to save the Office of Technology Assessment. Its budget was a minuscule (by federal government standards) $20 million, and it employed a grand total of two hundred workers.

Still, the action has symbolic value. Maybe there really is a change afoot. A bunch of other agencies are on the chopping block. Most of them are small, but there has been talk of eliminating giants like the Commerce Department, the Energy Department, and the Housing and Urban Development Department. We'll see. And of course, now and then, "reforms" are introduced; this agency announces it is eliminating X number of regulations; that agency vows to cut paperwork. In 1996, the Federal Aviation Administration reduced its personnel rules to 43 pages from 1,069. And, of course, the Republicans keep talking about requiring regulators to factor in the cost as well as the benefit of their mandates.

I think a more realistic goal would be to give bureaucrats more flexibility. *Give them the authority to make exceptions.* True, there would have to be some oversight to make sure they don't show favoritism. And the law would have to be carefully written to avert a new wave of litigation challenging any decisions they make.

To set the tone, the government could hire a couple hundred experienced former business executives to form a special strike force against red tape. We could call it the Federal Red Tape Erasing Unit. The guy who runs it would have the title of director of red tape common sense.

Yes, we would actually be creating a new bureaucracy. But it would at least sound like progress.

The strike force would be created by an act of Congress and would have the power to make instant decisions overruling regulations. For example, a poor little New Hampshire sawmill with only three employees would only have to install one rest room, not two.

That would be true progress.

We're saying they can overrule regulations by fiat. To paraphrase Marie Antoinette: Let them issue variances!

This is exactly what you'd do in industry if you had a similar problem: Get somebody in there to clean up the damn mess. Somebody who can say, "Yes, I know that the regulations say so and so, but that just doesn't make sense." I go back to my guy in the torpedo plant. You have to look at the big picture.

After all, you don't build a boiler without a steam vent. And a fireman doesn't apply for a permit to knock down the door of a burning building, nor does he fax a request to the owner in Florida to send him the keys by Federal Express.

Of course, our theoretical guy in charge, the director of red tape common sense, would need to be immune from prosecution or legal liability for his actions. Just as assuredly, the 820,000 lawyers in this country wouldn't take that lying down; we might have to amend the Constitution. It could be one of the great trinity of amendments of the waning years of the twentieth century: an amendment banning desecration of the flag, an amendment permitting prayer in public schools, and an amendment exempting the director of red tape common sense from libel suits.

But now we are dreaming. By the time that happened, the number of lawyers would have doubled to 1.64 million. What would we do with them?

Our director of red tape common sense wouldn't have free rein.

There would be an oversight board to make sure he and his troops didn't get carried away. There we go, we've got yet another new bureaucracy. Even in the midst of a diatribe against bureaucracy, we can't resist the urge to set up a new agency.

The director of red tape common sense wouldn't be allowed to overrule basic law. The Red Tape Erasing Unit couldn't tamper with certain benefits, such as Social Security or the right to family leave.

It couldn't eliminate the Food and Drug Administration's requirement that new medical devices be safe and effective. But it could step in where overzealous or vindictive bureaucrats are delaying or preventing the introduction of promising devices for petty reasons.

Then, of course, there would be exceptions to exceptions. Isn't this where we came in?

I suppose government ought to be run more like private industry. That's the world trend. Consider the 8 billion man-hours that we estimated above that the private sector spends on government paperwork. If our new strike force could somehow save half of those hours, and assuming an average wage-and-benefits cost of $30 an hour, it would have cut industry costs by $120 billion. Thus industry will be more profitable, and the government will take in more receipts by taxing those dollars.

Is all of this wishful thinking? Probably. The Federal Red Tape Erasing Unit would challenge the authority of too many entrenched bureaucrats. And for every business that was freed of some onerous bureaucratic burden, there would be a competitor rushing to his congressman to complain about unfair advantage.

It is a risk worth taking, but our society is unlikely to take it— not with 820,000 lawyers out there. As the character in the Pogo cartoon said: "We have met the enemy, and it is us." Still, it is a risk worth dreaming about.

Even so, there is one reform we might be able to pull off: making it easier to fire incompetent civil servants. We've been hearing about this for years, of course. As much as I oppose meaningless bloodletting in the private sector, I also believe that management has to retain the option to get rid of poor performers, malcontents, or unneeded workers.

Yet, it is all but impossible to fire civil service employees, the supposed "servants" of us taxpayers. And that invulnerability not only breeds arrogance in many of them but tends to blind them to the notion that actions have consequences. No matter what they do, they still get their paychecks and medical benefits and four weeks of vacation, so they have difficulty grasping the fact that some of their actions might cost a small business tens of thousands of dollars.

There are lots of good civil servants. I'd be all for giving these people a 20 percent raise and subjecting them to ordinary business practices. This way, you could eliminate the bad ones.

If the Republicans really want to balance the budget by the year 2002, one of the big factors they have to weigh is the growth of industry. And industry will grow much faster if it is unshackled from unnecessary regulations. That will require some risk taking. A good general doesn't go into battle with the sole goal of keeping casualties to a minimum. He goes in to win.

The casualties in this case would be a few bum decisions. But it would be well worth it. Hell, I figure the real cost to the economy of federal regulations is much more than the $500 billion annually business spends to comply with them. I'd say multiply that by five to get a rough measure of lost opportunities. That's $2.5 trillion, more than a third of our gross national product of about $7 trillion in 1995.

I have no definitive answer to the problem of bureaucrats. But we should all be trying to think of solutions. Here is my contribution to the debate—idle thoughts on idle people, so to speak.

1. FIGHT FIRE WITH FIRE. Remember the movie *Ghostbusters*? This country needs a team of bureaucracy busters. So let's set up the Federal Red Tape Erasing Unit that I discussed earlier, headed by the director of red tape common sense. He'll need a deputy, of course, a couple of assistants, a secretary, some field workers, a support staff. And let's see: They'll all need office space, and desks, and file cabinets, and, of course, lots of paper.

2. CREATE A NEW ECONOMIC INDICATOR. This would be a government-sponsored system for measuring the impact of bureaucracy on America's economic vibrancy and international competitiveness. We could call it the "amoeba indicator." The agency in charge would also estimate the total cost of bureaucracy and the average cost to each taxpayer. And, for comparison's sake, it would calculate the bureaucratic drag on the economies of our major trading partners.

Why has nobody thought of this before? Throughout the ages, bureaucracy has been blamed for the demise of empires, including the Roman Empire, the British Empire, and the Soviet Empire. Whittling

Slicing the Baloney

down the huge, unseen costs of bureaucracy might be one of the great unheralded growth opportunities for the U.S. economy. Reducing bureaucracy is arguably more important to the future of our country than cutting the budget deficit, cutting the trade deficit, or cutting the welfare rolls.

3. TRAIN PEOPLE TO BECOME BUREAUCRATS. Let's face it: Bureaucrats will always be with us. But does anybody study in college on how to be a bureaucrat? Maybe our schools of higher learning should offer courses. The idea would be to make bureaucrats more efficient and more responsive to the concerns of their employers (i.e., taxpayers).

4. SET UP TEMPORARY EMPLOYMENT AGENCIES FOR BUREAUCRATS. No, I'm not kidding. We have temporary agencies for almost any profession you can think of: accountants, bankers, maids, secretaries. Why not an employment agency for part-time bureaucrats? It could be called Bureaucrats Incorporated. The IRS could hire one hundred thousand bureaucratic temps at tax time. In time, agencies could shrink to a lean core of full-timers, constantly dipping into the private sector for assistance in busy times. Those who sign on for temporary or part-time work could range from retired academics and laid-off middle managers to young up-and-comers in any profession who need extra money or training.

I confess to indulging in a bit of hyperbole in this chapter. So let me back up a little bit. Many regulations are justified and necessary. Who can argue with the FDA's mission (as opposed to many of its actions) to make sure prescription drugs are safe and effective? Who can oppose regulations aimed at reducing brown-lung disease in textile workers? And while red tape—all those forms and procedures that bureaucrats force businesses to fill out and follow—can be cumbersome, nobody's come up with an alternative as of yet.

The real reform would be mandated cost-benefit analysis to judge the true worth of regulations to the economy. It isn't always easy to predict the benefits or estimate the costs, but there should be some effort. Harvard's Center for Risk Analysis estimates that reallocating resources to more cost-effective regulatory programs could save sixty thousand lives a year. Robert Hahn of the American Enterprise Institute analyzed ninety-two regulations issued in the 1990s and concluded that the benefits exceeded the costs in only seventeen of them.

Does it make sense for the federal government to spend more cleaning up out-of-the-way waste sites than all the money it devotes to research on cancer, heart disease, and AIDS combined?

Realistically, red tape is here to stay. It is as old as civilization, and it flourishes in our great country as freely as it ever flourished in ancient Egypt. For all of our Founding Fathers' determination to eradicate the bureaucratic excesses imposed by the British monarch, Alexis de Tocqueville took due note in his famous 1840 book *Democracy in America* of the extent to which the bureaucratic mentality endured a mere half century later:

"The American government covers the surface of society with a network of small complicated rules, minute and uniform, through which the most original minds and the most energetic characters cannot penetrate."

Remember the quaint notion of the march of civilization? It supposedly moved along, unstoppable, like Old Man River. In truth, civilization is more like a series of clearings in the jungle. The jungle—in this case bureaucracy—is always fighting to take back lost terrain.

15

How the Feds Fiddle with Our Future

There's a scene from the old Jack Benny radio comedy show that reminds me of my brush with America's antitrust watchdogs. One night, the notoriously stingy Benny is walking along a dark city street when he is accosted by a gunman.

"Your money or your life," the gunman rasps. There's a long silence. "I said, your money or your life," the gunman repeats, raising his voice. There's another long silence. "I said, your money or your life!" shouts the now exasperated gunman.

Benny finally replies, "I'm thinking, I'm thinking."

The Justice Department held a gun to our head for two long

years. Like Jack Benny, we were thinking, we were thinking. But in the end, like Benny, we decided to hand over the money—in our case, $1 billion worth of companies that the bureaucrats insisted we sell off. By then, survival seemed a wiser choice than suicidal defiance.

The government would appear to be up to its old tricks lately. In 1995, it fussed and fretted over the expansion plans of one of America's more innovative high-tech companies, software giant Microsoft Corporation. Like us, Microsoft seemed to them to be getting too big for its britches.

That's always been the problem. The antitrust authorities, while sometimes doing a laudable job of breaking up business monopolies and punishing price-fixing, too often have strayed beyond their intended statutory authority, which is to combat unfair trading practices, and have attacked success and bigness as an evil in itself.

That bias made us vulnerable. From the moment I took over ITT, with most of our stockholders (85 percent) marooned in the United States away from the largest part of our business overseas (some 90 percent), my strategy had to be growth, principally in the United States. I made no secret of my plan to double profits within five years. So I set about building one of the greatest conglomerates this country has known.

Consider: In 1959, the first full year I ran ITT, its earnings were $29 million. In 1977, my last full year, they were $562 million. Sales in the same period went from $765 million to nearly $28 billion. The number of shares outstanding increased from 15.5 million to 135 million. The earnings per share rose from $1 to $4.20. The worldwide workforce had nearly tripled, from 136,000 to 375,000.

A pretty good record, you might say—unless you have something against growth. And a fellow by the name of Richard W. McLaren, the Justice Department's assistant attorney for antitrust in the Nixon administration, had a lot against it. For reasons unknown.

We did not constitute a price-fixing cartel. We were breaking no laws. No matter. McLaren was of a particular bent of mind: Conglomerates were economic octopuses, strange predators feeding on every corporate entity in their paths in a single-minded quest to take over the country.

It was pure nonsense, but that was the way he thought. And when we announced our plan to buy the Hartford Fire Insurance Company for $1.5 billion in 1968, an enormous sum in those days, McLaren hit the roof.

To this day, I have no idea what motivated McLaren. He was a rather pompous lawyer from Chicago whom nobody had ever heard of. And, suddenly, he was able to take center stage and get quoted in the *New York Times* and the *Wall Street Journal*. That elevation could have been part of it. It's also possible that people in the insurance industry or in other fields that we had entered recently were getting through to him with the message that ''More is less''—more competition against them was less than desirable. But I doubt that.

In any case, we learned that McLaren was telling his associates privately that he thought we were just plain too big. He never stated that publicly, of course. If he had, he would have revealed his investigation as the personal publicity vendetta that it was, devoid of any real appreciation of antitrust law.

I had already had a taste of the Justice Department's sense of justice in our bid for the ABC television network in the mid-1960s. In December 1965, we agreed to buy ABC for $400 million. A few months later, shareholders of both companies approved the merger. The Justice Department voiced no antitrust objections—and how could they? ABC was the weakest of the three networks. And though we were big and growing, we were hardly a colossus: Revenue in 1966 was a bit over $2 billion, having doubled in four years.

Approval by the Federal Communications Commission seemed a sure thing—until an antibigness minority kicked up a fuss about the need to preserve ABC's ''independence.'' But in December 1966, the FCC voted 4 to 3 for the merger, anyway. The most vocal opponent railed against the decision. The resulting public furor prompted the Justice Department to intervene.

But again, after much back-and-forth, the FCC voted 4 to 3 in our favor. Despite this, the Justice Department then filed suit to block the merger. There was more back-and-forth, and suddenly, it was December 1967—two years after our original agreement, and coming up on a deadline that allowed either party to the agreement to cancel.

I had to cancel.

Why? I had been fighting too long for a property that wasn't crucial for ITT's development. The ''on again, off again'' jockeying of the FCC and the Justice Department were unsettling to the company and its stockholders. The endless delays had further reduced our acquisition activity to a shambles. We were at that time holding friendly talks with Holiday Inns, the biggest motel chain in the country, but held off making an offer on the advice of our lawyers. They feared it would muddy the waters of our ABC bid. Looked at from the 1990s, doesn't that seem a bit odd? Would ownership of motel rooms pose a competitive threat to other TV networks? What was going on here?

I can't tell you what the Justice Department argument was because I never understood it. All I know is: (1) the Justice Department had no problem with the merger; (2) the FCC approved it; (3) the Justice Department decided it had a problem, after all; (4) the FCC approved it again, anyway; (5) the Justice Department moved aggressively to block it.

All of which raises a question that I suspect a lot of companies would like answered: Why are two departments of government administering antitrust laws, and who is on top? It's like a two-headed duck that doesn't know which way to walk or how loud to quack.

In many other merger cases, the choice of regulator is between the Justice Department and the Federal Trade Commission, or FTC. The prospective corporate partners can't be sure in advance which agency will review the case. It matters. The Justice Department, tough as it is, will generally drop an investigation if it can't get a court injunction to halt a deal. The FTC, by contrast, won't; it will pursue an administrative case that can last as long as five years. (Maybe they need the work; ambition and the desire for growth aren't limited to companies in the private sector.)

When it came to pursuing a case, the Justice Department's McLaren was no slacker, of course. He tried to tie our previous acquisitions and our bid for Hartford into some vast competitive intrigue. The translation into plain English of his philosophy for corporate success was as follows: Growth must come in small bites. Chew your food twenty times before you swallow.

But, of course, he couldn't announce fastidious corporate chewing as government policy. He had to hunt around for a more refined legal basis. He never found one, so instead he and his antitrust associates literally turned to obfuscation.

They talked at great length about population growth trends. They gave a statistical rundown of concentrations of industry over the ages, including a table showing that the twenty largest companies in the United States had a bigger share of industry than the twenty largest companies had in 1840. They made strained comparisons of ITT to giant shopping malls that were shuttering quaint boutiques in New England villages.

All this evidence was marshaled with great fanfare—and it was all irrelevant. Antitrust law isn't designed to diffuse corporate power or uphold somebody's nostalgic vision of the good old days when you could buy nickel Cokes at Cooper's Corner drugstore. It is designed to assure fair competition.

Lest I forget: The wonderfully absurd theory of "potential antitrust behavior" was also invoked. This held that, even if ITT had committed no breach of the law, it had the "potential" to squash competition by virtue of its size. By that logic, I retorted, we should arrest a man for carrying golf clubs; clearly he is a "potential" murderer. Indeed, tens of thousands of men and women walk about this land of ours every day, carrying golf clubs. Arrest them all, before they kill!

We argued until we were blue in the face. There's nothing in antitrust law that says you can't get too big, we said. Antitrust law forbids restraint of trade, pricing discrimination among customers, or other actions that reduce competition. We also pointed out that we weren't anywhere near the biggest company in the United States, particularly with over 50 percent of the company still abroad; not by a long shot. Antitrust law, furthermore, is not about size—it is about patterns of behavior. Even so, McLaren just thought we were getting too big. I don't think he understood that conglomerates, by their nature, are especially suited to growth, but without concentration of power in any given industry. He pressed on with his case, under the supposedly probusiness Nixon administration.

We were being penalized for our efficiency, we said. We were perhaps one of the most efficient companies in the country. Hadn't anybody noticed, we wondered, that we were one of America's top twenty exporters at the time when everybody seemed to be concerned about our country's widening trade deficit? Apparently not.

We had never made a hostile bid! And when we acquired a company, we made it grow more than it ever could have grown before. We saved some from failure. What was wrong with all that?

As for McLaren & Company's endless stewing over the dangers of "concentration of power," I have this question: Aren't efficient companies exactly the place where power ought to be concentrated? Would it be better to concentrate power in the hands of bumbleheads?

And if power corrupts, the American people should take another look at the Department of Justice.

Indeed, the irony of all this was that we were doing the very opposite of what the government accused us of doing. We *increased* competition, because we by policy only bought medium-sized or second-level companies in their industry and thereby forced the dominant players, and everybody else for that matter, to be more competitive and to hustle a little harder to deliver quality goods and services at reasonable prices to consumers.

We always shied away from buying the biggest company in any industry; we weren't so naive as to think that wouldn't set off alarm bells. To be sure, acquiring a market leader would have been perfectly proper in a competitive industry, but in the climate of the times, it would have invited endless government scrutiny. So we'd buy the number two (Avis being a famous example) or number three or number four, and make them better. It was also a far less expensive course of action. We then put pressure on the number ones. In a world ruled by common sense, that would be viewed as highly positive.

One irony led to another: The Justice Department was actually doing the opposite of what it was supposed to be doing. It was squelching, not advancing, competition.

To us, the notion that big is bad and small is beautiful was a simplistic statement and an even more simplistic policy. It might hold true for collectors of miniature photographs but not for a business trying to survive in a competitive world.

McLaren really was stretching things. At one point, he tried to establish a nefarious link between Hartford Insurance and a company we owned that made sprinkler systems for office buildings. He argued that Hartford could undercut its competitors in buildings that had ITT sprinklers. He produced no evidence for such a conspiracy, for the good reason that none existed. Even so, Mr. McLaren insisted on addressing the *"potential"* as though that proved his point of improper action. There's that word again. For no abuse existed.

He and his associates put us through two years of hearings and filings and testimony and never found a damn thing except one, which was so trifling as to make a mockery of the whole process. Some kid barely out of his teens who worked for an Avis outlet in Puerto Rico had sent a letter to some local group putting pressure on them to rent Avis cars.

It was literally the only thing McLaren could find. It turned up time after time in the hearings. Otherwise: nothing! You might think that would be embarrassing for McLaren and the government.

Not at all. Because the issues of antitrust are so arcane, the suit, once it was brought, went on interminably, like the battery-powered rabbit in the TV commercial.

We pleaded our cause to John Mitchell, the attorney general. For a long time, he refused to see us. Finally, I got ten minutes with him, but he really wasn't interested. He said okay, thanks. We also talked to one of Nixon's top aides. Our message was: For God's sake, get this straightened out. Nothing ever came of either meeting.

I came to appreciate more fully Revolutionary America's rallying cry of "No taxation without representation." We were paying millions in taxes, considered ourselves to be unfairly treated, and yet couldn't find redress.

The pressure on us to settle grew, not from any proven infractions, but from the prolonged uncertainty. The stockholders were asking, "What the hell's going on? What is it that we're buying or selling?"

Like Gulliver in Lilliput, we were prostrate. Just as the Lilliputians pinned down the shipwrecked English sailor with thread-sized cords, the Justice Department bureaucrats pinned us down with tangled strands of red tape and legal theory.

What did our lawyers make of all this? A lot of money. And since this had gone on for two years and they saw no way of settling on the merits, they ultimately recommended we settle so we could go back to running the company. So we settled.

For the antitrust authorities, Hartford was just too big a prize to let us snag without attaching severe restrictions on our growth. And the settlement surely did that. We were barred from making any more major acquisitions in the United States for ten more years. And we were also required to give up Avis (car rentals), Grinnell Corporation (fire sprinklers), Canteen Corporation (vending machines), and several other companies with a total value of $1 billion. Several years later, Avis was sold for ten times the price we were paid for it. There were absolutely no antitrust infractions between these companies and our ownership of Hartford at all. It was a small-town prejudice against bigness that infused the government that did us in.

ITT was like a powerful sedan and McLaren like a highway cop who ticketed us on the theory we might exceed the speed limit next month. I tell you, trying to straighten out a misled public official would be a lifetime career.

We settled because our job was to run a company, not provide textbook cases for the misapplication of antitrust theory. After two years, it was the only logical solution. After all, this was a war between the head of an entrenched government bureaucracy with a bottomless supply of public funds to finance its fishing expeditions and a corporation with stockholders to satisfy and genuine business to attend to.

We needed to get on with it.

It was a tough decision. Making acquisitions was our way of life. To rebuild itself in the United States, ITT had gone into at least sixty different businesses. This had required enormous energy and hard work.

We were submitting to blackmail. But what could we do? The investigation was exhausting our attention. We calculated that a court fight would drag on for at least two more years and maybe longer. And even if we won, the case could be remanded to a lower court and start all over again.

This whole episode, in my opinion, should stand as a legal monument to the vanity of Justice Department antitrust chief Richard McLaren and to the peculiarity of his legal doctrine of "potentiality."

ITT did not engage in anticompetitive practices, it did not attempt to restrain trade, it did not collude with any other company to fix prices. It was not a monopoly or a cartel or a trust.

It was a conglomerate.

Mind you, I'm not against enforcement of antitrust law. I'm for it! I think the government should vigorously attack anticompetitive practices. It should crush attempts to restrain trade. It should break up business monopolies or cartels. It should bust trusts. It should punish price-fixing. At least when the Justice Department launched a criminal inquiry into Archer-Daniels-Midland Company in 1995, it was investigating allegations of a clear, specific violation of American law: a conspiracy to rig prices. (In 1996, Archer Daniels admitted it conspired with competitors to jack up the price of a livestock-feed additive and a flavor additive, and it agreed to pay $100 million in fines.)

But it shouldn't invoke antitrust law to disrupt or drag down an honest business engaging in purely aboveboard activities, simply because some high-level bureaucrat has a "bad feeling" about the company or fears it has become too successful.

Even today, the Justice Department sometimes has difficulty distinguishing between bigness and badness. Take Microsoft, the software giant.

Did Microsoft chairman Bill Gates really threaten the financial-software market with his proposed $2 billion acquisition of Intuit in 1995? The Justice Department feared that the combination would beat up Intuit's competition. But Intuit was already beating up its own competition. Nobody accused Intuit's founder, Scott Cook, of engaging in predatory pricing or taking unfair advantage of anybody. There's no basic invention involved; Intuit simply makes easier-to-use financial software for individuals and small businesses. There is no guarantee somebody else won't come up with a better product. Scott Cook once said he had a bigger rival whose loyal customers were proving next to impossible to win over. And then he held up a ballpoint pen.

No, what the Justice Department was really saying was that it didn't want Bill Gates to become any more powerful. They continue to view any company that has become big and that doesn't have an equally effective competitor as a "potential" antitrust problem. There's that word again.

Bill Gates got to where he is not by antitrust behavior, but by doing a good job: Even so, rather than engage in a prolonged fight, he threw in the towel. (Would that I had seen the light as early on as he did!)

Well, no sooner had the Justice Department quashed the Intuit takeover than it contested Microsoft's plan to include an on-line service in its Windows 95 operating software package. It was the automatic tie-in that bothered our antitrust watchdogs, or "bundling," as they called it.

What rubbish! Every car that is ever bought is "bundled" into the seller's dealer network. If you buy a Ford, you're going to have to buy replacement parts from Ford, you will in all likelihood sign up for a loan from Ford credit, and you will get free or low-cost repair work done by Ford mechanics. Sure, it locks you in to Ford, but it also provides you with more efficient service than you'd otherwise get.

Every patented drug is a tie-in for eighteen years. By law, the inventor of any product gets exclusive right to make and sell it for that long. It doesn't mean competitors can't try to come up with a different product that will do the same thing; it just protects his investment and rewards him for his innovation. Tie-ins aren't unusual.

There's nothing wrong with them. They are the best way to provide the most efficient service to customers.

The wording of the Justice Department's legal brief was revealing. "The government believes that Microsoft's forced inclusion of the Microsoft Network access software with Windows 95 might, under certain facts, violate the antitrust laws," the department said.

Now think about that word "forced." Microsoft was automatically including the on-line software in its operating software. Car companies use the term "standard equipment" to describe features that are contained in every car, as opposed to those you pay extra for.

Does this mean they are "forcing" consumers to buy cars with air bags or tinted windshields? If General Motors had half the U.S. car market but suddenly decided to put air bags in every new car, would the Justice Department scream about the "forced inclusion" of the safety devices?

Microsoft made an interesting point in its defense. It wondered how a company with zero market position could pose such a monopoly threat.

Earlier in 1995, the Justice Department had actually sided with Microsoft, reaching a settlement that absolved the company of broad antitrust charges brought by some of its competitors. That saga took a tragicomic turn when federal judge Stanley Sporkin rejected the consent decree by saying that Microsoft's practice of announcing the future availability of a product—presumably to stop people from buying competitors' products currently on the market—was "terribly bothersome to this court."

There it was, in black and white. Microsoft was guilty, not of violating any particular law, but of bothering Judge Sporkin. (Later, an appeals judge ruled that Mr. Sporkin had overstepped his authority; still later, another judge approved the original settlement.)

And yet innumerable companies, notably International Business Machines, have been doing for years what Judge Sporkin found "bothersome" and what consumers have come to expect as their own protection.

In the summer of 1996—here comes the Justice Department again! This time, to investigate charges Microsoft was trying to crush a company called Netscape. Don't believe it.

Microsoft is only the most vivid recent example of the Justice Department's ingrained antipathy for bigness. IBM also got beat up because they were too successful. That was in the sixties and seventies and early eighties, before they got unsuccessful, and then very unsuccessful, to the point where everybody thought they might go belly-up. Then, of course, they got successful again, and recently seemed to be close to becoming very successful again. If they ever get very, very successful again, I guess it will be only a matter of time before the Justice Department comes calling.

In the early seventies, the FTC accused Xerox of trying to monopolize the market for office copiers. While the FTC was creating difficulties for one of America's most innovative companies, the Japanese were busy making high-quality, low-cost copies of Xerox's copiers.

And look at pricing on airplane tickets. The government broke up that industry, and now the airlines are broke all the time. Is that good?

It's not just big companies, either. In 1995, the FTC accused car dealers in San Jose, California, of a conspiracy to restrain trade because they had pulled advertising from a newspaper that had run an article trashing car dealers. It seems that the perpetrators were "depriving consumers of truthful information."

Think about that one for a moment. In a supposedly free country, with a Bill of Rights that the last time I looked still guaranteed freedom of speech and the press, businesses are told they can't *not* advertise certain goods.

And by worrying about depriving consumers of information about products, what does that FTC action tell us about Big Government's opinion of the citizenry's ability to think for itself?

The car dealers insisted there was never a conspiracy. But what if there was? And why call it a conspiracy? That's a loaded word. Why not call it a boycott? What's wrong with a boycott? Remember when blacks in the South boycotted businesses that they believed mistreated them? Was that a conspiracy? Sometimes consumers, or even investors, will boycott companies that they believe misbehave in some way, either by engaging in the tobacco trade, or by doing business with Third World dictators, or by harming the environment. You don't have to agree with them to acknowledge their God-given constitutional right to make a protest.

The FTC said the mass pulling of advertisements had a "chilling effect" on the newspaper in question. Well good God in the morning, that's what it was intended to have. I recently canceled my subscription to the *New Yorker,* as some others perhaps have, because of what

I see as its increasing vulgarity and left-wing stridency. I stopped getting the magazine long before it published a cover depicting the Easter Bunny being crucified on a tax form, but I understand that little witticism didn't sit well with some folks. Will the FTC investigate disaffected readers for conspiring to withhold revenue from Newhouse Publications? Will we be taken to task for actions that sent a chill through the heart of Tina Brown? (Think about that one!)

The real chilling effect comes from the Justice Department and the FTC. Recently, Gibson Greetings rejected a takeover bid from American Greetings, even though it had recently suffered numerous business setbacks, because it feared "overwhelming antitrust problems."

Somehow, greeting cards strike me as a market not terribly difficult to break into. I'll bet you could walk around any major city and browse through the card displays in all the drugstores and news shops and find one hundred different brands on the racks. But Gibson feared a federal onslaught if it merged with another company.

It's sad. It's more than sad. It's chilling.

Or how about this one: The Clinton administration in 1995 boldly launched an investigation of the U.S. Catholic Conference, the National Conference of Catholic Bishops, and fifteen book publishers for price-fixing in the new catechism of the Catholic Church.

Laugh if you will. The overkill isn't really all that funny. In today's global economy, shouldn't we concentrate on making U.S. companies the best, not on crushing them just because some ideologue in the Justice Department thinks they are getting too big for their britches?

I share the lament of Jonathan R. Macey, a professor at Cornell Law School: "Our most notable corporate success stories—including Microsoft—are routinely attacked by the government at the height of their success." Like the mythical Sisyphus doomed forever to roll a boulder up a slope in Hades, only to have it roll back down again, our corporate success stories push their way to the top, only to get shoved back down.

Instead of cracking down on the winners, the government ought to tell their competitors: Stop whining and go out and work harder.

The Justice Department's antitrust policy reminds me of the apocryphal story about a poker player with four aces who bets his hand for a big pot against a three and a six of hearts, a seven of diamonds, a nine of spades, and a jack of clubs.

"I win," says the guy with the seemingly terrible hand, pulling in the loot. "Hold on," the guy with the four aces says. "I've got four aces."

"Can't you read?" asks the first guy, pointing to a sign on the wall: "The top hand in this house is a yazoo, consisting of a three and a six of hearts, a seven of diamonds, a nine of spades, and a jack of clubs." The second guy grumbles but stays in the game.

Several hours later, he gets a yazoo, and bets to the hilt. "I win," his opponent says, showing a pair of fours and scooping up the pot. "Whoa!" says the guy with the yazoo. "Look: a yazoo."

"Can't you read?" asks his opponent, pointing to another sign on the wall: "Only one yazoo per night."

The Justice Department says its goal is to promote competition. But its method resembles racetrack handicapping, putting weights on the fast horses to keep them back with the laggards and thereby slowing down the whole group. This reduces competition to the lowest common denominator—at a time when America is worrying about recession at home and ever-fiercer competition abroad.

Once you get nailed, you really get nailed.

Judge Harold Greene was still monitoring the Baby Bells twelve years after the original breakup of AT&T, all the way up to the recent deregulation of the communications industry. Judge Edmund Palmieri kept tabs on the big movie studios until his death in the late 1980s, more than three decades after they were forced to give up their theaters.

And Judge David Edelstein tracked IBM for almost four decades to make sure it didn't violate a 1956 antitrust settlement. Over the years, it became increasingly clear to just about everybody that Mr. Edelstein was biased against IBM and that he was resisting pressure to reassign the case. Finally, in 1995, an appeals court ordered him off the case, ruling unanimously that "a reasonable observer would question the judge's impartiality." And in 1996, IBM was freed from most of the old restrictions.

And yet the law remains so vague and enforcement of it so fickle that nobody can predict when or if his or her company will become a target. I don't know of any areas of the courts so completely without any definition of what the law is.

This ambiguity opens the government up to political pressures of all sorts. If there were enough of a popular outcry against Wal-Mart for hurting local businesses, I have no doubt that the Justice

Department could find antitrust grounds for slowing or stopping its expansion.

At bottom, U.S. antitrust policy is fueled by a simple mistrust of power. It is true that power can corrupt the human heart. But that is a personal truth that shouldn't be used as a weapon against businesses that aren't committing any legal offenses. Corporate power, properly handled, is just a competitive tool.

Maybe we ought to rename the Justice Department the Just Dis' Us Department. (For those not in the know, "dis" is an inner-city street term that is short for disrespect and means "to insult.") While we're at it, we could have a contest to rename the antitrust division. How about the Ante up Division? (Everybody's gotta live.) Got any suggestions?

What is the solution to this mess? The short answer is to set up an independent arbitration panel. We could give companies a choice: the Justice Department, the FTC, or the arbitration panel. That in itself would be a major antitrust breakthrough. It would end, once and for all, the Justice Department's monopoly on competition policy. Or it would force the Justice Department to retreat from its world of fantasy, and into the real world.

16

Coming Soon:
1 Million Lawyers

"The American legal profession is losing its moral compass. In the last twenty years, the profession has moved further than ever toward becoming merely a business, with no other ethic than that of the market."
—Anthony T. Kronman, dean, Yale Law School, 1995

Our general counsel at ITT, Howard Abel, told me a wonderful story. Before he joined us, he defended a company against charges of negligence that had supposedly resulted in extreme pain and suffering for the plaintiff. The "victim" put on quite a show in the courtroom, hobbling around and grimacing as if each movement were an ordeal. The joys of life, it seemed, had been snatched from him.

Howard didn't believe a word of it. But the jury did, and awarded him a huge sum of money. Afterward, Howard went up to the plaintiff and said, "Okay, you won. But I'm going to keep an eye on you. And you'd better watch out, because if I catch you playing golf or driving a car or engaging in any other physical activity, I'll reopen the case."

"Don't bother," the man told him. "I'm taking the first flight to France and going straight to Lourdes. You're going to see the damnedest miracle."

I'm half expecting somebody to sue the furniture industry for repetitive stress syndrome. Picture the headline:

MAN SUES BED MAKERS, CLAIMS THAT YEARS OF GETTING UP, OFTEN ON WRONG SIDE, HURT HIS MUSCLES AND HIS MORALE

Perhaps that one wouldn't surprise you any more than dozens of other headlines you've read. I like the inmate who filed suit to force prison authorities to serve him chunky peanut butter instead of creamy peanut butter. Or how about the woman golfer who won forty thousand dollars from her country club for injuries she received when the ball she hit bounced off a railroad track and hit her in the face.

Lawyers would be almost comic if they didn't cause so much unnecessary distress. In 1995, a self-styled civil-rights activist filed a complaint against a new school for immigrants in New York City, claiming it created "education apartheid" and did all sorts of psychological damage to the students. No parents, students, or anybody else joined in the complaint.

So are there too many lawyers? We're heading fast for the 1 million mark. Already, there are 820,000—or 310 for every 100,000 Americans in 1994, up from 255 per 100,000 eight years earlier.

Since the U.S. population only increases by about 1.5 percent a year, if that rate of increase continues for a few more centuries we'll end up with more lawyers than people.

An estimated 60,000 lawyers live in New Jersey, one for every 117 people. If they, and their spouses and children, moved into their own community—perhaps it could be called Sioux City—it would be the most populous metropolis in the state.

After the Republican landslide in the congressional elections of 1994, members with business backgrounds outnumbered lawyers for the first time in decades, 191 to 170, but lawyers still made up a majority of 54 out of 100 in the Senate.

All this lawyering is more than just a financial drain on America's productive sectors. Even more fundamentally, it is eroding

Americans' confidence in our court system. People feel it no longer truly serves the cause of justice, but rather the interests of our smartest lawyers. A lingering sense of grievance is affecting more and more people. Rational people will seek long-term improvements. Fanatics will be tempted down other paths. If any good comes from the O. J. Simpson trial it is the stark picture it drew of some of the weaknesses of our court system.

Richard Epstein, a professor of law at the University of Chicago, cites statistics indicating that the optimal number of lawyers in the United States is 60 percent the current number—and that each lawyer in excess of the optimal number reduces the gross national product by $2.5 million. Let's see: That means there are 328,000 too many lawyers, each costing the economy $2.5 million, for a total drag of $820 billion. To say nothing of the rafts of headaches.

Litigation in the United States is a mostly nonproductive activity driven by a quest for legal fees. It is swamping the courts. It is sapping the energy from our most productive sectors. It is putting our American industry at a competitive disadvantage. However, not all is lost! The producers of legal-size paper are doing quite well.

I would like to show an ounce of consideration. Some lawyers work hard. Some do pro bono work. We all need lawyers (mostly to protect us against other lawyers). And lawyers provide us with an interesting national pastime. One of the commonest forms of public expression in this country is: I'll sue you, you bum.

We're not ostracized for suing. Often we're commended. If a dog bites your ankle—sue! In New Jersey, dog-bite cases are ho-hum, five-thousand-dollar affairs. The owner shrugs; the insurance company will pay. The insurance company shrugs; it's only five thousand dollars, and besides, their customers will pay. The lawyer and the victim split the proceeds. The lawyer for the defense gets paid, too. The fact is, our society is open to legal blackmail. Only it's never called that. It's called "exercising your rights."

Remember Parkinson's Law: Work within a bureaucracy expands to fill the time available for its completion. I'd like to offer a variation on that theme: The number of "victims" in this country expands to fill the chairs in the fast-growing number of lawyers' offices.

Here is a basic dialogue:

LAWYER: You've been injured. You know that?

POTENTIAL CLIENT: I have?

LAWYER: Yes. Let me explain. (He describes the pain and suffering that the potential client has endured, or might conceivably someday endure as the result of negligence on the part of a corporation or individual with hopefully deep pockets.)

POTENTIAL CLIENT: Hmm. I don't know . . .

LAWYER: Furthermore, you're entitled to a lot of money.

POTENTIAL CLIENT (BRIGHTENING): I am?

LAWYER: Now, if you'll let me handle it for you . . .

Is the lawyer creating a lawsuit? Nah. He's only reading the victim his rights.

Lawyers have discovered the earning power of confusion. They paint endless shadings between guilt and innocence. And they prolong the trial until everybody is befuddled. One of their specialties is the class-action shareholder lawsuit. Here's how it works. If any company's stock takes a sudden plunge, a law firm pulls a canned legal complaint out of its computer and fills in the blanks. Because the information superhighway gives it instant access to documents the company has filed with regulatory authorities as well as to company announcements and press releases, it slaps any positive pronouncements into the lawsuit as evidence of "fraud" and rushes to the courthouse to be the first to file. It knows full well how many others are playing this game. In fact, the judge helps them coalesce around his role as the final arbiter on the split of the fees.

The most vulnerable targets are young, fast-growth, high-technology companies whose stocks by their very nature are volatile. Suddenly, their energies are diverted from creating a new software or developing a new cancer treatment to fighting a new legal battle.

These class-action lawsuits are often logically absurd. A company's shareholders are by definition its owners. Thus, in a class action, if everybody joins in, shareholders are suing themselves.

But you can create all sorts of classes of victims. How about a separate class of investors who were wiped out in margin calls? I'm not even a lawyer, and I can think of myriad possibilities.

Granted, a small number of these suits are justified. But for the most part, strike lawyers are like hunters who stalk deer at night with the headlights of their car. It's time to revoke their hunting licenses.

There was such an outcry against frivolous securities lawsuits—even the Beardstown Ladies, authors of a popular how-to investment book, got up in arms—that Congress passed a law in 1995 over President Clinton's veto to limit them. How effective it will be in the long run remains to be seen. Within months of the law's passage, trial lawyers in California were pushing for a ballot initiative that would make it easier to press fraud claims in state courts. (There's hope, though; the measure lost by a landslide in the November 1996 elections.)

In 1996, Clinton vetoed a much broader tort reform to limit civil lawsuits against companies for defective products and doctors for malpractice. That's a rich field to plow. Lately, I've been reading about something called "multiple chemical sensitivity." Victims claim everything from dizziness to brain damage for having to breathe the horrendous toxic fumes of all the perfume, cologne, hair spray, and other artificial fragrances people wear, including clothes that have been washed in scented soap! It has become a movement with its very own Chemical Injury Litigation Project. Before long, whole new industries will be up for grabs.

We've come a long way from whiplash. And even that is a questionable ailment. A study of accident victims in Lithuania, where personal insurance is rare and suing for automobile injuries unheard of, shows that whiplash and the attendant pain and suffering are nonexistent in that country. Could it be that the affliction is the figment of the legal imagination?

Another trap that lawyers like to lay is the wrongful-dismissal lawsuit. Some time ago, a small company that I am connected with hired a sales manager. It didn't work out, but instead of firing him, we transferred him to another position. And, mind you, we didn't cut his pay or change his title. But he sued us—on the ground that we had made him fearful that he *might* be fired. Can you believe it? The employee actually wasn't a bad fellow—he just ended up with a lawyer who specialized in this sort of thing. The lawyer had learned we were about to float a stock offering, and probably assumed we would agree to a quick settlement to avoid bad publicity. No doubt he suggested to our employee that he could collect substantial dollars that would well exceed his fees.

It might have been easier for us to pay the money, with Uncle Sam picking up 40 percent of the tab in the form of a tax deduction on the cost. But we decided to fight. It was the principle of the thing. We had gone out of our way to help this guy twice—first by hiring him, then by transferring him to a new position. We didn't take kindly to being sued for our efforts.

So we put the whole thing in our proxy and informed our shareholders that, no, we weren't about to reward this kind of blackmail. It took some testimony, but the judge sided with us.

If more companies stood up to legalized extortion, there might be less of it. And yet, I understand why so many companies settle. The haunting truth is these cases can drag out for years.

This sort of nuisance lawsuit is all too common in American courts. Nothing like it exists anywhere else in the world. A friend tells me a revealing story about an American woman who married an Italian banker after she graduated from college in the late 1970s, moved to Rome, and started a family. In 1992, her husband was transferred to the United States. That summer, she had a baby—her fourth child—in a New York City hospital. Everything went smoothly, except that afterward she had a slight tingling in one of her legs. Her kindly American doctor assured her the symptom was commonplace and would soon go away. Still, she asked my friend for advice: Should she sue?

"Why, no, I don't think so," he replied. "It doesn't seem to be any sort of harmful or permanent condition." She persisted. What if the tingling didn't go away? What if there were complications down the road? And, more to the point, how much money did he think she might win? Did he know any good lawyers?

"What if this had happened in Italy?" he finally asked her. "Would you sue the Italian doctor?"

She looked at him as if he were crazy. "Of course not," she said. "People don't sue for stuff like this in Italy."

Companies sometimes have to fight for their survival against avaricious tort lawyers. Dow Corning, the maker of silicone-gel breast implants, declared bankruptcy in 1995, even though it had agreed to pay $2 billion as part of a huge settlement—and even though there's no scientific (as opposed to anecdotal) evidence that breast implants cause any harm.

Plenty of people have found a mouse in their soft drink that wasn't there until they put it there. ITT's Hartford Insurance once settled for $7 million with a guy who suffered an electric shock using a power tool. The insulation had worn bare after many years of use.

Shouldn't he have noticed? Shouldn't he have bought a new cord? No company yet, to my knowledge, has ever built anything that will last forever.

The defense might show why the victim of an accident contributed to the cause of the accident. But the plaintiff's lawyer will say: "That may all be true. But he's dead." And the bereaved relatives will say: "To soothe our pain, we want *money*."

Some cases are ridiculous. Remember the woman who won $2.7 million from McDonald's because she claimed the coffee was too hot? She scalded her legs when she spilled the coffee in her lap. I'm sorry she injured herself. And it may or may not be that McDonald's coffee was unusually hot. But the fact is, coffee is hot.

The final settlement was much smaller, but the publicity set off a rash of copycat lawsuits. That prompted some big fast-food and coffeehouse chains to post warning signs reminding their customers that . . . coffee is hot.

Or remember the case of the car owner in Alabama who got $2 million in punitive damages because BMW, the manufacturer, had painted over some minor scratches on the way from the factory to the showroom? The jury decided the repainting job had reduced the value of the car by $4,000. Fair enough, I suppose. Then it added punitive damages of $4 million! That's a lot of paint and suffering. A state court later lowered that amount to $2 million. BMW had to stop delivering cars to Alabama; dealers wouldn't accept them for fear of getting dragged into a lawsuit.

What if BMW had discovered the scratches before the car left the factory? It would have repainted the car in the factory as part of the ordinary manufacturing process. Thus, the car would have been in exactly the same condition as it was sold in, yet there would have been no ground to sue.

And what if the paint job was a good job (and, indeed, I assume that it was)? Did it really detract from the BMW's value? Suppose it was better than before?

The award was so egregious that the Supreme Court in 1996 gave a rare victory to business and struck it down as so outlandish that it violated the constitutional right to due process of law. It was the first time in more than a decade the nation's top court overturned an award as excessive. But while companies cheered, plaintiffs' lawyers vowed they wouldn't be deterred from pushing ahead with lawsuits and described the court ruling as an aberration.

But put aside the unfairness issue for a moment. The fact is, it is impossible to predict what a jury might decide or how much money it might award, especially if the plaintiff's lawyer is skilled at playing on jurors' heartstrings.

So companies simply have to err always on the side of caution. They must take extraordinary precautions to show they have put the consumers' interests first. BMW probably ought to have put a sign in bold letters on the windshield that said, "Several Square Inches of This Car Have Been Repainted."

Some will say, "Well, at least with so many lawyers around, the little guy is protected against genuine abuses." Poppycock. The frivolous cases clog the courts, forcing people with legitimate cases to wait for years.

There ought to be some penalty for filing frivolous suits. Why not stipulate that plaintiffs' attorneys who lose their case must pay a "social tax" of 25 percent of the damages they sought? You need a harsh response to socially destructive lawsuits or they'll go on forever.

Forcing the litigants to pay the winners' legal fees—that's not enough. So how do we get their attention? Maybe they should pay six times the legal fees, with everything above the actual legal costs going to reimburse the defendants for their lost opportunities, or at least for all the time they have wasted dealing with this nonsense. Add to that three times legal fees to compensate them for the damage to their reputations. Now we're getting a little bit closer to matching the plaintiffs' rewards. Call it a leveling of the playing field.

Maybe Congress should pass another law: Cut the number of law-school graduates by half and allow subsequent increases no greater than the growth of the general population. For good measure, perhaps it should make sixty-five the mandatory retirement age for lawyers.

Why is legal reform so difficult to achieve? Because it has to be approved by so many *lawyers*. Indeed, whenever a new proposal makes the rounds of Congress or a state legislature, I would urge Americans to follow the course of reason: Don't hold your breath.

Every time you or I make a dollar in salary, interest, dividends, or capital gains, it gets reported to the IRS. But there's no law that says trial lawyers have to report any of the tens of billions of dollars they get in their cuts of legal settlements every year, because their lobby has blocked passage of such a requirement by Congress. Of course, there is a law that says they must pay taxes on those earnings—but the potential for abuse is obvious. Meantime, the IRS estimates that 10 percent of all lawyers never even file tax returns. These scofflaws should be disbarred for life.

Is it possible that Congress, and the states, have passed so many laws to give lawyers something to do? For them, fourteen new laws are fourteen new opportunities. They'll try new cases under the new laws setting new precedents that embellish previous cases. What opportunity for growth (in fees). New laws can be likened to a corporation's new products. How else do you grow?

Every new state or federal law or local ordinance opens up fertile new ground for plaintiffs' lawyers. Everybody got a laugh about the strip club that was threatened with a fine for failing to install a wheelchair lift for its stage, in violation of the Americans with Disabilities Act.

Then there was the Topeka, Kansas, motorist who was fined for not wearing a seat belt. He sued the city, claiming it violated the ADA by refusing to accommodate his particular disability, claustrophobia.

One way to deal with the abuses would be to establish arbitration panels to hear disputes. The country is already, in fact, moving in this direction. They could be made up of fair-minded professionals who are trained to think. Some members would probably be retired judges.

But wait! I hear you say. What about our tried-and-true jury system, where upright citizens carefully weigh the evidence and, following their consciences, render a verdict? Ladies and Gentlemen, I give you the O. J. Simpson case.

Back to my suggestion. Congress should pass a law giving the judge in a civil trial the right to order the case into arbitration, especially if he thinks that it is a frivolous or contrived suit or if the issues are so complicated a layman would have trouble understanding them.

Imagine standing before eight bus drivers and saying, "Let me explain to you about software-patent infringement. . . ." It happens all the time. Strike-suit lawyers love it. Our arbitration system, by contrast, would have access to a large pool of specialists, so that in such a case it could tap into one or two patent-law scholars.

The law should define the arbitration panel's powers. The panels would then listen to both sides, minus the histrionics, and render a decision. Quickly, without tying up the corporation for months. This would certainly help to unburden our court system.

Of course, you can be sure of one thing. Lawyers would never agree to this. They would fight like crazy. Why? Because here is somebody taking away their license to obfuscate. They will surely come up with six thousand reasons why it can't be done.

It is their job to protect the poor and downtrodden, they will say. It is a role cut straight out of Robin Hood, except that they get a large percentage of the proceedings. They are Robin Hoods in Armani suits.

Besides, they will say, there were only three hundred class-action shareholder lawsuits last year. That's not very many.

Except that there were only one hundred five years ago.

Already, though, the parties to a civil dispute have the option of going to arbitration—and they are doing so in increasing numbers. The nonprofit American Arbitration Association is the biggest provider of such dispute resolution, handling about sixty thousand cases a year. But for-profit companies are being formed, too, hiring retired judges and other specialists to perform the same service for a fee.

One of the delicious ironies of this process is that more and more clients are suing their plaintiffs' lawyers for malpractice for failing to win malpractice awards.

Not long ago, some Bank of Boston customers involved in a class-action lawsuit involving claims of mortgage-escrow overcharges discovered that the settlement their lawyers reached would actually cost them more than they got back—while the lawyers walked away with $8.5 million in fees.

What did these customers do? They sued their lawyers, of course!

Lawyers, though, often walk away with big bucks while their clients end up with peanuts. A judge in Alabama just awarded $2 million in legal fees to nineteen lawyers who won a $1 judgment for consumers in a gasoline price-fixing case.

The *Forbes* list of the highest-paid lawyers in America is instructive: Joseph Jamail, with $90 million in 1994 income, and John O'Quinn, with $40 million, were instrumental in verdicts that drove two giant corporations, Texaco and Dow Corning, into bankruptcy. Wayne Reaud, with $26 million, and Walter Umphrey, with $19 million, both specialize in asbestos lawsuits. Mr. Reaud told *Forbes,* "The Lord has let me make money from doing this." All four men are based in Texas, a state notorious for its sympathetic stance toward the plaintiffs' bar.

It goes without saying that lawyers are an integral part of any legal system. No democratic or prosperous society can function without them. Indeed, the oft-quoted Shakespeare line from *Henry VI,* "The first thing we do, let's kill all the lawyers," was uttered by a bad guy.

In the United States, most lawyers actually serve legitimate purposes, from writing contracts to defending the accused. It's just that there are too many of them. It's like the Hydra, only worse. You'll remember the Hydra was the snake with nine heads of Greek mythology; every time Hercules cut one head off, two more appeared.

I wonder if I should have said that: Will somebody sue me? Will someone else rush to my defense and plead my insanity? It may be far-fetched, but stranger things have happened in today's litigious climate.

The impact on corporate America of too many lawsuits is the same as the impact on our cities of too many cars: gridlock. And, as trade barriers between nations fall and more Third World countries join the global economy, America's competitive position will erode.

The simple fact is that lawyers make the laws as well as administer them. They dominate Congress and most state legislatures. And, of course, they become judges. It is their responsibility to fix a system that is badly in need of repair.

That, of course, is a magnificent theory, worthy of a lawyer.

A Cold Look
at Some Hot
Issues

17

Pssst! Wanna Buy a Derivative Cheap?

When it comes to financial scams and skullduggery, over the years I've seen it all.

After all, I've been observing Wall Street since the days when Calvin Coolidge sat in the White House. Seven decades later, I'm still at it. I have talked to investors, investment bankers, and other deal makers almost daily. Over these years, I've bought, managed, and sold more companies than I can remember. I've cooperated with, clashed with, negotiated with, and gone hunting with some of the great movers and shakers of American business and politics.

And I've watched with wonder as each new scandal unfolds,

from Swedish "Match King" Ivar Kreuger's bid to corner the world market in kitchen matches in the 1920s to John G. Bennett Jr.'s matching-funds charity scam in the 1990s. And I've tried to make sense of them, to figure out what motivates the culprits to perpetrate such spectacular rip-offs, and what induces the victims (often savvy businesspeople) to let down their guard and be taken in by them.

If Laurance Rockefeller and William Simon could be fooled by Mr. Bennett's New Era Philanthropy con, who is immune to the allure of the fast-buck artist? Maybe it's even worse than P. T. Barnum thought; there's not a sucker born every minute; there's a sucker born every time somebody's born.

The real cause is greed. That's why gambling is so big—people want to get something for nothing, and get it quickly. But the odds of getting rich in gambling are long, and cleverness counts for almost nothing. By contrast, the odds for the perpetrator improve markedly if he engages in a little deceit, and even more if he is smart about it.

I've puzzled over the evolution of the Great American Swindle. Are today's hoaxes different, somehow, from yesteryear's? Are they more sophisticated? Is the public's reaction more muted? What has changed?

And I think I have at least a partial answer. People haven't changed. It's just that cheating them out of their money has become so commonplace it barely merits ink in the papers anymore. It fits into a larger pattern of selfishness and immorality in our society.

People are so inured to wrongdoing, legal and illegal, that they simply tolerate it on a grand scale. Many have lost their capacity to be outraged; the rest have high blood pressure.

They lose track of the number of special prosecutors appointed to investigate suspected transgressions by political figures. They read endlessly about big-time money grabs—from the savings-and-loan fiasco to the junk-bond excesses of the 1980s.

Is it nostalgia that makes me think that Americans set higher standards for their public figures in the first half of this century? Maybe, but I contend that retribution was sharper back then. Murderers were hanged. In some states we are just getting back to that.

People lived by a code of honor. When Jay Gould and his confederate Jim Fisk tried to corner the gold market in 1869, John Brown, of the then powerful firm Brown Brothers & Company, put his bank's *entire capital* at risk to block their machinations.

There's a story I heard: Jack Dreyfus, the founder of Dreyfus and Company, once made a verbal agreement to sell the firm to somebody in the Middle West for a given price. Jack had a change of heart, but decided as a matter of his honor, he must go through with the deal.

He had given his word.

The buyer, though, decided to try to knock the price down. He said, "I think I should offer you X instead of Y." Jack said, "Thank you. Now I don't have to sell it to you under the terms we discussed. I withdraw my offer."

Contrast that to the way some Prudential Securities brokers took their clients on a $1 billion ride in the 1980s by putting them into high-risk limited partnerships. Prudential ultimately paid $700 million in fines and penalties imposed by the federal government.

Some years ago, a magazine asked a large number of prominent people which they would choose: to be guilty of a serious crime and have a good lawyer, or to be innocent but have a bad lawyer. Most chose the former.

Derivatives are just one of the latest mechanisms for whetting man's greed, or just plain foolishness.

You have to be fairly smart to manipulate derivatives. Anybody can cook the books. Cooking derivatives requires a special talent of a higher order. And the people who have abused them in a big way in the past couple of years have all been smart; like Robert Citron, the treasurer who drove one of the richest counties in America into bankruptcy, and Nicholas Leeson, who brought down the 233-year-old Barings investment house in London by concealing losses of nearly $1 billion in futures trading.

Derivatives are specially designed investments whose value is determined by—or "derived" from—the performance of some underlying asset. They can be simple or complex, and are used for various reasons, including hedging risks, betting on the direction of a market, or reducing the cost of borrowing. In a way, the interest rate you earn on a savings account is a derivative of the cash you put in the bank.

But the financial world has devised so many complicated derivatives over the past few years that you need to be on the top 1 percent of the learning curve to understand them. Investing in derivatives is a little bit like playing pool. In the simplest shot, you hit the cue ball against the ball that you want to go into the pocket. That's generally pretty easy. But it gets more intricate in combination shots, where the cue ball sets off a chain reaction, hitting a second ball at just the right angle, so that it will hit a third ball at just the right angle, and so on, until, if your aim has been accurate and your strategy sharp, the final ball goes whizzing into the pocket.

If you've ever played pool, you know that kind of accuracy is hard to come by. Each time you add one more ball to the equation, you increase the odds against you by a factor of fifty. That's because the most minute error in the angle of the first collision will create a big error in the angle of the second collision, and that in turn will create a huge error in the third collision, and so on.

Likewise, in a complicated derivatives transaction, a small miscalculation in the first phase can create a big miscalculation in the second phase, which in turn can create a huge miscalculation in the third phase, and so on. Derivatives are often called "exotic," which is another way of saying the layman can't understand how they work. For example, there are securities you can invest in that are basically backed by either the interest or the principal of various pools of residential mortgages, and betting on them requires a willingness to predict repayment patterns (and thus, presumably, the evolution of the economy), as well as the direction of interest rates.

The people who have lost a lot of money in derivative deals claim they didn't understand them, that the mysteries of such operations were not explained to them—or at least the downside wasn't. Thus Procter & Gamble sued Bankers Trust over derivatives losses of $102 million, claiming it was a naive victim, and the home office of Barings expressed astonishment at the damage a single trader in Singapore was able to wreak.

Really, now! The fact is, at Barings, at Procter & Gamble, in Orange County, California, and in numerous other cases, people were betting on low interest rates. When interest rates went up, they were all driven to the brink. The multiplier effect again. All these supersophisticates should have foreseen it. But they didn't.

Some people really are victims, of course. Lots of towns and counties, universities, small companies, and even individual investors have been burned by derivatives because they really didn't understand their downside. Of course, they were quick to grab investments that promised better-than-average returns without asking too many questions.

But how about the guys who were selling them? I doubt that Merrill Lynch or Bankers Trust or any of the other firms that peddle derivatives said: "If you buy this, you'll make an extra one percent, but if interest rates go up you'll lose your shirt." (Bankers Trust settled the dispute with Procter & Gambler in 1996.)

When people do lose their shirt, the financial world looks on horrified (and maybe secretly enjoys the spectacle). It tut-tuts about the recklessness of people like Leeson of Barings Bank.

But suppose Leeson had been successful. What if he had *made* $1.4 billion instead of losing it? Would he have been hailed as a genius? Of course he would. And he would have gotten a big bonus. Or flip the question and ask: What if George Soros had *lost* a billion dollars instead of making a billion by speculating against the British pound? Would he be looked down on as a loser? Of course he would.

Instead, our poor Mr. Leeson had to make a dash across three Asian countries with his twenty-three-year-old bride—in a Porsche, no less. That's going out in style. He ended up in a Frankfurt jail, then a Singapore jail. Oh, have a heart. It was only $1.4 billion.

Besides, what ever happened to *oversight*? I just can't imagine giving anybody anywhere the ability to put billions of dollars into play without having somebody supervise him. But that's what happened at Barings. That's what happened at Daiwa Bank when Toshihide Iguchi lost more than a billion in unauthorized trading of U.S. Treasury bonds in 1995, and at the Sumitomo Corporation when Yasuo Hamanaka lost $1.8 billion playing the copper market over ten years. Mr. Leeson and Mr. Iguchi and Mr. Hamanaka had carte blanche. They just went ahead and did it.

Back in the forties, I remember a teller stole something like eighty thousand dollars from the safe of his bank. It was a huge amount of money at the time, especially for somebody earning thirty dollars a week.

The judge freed him. He said the bank should never have put somebody making such a paltry salary near so much money. I am not sure he was right—but he had a point.

I guess financial scandal will always be with us. My mind drifts back to some of the champion swindlers who were short-term sensations and gained a minor place in history for far smaller transgressions than those recorded today. Is that progress?

CHARLES PONZI, whose last name has become synonymous with get-rich-quick pyramid schemes that use money from new investors to make interest payments to early investors. For a while, the supply of new suckers is sufficient to keep the original suckers happy. It becomes a frenzy of greed. Inevitably, though, the structure collapses. Ponzi raised about $15 million in 1920, and spent several years in the brig for larceny and mail fraud.

He died, broke and blind, in a Brazilian poorhouse in 1949.

IVAR KREUGER, the Swedish match king, who enjoyed the respect and confidence of international finance. Until he wound up with a vault full of blotting paper that should have been bonds.

Most distressing.

Kreuger tried to corner the world market in matchsticks, of all things. At his height in the late 1920s, he was said to control three-fourths of world production, even selling his "little wooden soldiers" to African tribal chieftains.

But his matchstick empire-building was just a cover for a Ponzi scheme. The match trade didn't make him much money, so he issued stocks and bonds, transferred the proceeds to his native Sweden, and used the capital to pay dividends. He was a colorful character, striding through the halls of power in Europe and America. Herbert Hoover even made him a financial adviser.

In the end, he was caught up for cheating investors out of $500 million and shot himself to death in a Paris gun shop.

F. DONALD COSTER of the McKesson & Robbins drug empire. He wound up with empty warehouses that should have been full. And even the warehouses were fiction.

That's carrying things a bit far.

Mr. Coster's real name was Philip Musica, a man who had a couple of convictions under his hat when he set up a hair-tonic company in Mount Vernon, New York, in 1923. The company sold hair tonic, but the real profit was in selling alcohol to bootleggers. Mr. Musica/Coster merged his company with the ailing McKesson & Robbins in 1926 and poured huge amounts of money into fictional drugs stored in "warehouses" that were in fact tiny offices.

He shot himself to death in his Connecticut mansion in 1938.

ALFRED LOEWENSTEIN, a Belgian financier and the world's third richest man when he disappeared from his private Fokker VIII four thousand feet over the English Channel in 1928. They tell me that pushing open the door of a plane flying at over two hundred miles an hour would require Herculean strength. But he apparently managed it. Did he have any help from any of the six other people on board—two pilots, two stenographers, a valet, and a male secretary? Or was the whole thing an unfortunate accident, as the authorities ruled? Imagine, a notorious stock manipulator beset by business problems; a billionaire known for his shady associates and shady past (he was drummed out of the Belgian army for profiteering); a man with a beautiful but estranged wife, numerous enemies, and a cartload of million-dollar insurance policies, accidentally tumbling out of a plane! The body was supposedly found and hastily buried, but some had their doubts. Perhaps he survived and is peacefully living in a sod hut in the Kent countryside. We shall never know. The reports of sightings à la Elvis have long since subsided.

RICHARD WHITNEY, who headed the New York Stock Exchange for five years in the 1930s, pledged his customers' securities as collateral for loans. I used to see him on the floor. He was imprisoned in 1938 for stealing securities from clients, including a pension fund for families of stock exchange members. A tragic case considering his other meritorious activities.

BILLIE SOL ESTES, a close associate of President Lyndon B. Johnson, who was convicted in 1963 of mail fraud and conspiracy for selling $24 million worth of mortgages on nonexistent fertilizer tanks. He was paroled halfway through his sentence, but sent back to jail on charges of fraud and tax evasion. In 1984, he resurfaced, this time to make the wild claim that when Johnson was vice president in 1961, he ordered the murder of a federal official to silence him about Johnson's supposed involvement in a fraud.

BERNIE CORNFELD with his world-girdling mutual fund company, Investors Overseas Services based in Geneva, and its main vehicle, the Fund of Funds.

Boy, was it ever a fund of funds! In the 1960s, Bernie gained control of several funds and sold them as a package—charging a 20 percent fee. Not surprisingly, his investors lost millions while he (and a lot of his salespeople) got rich. In his heyday, Bernie flew about on his private helicopter or jet when he wasn't reputedly entertaining scantily clad women at his French château or escorting them around town in his Rolls-Royce.

But then, law-enforcement officials turned the heat on, and Bernie hopscotched from one refuge to the next, always one step ahead of extradition. He ended up spending eleven months in a Swiss jail, emerging with a full beard and a bevy of bathing beauties. Alas, as I pen this, I read in the papers that he has just succumbed to his last extradition, to that great mutual fund in the sky.

ROBERT VESCO, the former financial whiz kid who became a fugitive from U.S. justice and until recently was living high on the hog (several homes, a yacht, a private plane) in, of all places, Castro's Cuba. A high school dropout, he began building a business empire of mostly small companies in the late 1960s. One of his acquisitions was Mr. Cornfield's Investors Overseas Services in 1971. The SEC accused him of looting $224 million from various IOS-managed mutual funds. Since he fled this country, he has been suspected of selling arms to Libya and being involved in the Latin American drug trade. The Castro regime convicted him of economic crimes in 1996 and sentenced him to thirteen years in jail.

ANTHONY "TINO" DE ANGELIS, a former butcher who became the author of one of the great scams of the second half of the twentieth century, the Great Salad Oil Swindle. His Allied Crude Vegetable Oil Refining Corporation used the contents of mostly empty storage tanks in Bayonne, New Jersey, as collateral for loans totaling $150 million. Allied and more than a dozen creditors, including an American Express unit, went bankrupt in the 1960s. Mr. De Angelis went to the pen. He got out, defrauded some pig farmers in Indiana, and went back in. He got out again and, in 1992, at the age of seventy-seven, was arrested again and went back behind bars. Some guys never give up. When he wasn't in jail, he liked to ride around in a chauffeured Cadillac and give away cash and bikes—two thousand bikes in all, mostly to kids.

ROBERT MAXWELL, press baron, who drowned in the cold waters off his yacht in the Atlantic in November 1991 as his media empire crumbled under a mountain of debt. In an ironic twist, one of his own newspapers, the Sunday *Mirror* of London, proclaimed SUICIDE in a huge banner headline, thus contesting a Spanish autopsy blaming the death on a heart attack. A natural cause, of course, would have enabled the beneficiaries of his $36 million life-insurance policy to collect.

The drama wasn't over, either; barely a year later, Mr. Maxwell's son Kevin won fame and a place in the *Guinness Book of World*

Records for the biggest personal bankruptcy in the history of the world up to that date—around $600 million.

Heaven knows, this is only a partial list. We could also talk about Michele Sindona, convicted of siphoning $15 million from the Franklin National Bank, which collapsed in 1974; Joseph Ossorio and David Heuwetter, convicted of cheating major banks out of billions in a scandal that resulted in the failure of Drysdale Government Securities in 1982; Marc Rich, the commodities trader indicted in the biggest tax-evasion case in U.S. history. . . . Ivan Boesky and Martin Siegel . . . Charles Keating . . . John de Lorean . . . Dennis Levine . . . Peter Brant and Foster Winans . . . But there are so many others.

In late 1996, a Long Island, New York, car dealer got five years in prison for bilking General Motors out of $422 million. It seems odd that the world's biggest car maker somehow failed to notice such a huge cash drain—but it did. Not long after, an investment adviser *working out of her home* in New Jersey pleaded guilty to stealing $65 million from clients—including friends and family members.

What are the hallmarks of scams? One thing strikes me: They are usually orchestrated by charismatic, high-living fellows who in some cases mean well and are blinded by their own visions. Some, of course, merely have larceny in their hearts.

A few years ago, I organized a friendly leveraged buyout of a company called Ticor. It was the largest title company and one of the largest mortgage-guarantee companies in the United States at the time. It was based in Los Angeles. It operated out of a great big building, twenty-four stories high.

My partners and I led investors in a $271 million leveraged buyout of Ticor from Southern Pacific. Four of us together put up less than $2 million. We then sold off about $50 million of companies that had nothing to do with the mortgage business.

It was a classic LBO: no acrimony, no delays, just a good business transaction. Ticor was well respected and staffed with veterans in the field. On mortgages it conservatively insured only the top 20 percent against sizable cash down payments. It had a superb record.

Looking back, I can see now that in one case it was too superb. It turned out that Ticor was writing insurance for a Maryland Mortgage Company that submitted appraisals for insurance based on the 20 percent limit. Stated simply, the 20 percent was figured correctly, but the underlying appraisal was not. It killed a tremendous deal for us. We lost $260 million.

Maybe we should have picked up on it sooner. But we did our due diligence. Everything seemed okay. Price Waterhouse did our audit, including reviewing our assets, and found nothing untoward. But in industry, these things happen. It is easy to suggest after the fact what else should have been done. But unfortunately, business is full of risks. If you tried to cover every contingency, you'd price yourself out of the market.

What does all this prove? Only that very little can be taken for granted—and a continuing assessment of risk is most helpful, especially if the projected return seems too good to be true.

So I was more than a spectator on this one. I was a victim— and my precounted millions went out the door.

As they say, there's a sucker born every time somebody's born.

18

And Furthermore, Mr. President . . . (A Critical Look at Some Political Pieties of the Day)

There are many ways to define politics. Henry Albert Laurens Fisher said it was the knack of making people happy. Henry Brooke Adams said it was the art of ignoring facts. Sidney Hillman said it was the science of how who gets what, when, and why. Well, I say it is the skill at avoiding risk.

Take the budget deficit. Nowadays, nobody can hope to make it to the highest office of the land unless he wraps himself in the American flag, lifts a sword high above his head, and vows to slay the great dragon that is breathing fire over our fair land: runaway government spending.

The budget deficit has been denounced as the greatest economic evil since King George's Intolerable Acts triggered the American Revolution. Politicians declare that it will rob future generations of their economic birthright. Even though it seemed to be narrowing a bit in 1996, to a projected $145 billion from $164 billion in 1995, that is still $600 for every man, woman, and child in the country.

Many Americans have trouble understanding what the budget deficit is, exactly. The concept is simple enough: It is the excess of expenditures over income. Perhaps you have encountered this problem yourself: Your monthly bills add up to $5,000, say, but your take-home pay is only $4,000. Your household budget deficit for that month is $1,000. What do you do? Scrimp, most probably, until you get the expenses back in line with your income. Or maybe you feel you can't cut back on your spending, so you take a night job to earn some extra money. Or, you could do what the U.S. government does and just borrow $1,000 a month, year after year. Sooner or later, of course, the interest payments will become too much and you'll go bankrupt. Uncle Sam has no such problem; he just prints the dollars he needs to pay off creditors.

But even Americans who see the problem have trouble grasping why the budget deficit is so terrible. Anybody can figure out that inflation is undesirable, because they know that every time the price of milk or gasoline goes up, they have that much less money in their pockets. But what can they relate the budget deficit to?

It is too intangible. It is a dry and academic subject. After all, Americans undoubtedly reason, political pundits have been sounding the alarm bell for years—yet, life goes on. It is one thing to worry about sons or brothers exposed to bullets or bombs in a faraway war, and quite another thing to fret about balancing the national books. Fixing the budget deficit requires thinking about economic projections (which could be all wrong). Why bother?

That's why politicians like to pounce on the subject. Their fiery speeches urging an end to government profligacy always get applause. And yet they themselves know their talking is just that— talk. The budget deficit is too easy a target—easy because everybody more or less agrees something ought to be done, but also easy because very few people will hold the politicians' feet to the fire on the issue. The "worsening budget deficit" is like aging. It happens so slowly, you can hardly tell the difference between today and to-morrow.

There is a huge electronic sign on the side of a building near Times Square in New York City that flashes the increase in the size of the national debt, dollar by dollar. It goes one way: up! It had grown to $5,214,520,637,910 (that's $5.2 trillion!) the last time I looked in 1996, almost double what it was in 1989, when the tote board first went up. "Your family's share" of the debt had ballooned to $64,486 from $42,000 in the same period. Tourists stop and gape (the natives ignore it), though I have yet to read about anybody who canceled a contract to buy a new car and used the savings to reduce "his family's share" of the national debt.

Even so, it is quite dramatic to see the last six digits swirl millisecond by millisecond in a blur of flashing lights to ever higher figures. It costs the owners of this so-called National Debt Clock $500 a month just to replace the lightbulbs. Those flashing lights are a dose of realism that the public should have no trouble comprehending. That is, if the public *wants* to comprehend it.

If you don't happen to be in the area of Times Square, the widening deficit doesn't seem quite so ominous. Listening to politicians' scare stories about the damage it will do to the fabric of society is a bit like discovering another gray hair on your head: momentarily disconcerting, but hardly a threat to life and limb. Will it deprive our grandchildren of their economic security? Who knows? By then, maybe the minimum wage will be $150 an hour, and the government will decide to pay the deficit off through that tried-and-true deficit-reduction plan, inflation.

Most people assume we'll lick this problem just as we've licked every other economic problem that has come our way. Remember the "oil crisis" of the 1970s, complete with long gas lines and talk of $100-a-barrel oil prices? Everybody said OPEC had a stranglehold on the West. The great economic challenge facing the world was "recycling petrodollars" through the Western banking system. Well, oil was recently down to $20, and nobody pays any attention to OPEC anymore. And "petrodollars" have gone the way of Susan B. Anthony silver dollars—out of sight and out of mind.

Remember the great hue and cry about double-digit inflation and interest rates in the late 1970s and early 1980s? Today, we've got both of those ogres down to their lowest levels since Dwight D. Eisenhower sat in the White House. Remember the hand-wringing about America's economic decline in the mid-and late eighties? Since then, American workers have increased their productivity faster than workers almost anywhere else, and American industry has reasserted itself as the world's most competitive.

Remember the international "debt crisis" of the late eighties and early nineties? It went away. So did the S and L "crisis." So has every other economic crisis you can think of. America isn't about to be undone by this crisis or that. We're a bit tougher than that. After all, in just the past three generations, we whipped Hitler and Hirohito, destroyed the Soviet empire, and met the Japanese economic challenge.

The U.S. budget deficit is actually much lower than that in most other countries: 1.6 percent of our gross national product at last count, compared with 2.4 percent in Germany, 5 percent in France, and 9.1 percent in Italy. In fact, the deficit shrank to an estimated $120 billion or so in 1996, way down from nearly $300 billion in 1992.

Naturally, our politicians ought to show more gumption and make the spending cuts and even raise taxes to get the budget in balance. But that is a risk *not* worth taking for a profession that is obsessed with opinion polls. For all their posturing, politicians still dole out pork with all the trimmings and shy away from reforms that would really make a difference. And this has gone on a long time; the last time the federal budget showed a surplus was in 1969, when it was $3.2 billion in the black. But it swung back to a deficit in 1970 and has been there ever since. The last president who really had spending under control was Eisenhower, with surpluses in 1956, 1957, and 1960. Some people say Ike was a boring president and the 1950s were a boring decade. Let's bring back those dull days and stodgy budget surpluses!

But 1.8 percent is peanuts. It's like a low-grade fever. It should be monitored closely so it doesn't get too high, and it should be eventually brought down to normal. Let's not forget that we owe our national independence, at least in part, to deficit spending. It seems that Louis XVI of France borrowed money rather than raise taxes to finance his assistance to the American patriots. (Never underestimate the power of risk aversion on history. President Johnson was accused of doing the same thing in Vietnam. Some things never change.)

The American trade deficit is another favorite target of politicians. They're against it. But while they thunder with indignation, the Japanese quietly walk away with an enormous prize: a surplus of tens of billions of dollars a year—year after year after year after year, for two decades now, and the U.S. government has done almost nothing about it. Our deficit with Japan "shrank" to $59 billion in 1995 from

$66 billion in 1994. Maybe Washington will take decisive action—next year.

And even as the imbalance with the Japanese shows signs of contracting ever so slightly, the Chinese are filling the role of bad guy, creating their own huge trade surplus with us while pirating American films, compact discs, and other intellectual property. And what American industry gets from Washington is, again, mostly noise.

The truth of the matter is that, as much as we like to export, we enjoy importing even more. Americans have one of the highest standards of living in the world and we expect it to keep improving. (To be sure, poverty remains an intractible problem.) So our trade deficit just keeps getting wider.

Where will it all lead? America has enormous advantages—vast natural resources, a skilled workforce, a democratic government that, for all our complaining, functions well and is almost corruption-free, the biggest single market in the world, a technological lead in many areas over the rest of the world, developed capital markets, and on and on.

Not only that, but American industry has thoroughly reinvented itself over the past decade to compete in the global economy. While the politicians dither, American corporations have turned themselves from laggards into the most efficient producers of goods and services in the world. The process has involved a lot of risk taking, and pain, but once again the country rose to an international challenge, in some ways the most daunting in our history.

But it is also safe to say that other countries are growing faster than ours is. International competition is intensifying. Consider: India is now one of the biggest producers of movie cartoons and software. China's economy is booming—and its number one market is the United States. Pakistan is coming along. So is South America. There is enormous potential in Russia and Eastern Europe. Western Europe and Japan aren't letting up. Everybody wants to export, including us. For now, America has the advantage of its technological superiority, while industrializing countries have the advantage of low wages. But that could change. Already, China is beginning to export some high-technology goods.

We can't sit still. Yet, too often, we do. In our history, again and again, we have fallen victim to our own complacency. Think of the market crash of 1929, Pearl Harbor, *Sputnik,* the oil shock of 1973. We get caught off guard. How many technological innovations have we given away to the Japanese because we didn't act quickly enough to market them ourselves?

Our politicians have to recognize the need to show a little more backbone about warning of the dangers of overconfidence or complacency. That calls for real leadership. Is that easy? Nope. Could you lose an election? Yup.

Indeed, showing leadership in American politics is a lot like tightrope walking—only more dangerous. In both cases, there are people down below holding nets to catch you if you fall. But in politics, there is a Catch-22: If you make one false step, a lot of those people will walk away. If politics is the skill of avoiding risk, leadership is the willingness to take it, even if it means—horror of horrors!—falling in the polls.

Some politicians are proposing a simplistic solution that will backfire: protectionism. We tried that once before, in 1930, with the Smoot-Hawley Tariff Act that set import duties at their highest level in history. Many people believe it deepened and prolonged the depression.

Other nations will retaliate if we repeat that mistake—which is exactly what they did in 1930. World trade will slump, as it did then. All economies will contract. No, better to slug it out.

Make no mistake, we have to get both our big deficits—trade and budget—down or we will imperil our grandchildren's future. It might take ten, fifteen, twenty years. But that isn't all that long. Think back to what you were doing in 1981. To some of us, it seems like only yesterday.

There's a children's game called King of the Castle. Four boys hold up three boys on their shoulders, and those three hold two more. The more you add to it, the more unstable the system gets. That's what our deficits are like, more dangerous the higher they get.

Of course our toughest competitors are also slipping somewhat. Japan is suffering the problems of a maturing civilization—demands by its citizens that they have more leisure and more of the fruits of their labor. And it is running out of manpower. Western Europe is hampered by a tradition of worker entitlements that put it at a competitive disadvantage in the world economy. In France, most workers get six weeks or more of vacation and many retire on full pensions at the age of fifty-five. This sort of thing can't last forever. The Europeans will have to go through the same painful economic readjustments that we have made.

But watch out! Don't write Japan or Europe off in the long term. The Japanese have always been incredibly industrious. That won't change. And they are in a better position than anyone else to profit from Asia's economic boom. And even while Americans are congratulating themselves on their economic rebirth, and even if the Japanese are assailed by self-doubt as their economy slows, they are still running that $59 billion-plus trade deficit with us.

Europe, too, will remain a dynamic economic power. The Common Market—now called the European Union—counts well over 400 million inhabitants. In 1996, it added three new members: Sweden, Finland, and Austria. It retains very close ties to Norway and Switzerland. Poland, the Czech Republic, and Hungary, the three most prosperous East European countries, are knocking on its doors. So is Turkey, though that's a longer shot.

Then you have Ukraine and other former Soviet republics waiting in the wings. It's quite conceivable that the European Union could grow into a colossus of 900 million people, dwarfing our North American trading bloc.

But the Europeans' cultural differences, and their inevitable squabbling as they seek to solidify their ties, will give us a respite. A good thing, too, if only we will make the most of it.

Frankly, though, all the foreign competition should be good for us—*if* our political leaders are smart enough to understand the trends and bold enough to propose solutions to the American people. And *if* the American people, in turn, are resolute enough to work together for once.

To some extent, we're now competing against people who may until very recently have commuted to work on a bicycle and haven't been able to afford much more than a bowl of rice for lunch. But they have an incredible work ethic; they're smart; and they are moving fast into the next century. And, I might add, into the automotive age. China plans to produce 3 million cars in year 2000, up from zero in a few short years.

Let's hope that, like Saudi Arabia with its horde of petrodollars, the industrializing countries of the Third World will want to use their new wealth to buy into the good life rather than to create problems for other countries.

For Americans selling or investing abroad, there is a risk that is definitely not worth taking—paying off corrupt local officials, from the prime minister on down to some obscure customs inspector. Not only would such connivance be morally offensive, it would also violate U.S. law.

Of course, that puts us at a disadvantage to everybody else. In many Third World countries, slipping money under the table is a standard business practice. Just to get a document stamped, just to have your contract bid on, just to get an audience with a senior trade official, just to do about anything important can require the payment of a gratuity to some bureaucrat or intermediary.

A French company will pay the "fees" demanded by Saudi Arabian "agents." So will a German company or a Japanese company. But U.S. law forbids American companies to engage in bribery. Their competitors are certain to report them if they do. So we often lose out to European or Asian rivals. The Commerce Department in 1995 estimated that foreign companies used bribes to steal $36 billion worth of business away from U.S. companies.

A true story: A business colleague was in the office of a customer in Hong Kong and the representative of a Japanese company walked in with a bid for a project. The customer opened the envelope and took out the paper. "Hey . . . this is blank," he said. "That's right," the Japanese smoothly replied. "You put in the figure." I am happy to report that, for reasons other than price, his company didn't get the contract.

The Europeans aren't quite so blatant. Their approach is much more sophisticated. They have 187,432 rules, which all seem to work to their advantage. For example, if you want to sell, say, temperature controls, they have all sorts of tests that, lo and behold, European equipment passes but yours doesn't.

But in much of the developing world and "emerging market" countries, out-and-out corruption is the order of the day. South Korea's ex-president, Roh Tae Woo, was jailed a while back for accepting hundreds of *millions* of dollars in bribes. *Fortune* magazine found corruption so widespread it ran an "Asia Corrupt-O-Meter" to show the relative crookedness of officials in eleven big trading nations.

The "Corrupt-O-Meter" makes it almost seem funny. But it isn't. And it isn't just an obstacle for foreign exporters and investors. It is a threat to the economic vitality of developing countries. Corruption will ruin them unless it is quashed. Meantime, if Americans run the risk of losing out to less scrupulous economic adversaries, so be it. This is one of those cases where it really matters to do the right thing.

That brings me to another sort of risk that is not worth taking: exploiting poor countries under the banner of "free trade." Free trade is a fine-sounding phrase and a legitimate goal. And wealthy countries believe in it because they can afford it. Their technology makes it easy for them to tolerate it. But its benefits are relative. If a remote rain forest tribe makes hand-carved hardwood tables that Americans want, does it make sense for us to trade them tobacco that they don't need?

Free trade has achieved the sanctity of apple pie. It perhaps doesn't deserve such high moral status. We have to keep earning our way, not only by making goods efficiently that we can export at attractive prices to foreign buyers but also by helping poor countries that import our goods make and sell competitive values to us.

Otherwise, our trade with the developing world risks paralleling the Europeans' early exchanges of goods with the Indians. The Europeans offered sharp steel knives and brightly colored cloths for the Indians' land. In other words, they exchanged cheap trinkets the Indians were incapable of producing in exchange for the Indians' birthright. If I were a Third World leader, I'd say, "I'll engage in free trade with anybody who will give me back the value—not the cost, but the value—of what I give to them."

Picture a tribe on a lost island, living contentedly on fish and coconuts. The Americans (or Europeans, or Japanese) come and say, "Give us your fish and coconuts and your waterfront property so we can build tourist hotels on it; then, add work shifts in your factory at your wages to make articles for our consumers, and in return, we will give you TV sets and medicine to prolong your lives by ten years."

Well, sounds good. There was a song a few years back called "Bongo, Bongo, I Don't Want to Leave the Congo." And the song went on to explain how much better off the singer was *without* civilization. That was pure entertainment; in the global economy, nobody can live in pure isolation anymore.

There are values that never get factored into the economists' equations: In this case, the islanders' leisure time and emotional well-being and their island's natural beauty. Free trade has to be fair trade or it will never last. And fair not just in the sense of an even playing field but also in the sense of rich countries doing more to help poor countries elevate themselves.

There is no such thing as pure free trade, just as there is no such thing as a free lunch. It's a slogan. For rich countries, it can be a marketing cry that really means, "I get the profit, and you get the work." For poor countries, it can be a snare. Perhaps it should be renamed, "Let the buyer beware."

We rightly get mad at Third World countries that sell dope to us. But is that any different than selling cigarettes and soda pop to them when many of them can't afford soup? Maybe the country you're trying to sell cars to doesn't really need cars. Maybe donkeys—the same donkeys that the population has been riding for millennia—will do just fine.

True free trade exists between countries of roughly equal economic strength and productive efficiency, like the United States and Germany. But it loses its meaning if you're talking about the relationship between an advanced industrial power and an emerging economy.

The Chinese today are copying just about anything they can and shipping it to the United States and other rich countries. They're making toys and raw steel and shoes and watches. Before long, they will be making televisions and cameras, just as Korea is doing today. Sure, China has a huge trade surplus with the United States. But who is really benefiting? What we're really doing is selling our finished goods for China's cheap labor.

Economists have theories about "comparative advantage" and the like, but let me say this: One man can be stuffing himself silly with lamb chops and bread and corn and pomegranates and tapioca in the Ivory Coast and another man can be starving in Somalia, and economists will declare that the average African is enjoying a lean but balanced diet.

Wait a minute, some hard-nosed realist is likely to ask at this point: Am I my brother's keeper? The answer, I submit, is, "Yes." Now *that* is a risk worth taking!

Such high-mindedness is not beyond the grasp of politicians. I have known a few who actually put principle above expediency. But for most, reality sets in sooner or later, as they attempt to resolve the conflict between their deepest convictions and the less-than-high-minded will of the people. Soon, they are compromising left and right. For the cause of some greater good, they will join others in doing something that is semigood, that is, something that might be good, looked at from a certain angle, or at least is probably not bad, viewed from another angle.

Here is the fundamental way a politician operates: He appeals to the majority. And the majority, unfortunately, is exactly what the word says—it is the majority. Alas, the achievers are always—the minority.

Now the achiever has a burning desire to succeed and, in the process, perhaps, to get rich. Nothing wrong with that. So he works harder and he thinks harder. He does this all his life. He works until 8 P.M., or 9 P.M., or even midnight. He sometimes works on Saturdays and Sundays and he takes a lot of risks, a lot of heat, and a lot of aspirin. And he succeeds; perhaps he even gets rich.

Rich! Oh, boy! The politician knows that the rich, by definition, are in the minority. So he reaches into the rich man's pocket. Welcome to politics! Welcome to pork! Welcome to Washington!

Postscript:
Business Before Pleasure,
My Hat!

Business before pleasure, my hat! Business *is* pleasure. There is none greater in the realm of cerebral activity. Compared with running a business, or a division or department or just an office of a business, such widely recommended pastimes as golf, tennis, bridge, poker, gardening, playing the flute, and lying on the beach with a beer in one hand and a book in the other are cheap thrills.

"Business?" some will ask. *"Fun?"* I know the notion flies in the face of the stereotype of the business executive as harried and overworked and humorless. Well, maybe he is harried and overworked, but he's not humorless. If he's any good, his funny bone is in great shape.

All these books on managing: How terribly earnest and pedantic and shallow most of them are! No wonder people think of managers as dullards who are obsessed by number crunching and who lack a feel for the pulse and poetry of life. I myself find my eyes glaze over when management books blather on about "work processes" and "distribution operations" and "organizational integration" and "hierarchical gradations" and other such poppycock.

Managers read these academic tomes because they think they ought to. They think they might find some tips on how to do their jobs better. And, sometimes, they do. The authors often make one or two valid or even useful points. But they rarely give a glimpse of how much fun it is to take charge of an operation and run it your way.

Managing is like any game or activity that you're passionate about. It forces you to marshal all your skills for achieving specific objectives. And when you hit your stride, it's like acing a tennis serve or playing a Chopin sonata flawlessly on the piano. It's fun. It's what historian Arnold Toynbee meant when he said, "The supreme accomplishment is to blur the line between work and play."

Or what the Russian literary figure (and revolutionary socialist) Maxim Gorky meant when he wrote: "When work is a pleasure, life is a joy. When work is a duty, life is slavery."

Best of all, if you succeed, you win big: Not only in money, but in the respect and gratitude of those whose jobs you have created, preserved, and advanced, and in the sheer satisfaction of doing something well. If you don't succeed, of course, your name is mud. That's the risk you take. And, yes, I'll say it one last time: It's a risk worth taking.

Think of all those people who play bridge for dimes and quarters. They don't care about dimes and quarters; they care about having fun and winning. The same goes for the best managers, whether they're corporate executives or business owners. The money isn't all that important; playing the game is. If you enjoy yourself, you're more likely to succeed. If you succeed, the money falls in your lap.

So why the distinction between business and pleasure? I think it's based partly on misperception; people whose jobs bore or overwhelm them can't imagine someone with a much more demanding and time-consuming job enjoying it.

And of course, there are plenty of managers who simply dislike managing and who vent their frustrations on their colleagues or subordinates. They're misfits, and eventually they'll go into something else, but meantime they spread discontent.

I can't think of anybody having more fun than we had at ITT. And I do believe I met more interesting people on the job than I ever met at bridge or on the golf course. That's another advantage: Business attracts some of the sharpest minds and most adventuresome spirits. You meet 'em and you see 'em at their charmin' best.

Think of some of the most famous Renaissance figures: They were successful businessmen! Johannes Gutenberg, inventor of the modern printing press, had a metalworking business that also cut gems and made mirrors. The Medici family, the great patrons of the arts that ruled Florence for three centuries, gained its wealth as merchants and bankers.

To be more—I'm searching for some other word than "businesslike"—to be more practical about this, let's remind ourselves that we have to spend half our waking hours at work. Let's look at some of the pleasures.

I can hardly read a story about a successful businessman (or businesswoman)—or even a not-so-successful businessman, so long as he is struggling and hopeful—without thinking that he must be having fun. I believe it is their love of excitement that drives so many sports heroes, like golfing great Jack Nicklaus or football quarterback Fran Tarkenton, into business.

Likewise, seasoned deal makers keep going because they're having fun, not because they need the money. Take Sumner Redstone. He started off with a bunch of movie theaters and turned them into the biggest theater chain in the country. He bought Viacom, the second biggest media and entertainment company in the world, which is into movies, every kind of TV programming imaginable, video stores, amusement parks. He's got a swashbuckling style. Now in his seventies, he still loves doing deals. When he sold Madison Square Garden to ITT recently for $1.075 billion, he told the press, "My heart was in my mouth for the last fifty million dollars." And he clearly likes to be his own boss. That is apparently why he finally fired his right-hand man at Viacom, Frank Biondi Jr., in 1996, even though Mr. Biondi was considered one of the smartest people in the business. Explaining why it happened, Mr. Biondi said, "We weren't having as much *fun* as we did eight years ago."

The two things that separate ordinary pleasures and the pleasure of business are money and discipline. Ordinary pleasures don't make money, they *cost* money. And, while they require some discipline, there is no coercion. You don't have to get up at 7 A.M.

Suppose that, in some topsy-turvy world, you had to get up at 7 A.M. five days a week to play golf all day long. You'd end up hating golf. Worse yet, suppose somebody paid you to lie on the beach from 9 A.M. to 6 P.M. every business day. At 6 P.M. on Friday, you'd say, "Thank God that's over. I'm going to spend the weekend relaxing in the office. I can't wait to read Simison's report on raw-materials processing."

Sigmund Freud said there were two components to happiness and—surprise!—neither one was sex. Happiness, he said, was "Lieben und Arbeiten," love and work.

Recently, I read about a Wharton School of Economics study that supposedly shows that "workaholics" are less successful than their more laid-back co-workers. To which I say: bunk. I prefer the ancient wisdom of Proverbs:

Go to the ant, you lazybones,
Consider its ways, and be wise.
Without having any chief, or officer, or ruler
It prepares its food in summer,
And gathers its sustenance in harvest.
How long will you lie there, O lazybones?

Another sure sign that you're in the disciplined world of business rather than pursuing pure recreation is that you don't get a handicap in business. Toyota or Chrysler doesn't have to add a thousand dollars to the price of its cars to level the playing field.

Whether in business or recreation, pleasure comes from excelling at your task. To achieve excellence, you have to go through some shallow intermediary steps. But you accept them as part of the process. If reading all those reports at ITT had been an end in itself, I would have collapsed in ennui.

Fishing enthusiasts will sometimes get together to practice casting. If you told them their only objective was to see who could throw the line out the best, they'd leave in a hurry.

The pleasure isn't in casting, it's in catching the fish. The pleasure isn't in mixing the drink, it's in drinking it. The pleasure isn't in reading the business report, it's in applying it to your strategy for the company.

If pleasure comes from excelling, unhappiness comes from poor performance. The mediocre golfer throws his clubs away and swears off the game. The mediocre businessperson, needing to eat, sticks to the task but complains loudly about the rat race.

Why, then, do some people excel while others fail? A lot of qualities count—intelligence, drive, experience, eagerness, willingness to work hard, as well as a few less admirable traits such as charm and family connections. But for me, the key is *engagement,* by which I mean a passionate interest in what you are doing. From that flow all the other qualities that I have recommended in this book: an eagerness to work long hours, a willingness to take risks, a knack for seizing opportunities, a talent for innovation.

If you close your eyes and let your mind wander into the past, certain memories will rush up with such force and clarity that you almost feel you have transported yourself through time to the event itself. Sometimes I'll picture a hunt I was on a half century ago, and I can actually see a pheasant rushing through the brush in a flash of brilliant color. I can smell the forest floor and feel the autumn coolness and hear the report of my Browning gun, and the furious flappings of the bird's flight.

Yet I can't remember what I had for breakfast the day before yesterday. Was it eggs and toast? Cheerios? My mind's a blank.

Why the discrepancy? It has to do with engagement, of receptivity, of becoming so absorbed in your surroundings that you almost lose self-awareness.

If you're bored, then all the intelligence, experience, charm, and family connections in the world won't do you much good. But if you become engaged with your surroundings, your powers of absorbing and penetrating facts and solving problems shoot up by 1,000 percent. A 120 IQ will beat a 140 IQ every time.

You've noticed, perhaps, that some very smart people seem to languish at dead-end jobs while some less-than-brilliant lights move up the ladder of success very quickly. If you're engaged, not only will you succeed, you will take delight in what you do. You'll have fun.

Other rewards will fall on you to increase your satisfaction. As you get promoted to higher and higher positions, you'll gain more and more responsibilities. In other words, you'll be in charge—you'll be the boss.

Ambitious people have the most fun. Even if they start out in a low-level position, they know they're going to move higher—and the anticipation of their promotion carries them along.

As they gain responsibilities, they begin to savor the pleasures of being in charge. Few accomplishments give people greater satisfaction than running their own show. That's why so many men and women go into business for themselves. It's not the money; it's the fun of calling the shots.

If you move to the top of the ladder, you have to be careful or pride will take over and you'll get a little power-mad. Henry Ford was like an Asian despot. He was a law unto himself. The story goes that one of his senior executives once displeased him and he had some of his security guys haul him off to a private room in a hospital and feed him a huge dose of castor oil, with predictable results.

The key to enjoying business is growth—growth in size, growth in profits, and growth in your own responsibilities. If you succeed, you can take credit. If you don't, you can find an alibi.

There comes a point when you realize you're not working for money. Of course, that usually happens when you don't have to worry about money anymore. But it's a curious realization that usually has one of two results: You work all the harder because you realize your motivation is having fun, or, if you're not having fun, you retire.

If it came to a pinch, and you had a choice of keeping the job and losing the salary or keeping the salary and losing the job, you'd take the job.

I don't mean to stand in judgment of those who are having trouble with their jobs, who can't quite connect to them. It is a widespread problem. I'm familiar with it. But if you're struggling with a job you don't like, my advice is to try to find the interest in it.

Early in my career, when I was reconciling bank accounts, do you think that I was looking forward to a life of reconciling bank accounts? Of course not. I was hoping to go on to something else, something grander. But each time I reconciled a bank account, I got engaged, I found the interest in it.

The saying shouldn't be ''Business before pleasure''; it should be ''Business *with* pleasure.''

Index